"WATER UNDER THE BRIDGE"

by

Margarette De Andrade

CHARLES E. TUTTLE COMPANY
Rutland, Vermont & Tokyo, Japan

REPRESENTATIVES:
British Isles & Continental Europe:
Simon & Schuster International Group, London
Australia:
Bookwise International
1 Jeanes Street, Beverly, 5009, South Australia

Published by the Charles E. Tuttle Company, Inc.
of Rutland, Vermont & Tokyo, Japan
with editorial offices at
Suido 1-chome, 2-6, Bunkyo-ku, Tokyo

Library of Congress Catalog Number: 85-52408
International Standard Book Number: 0-8048-1430-9

Photographs reprinted with special permission from
  Museum of the City of New York

First printing - 1988

Printed in USA

Dedicated with deep affection and esteem to the first Manhattanite I met— my father, Jere J. Sheehan—whose recollections and valuable counsel in preparation of this modest work are gratefully acknowledged.

Introduction

The sayings "Water Under The Bridge" and "Water Over The Dam" are old fashioned adages conveying the idea of a terminated or continuing action. Manhattan Island — up to the time this story ends — never had any dams and presumably never will. But it has several bridges.

In 1947, when this sectional history was completed, the time was not ripe for its acceptance. We had experienced a devastating war which left no room for nostalgia. And so, "Water" was relegated to a file of unpublished articles and manuscripts.

Recently, while clearing out old files, I came across "Water" and it brought back to me some of the "dear, dead days of long ago" as it might do for those who are curious of what went before.

And so, nearly forty years after "hibernating," thanks to The Charles E. Tuttle Company, Inc. this modest work is now available to historians of Manhattan. It is hoped that they will consider it useful and that the reading public will find it an interesting saga of an integral part of a great city . . . perhaps even the Empire Borough of an Empire City of an Empire State!

Contents

CHAPTER ONE

The Battery Environs:
Shades of Yesteryear

To visit shrines in distant lands
May never me befall,
But I can walk where Jogues walked
Beside the Battery wall...
—Patrick Mac Donough

S HADES of yesteryear and phantoms of bygone days! If it is true
that "we are such things as dreams are made of" then the Battery,
as it concerns Manhattan must be a composite of all that has gone
before together with all that now exists. The people who used to frequent the Battery are as much a part of its present day life as though
they had temporarily retired and could be recalled into existence at any
given moment. They are still there, walking "beside the Battery wall"
as Jogues did; or searching the blue horizon, like Burr; or responding to
a gala welcome, like Lafayette. These and others are there, inspiring us,
encouraging modern Manhattanites to always forge ahead, showing us
the way to overcome obstacles in a world moving at a rapid pace.

There is something romantic about the Battery—a romance that has
found its expression in all mediums man has devised; oils, clay, words,
etc. It captivates one's imagination. The people of long ago remain
mere chimeras, it is true, but we are aware of them nevertheless, for the
objects with which they were associated remain—old streets, some old
houses, names which are derivatives of Dutch and Colonial Manhattanites and other links to a former era. Yes, the very trees and pathways
of Battery Park bespeak the presence of these oldsters.

1

There is nothing so romantic as an antiquity associated with objects, nothing which so captivates the imagination as an old house or an ancient jewel, or any object for that matter which has been handed down from succeeding generations. One enjoys going back through the years, seeing events as these objects saw them. On the other hand, there is something thrilling about newness which causes one to pause in his daily task, to gaze with interested wonder at the newest skyscraper under construction, the latest dance step or the last word in motion pictures or theatrical productions. Some of the districts of Manhattan are like this, romantic in their associations, yet thrilling in their very modernity.

The Battery Park section is one of these districts for despite all its sophistication there is still an air of quaintness about the Park and downtown New York. Shades of yesteryear inhabit the place. Interspersed with skyscrapers and the very modern buildings are yet to be seen a few landmarks of a former era. The winding streets, some retaining the cobblestones of bygone days, the flatroofed, low buildings breaking the lines of majestic skyscrapers suggest antiquity, even though this is one of the most modern sections of Manhattan. From Indian trail to the crossroads of the world, embodying great historical epochs of a nation, here the very pulse of Manhattan beats. When New York is ailing the pulse beats slower, when times are good the pulse beats faster, thus lower Manhattan serves as an index of the general condition of uptown districts.

When we were small—Gladys, Buddy and I—the Battery seemed so far away—almost remote. We lived in West Thirtieth Street, but in our childish minds the Battery was another planet, as far as we were concerned. This was not due to lack of conveyances, I should hasten to add, for there were "els" and subways and street cars. It was due more to a childish imagination which seems to magnify distance.

It was a pleasant diversion to go there once in a while; to see the ocean and scent its characteristic odor; to gaze at the Statue of Liberty standing like a sentinel guarding the entrance to the harbor—with barges, freighters, ferries and ocean-going liners scurrying back and forth, hither and yon. This latter sight invariably evoked a barrage of questions directed at my mother. Fortunately, Buddy was too small to express himself coherently, being a mere babe in arms at the time, but I am sure his silence was made up for, and amply, by the questions which were fired at my mother by two imaginative girls. Had she carried an encyclopaedia with her on these occasions, it would have been to little avail, for questions appeared before a sufficient time interval had elapsed to allow for a proper answer to each. Surviving the avalanche of interrogations, off we would go to the Aquarium to revel in its fascinating exhibits of varicolored peculiarly shaped specimens of marine life. Ah! The good old days!

And today as we look at the innumerable office buildings making up the famous skyline one sees from approaching liners, we cannot help but marvel at the thought that this is only a fraction of the land Peter Minuit bought from the Indians for $24.00 worth of trinkets on that historic May 6, 1626. Could he but return what would he think? This virgin forest wherein lurked the red man ever ready to kill the wary colonist—now converted into the greatest financial district in the world.

Or Father Jogues or Burr—what would they think were they suddenly plunged into the whirlpool of activity which centers around the Battery Park? When Father Jogues used to walk "beside the Battery wall" the wall was much nearer to State Street than it is at present; most of the land comprising the Park having been filled in since his time. Incidentally, the good Father was the first Catholic priest to enter Manhattes Island, as it was called when he wrote his "Description of New Netherland." But feeling that his real work lay out in the wilderness among the Indians, the Jesuit missioner did not tarry long around the Battery. The next time this noble soul appeared at the Battery was when he arrived aboard a sloop after having been ransomed from the Mohawks at Rensselaerwyck. His appearance bespoke more convincingly than words the suffering he had endured at the hands of the Indians as he had been kept as a slave and tortured beyond description. Father Jogues went back to Europe but returned to the New World in 1646 when he ratified a treaty between the Mohawks and the Canadian Government. He then remained to carry on his work with the Indians founding the Mission of the Martyrs in Indian country, but for some reason the people for whom the missioner had sacrificed the comforts and conveniences of civilization grew distrustful of him and tortured him as a sorcerer. Finally, the Jesuit was killed. His head was affixed on the village palisades and the trunk of the body was cast into the Mohawk River, flowing through territory which Jogues had explored. Father Jogues was canonized in 1930.

Facing the wall is the "pseudo" park which in summer is the haven of people who come from neighborhood tenements to enjoy the sea breeze. It was so when I was a youngster; it is still so. It seems that no matter how hot the rest of Manhattan is, one can always be sure of a refreshing breeze at the Battery, especially during the hot summer evenings. Here one may sit for hours watching the boats pass to and from the sea, just as the tragic Aaron Burr, in times long past, used to watch and wait for some news of his faithful daughter, Theodosia.

It is not difficult to visualize Burr, politician and financier, as one of the shadows of long ago. His slight frame silhouetted against the

Battery shoreline, the prominent forehead furrowed with lines of worry and despair, questioning and hoping for some assurance that his daughter was still alive. Burr was a man of many loves, but on no other did he lavish such affection as he did upon his daughter. On the day before the duel at Weehauken, which ended in Hamilton's death, and began the series of events climaxing in Burr's disgrace, Burr wrote to Theodosia, after directing that she should burn such letters as would injure any person ("more particularly applicable to the letters of my female correspondents"): "I am indebted to you, my dearest Theodosia, for a very great portion of the happiness which I have enjoyed in this life. You have completely satisfied all that my heart and affections had hoped or even wished. With a little more perseverance, determination, and industry, you will obtain all that my ambition or vanity had fondly imagined. Let your son have occasion to be proud that he had a mother. Adieu. Adieu."[1]

After the duel, Burr's affairs became more and more involved, eventually culminating in his trial for high treason. Burr was one of those people whose destiny it is to be always pursued by trouble. His life, exciting and dramatic, knowing the adversity of poverty and the opulence of riches, was never calm, never free from the invisible webs of intrigue, of danger and of public antipathy. Adversity followed him with a relentless fury.

Theodosia was married to a prominent southern planter, Joseph Alston by name, who later became Governor of South Carolina. She was brilliant and accomplished, inheriting her father's charm and keen intellect. After his trial for high treason, Burr fled to Europe to escape the scorn of his countrymen, for, though he was not convicted, he was made to feel the contempt of his former friends.

Theodosia was loyal and untiring in whatever she could do to help her father out of the predicaments which befell him; mitigating the feeling which existed against the former Vice President became of paramount importance to her. She was somewhat successful in this and when the wave of anomisity had abated, Burr returned from his European exile. At the time of Burr's arrival from Europe, Theodosia was in South Carolina with her husband and son. She embarked from that State to pay a visit to Burr. The vessel upon which she sailed was never heard from, though it was believed to have foundered off Cape Hatteras.

In the months that followed, Burr haunted the Battery, always hoping that the Fates would be kind to him and that his beloved Theodosia would eventually arrive. But she never did! And many an evening at dusk, when spirits are supposed to be abroad, it has been easy to imagine Burr's presence in the Battery, facile to believe that his desolate

4

spirit has left some evidence to manifest itself about the scenes of his unhappiness.

Battery Park is particularly interesting during the early morning of a week day, for then one may see the ferry boats, and subways sending forth the daily mass of clerks and bookkeepers who carry on the financial affairs of a great metropolis. If one wishes to be very observant he may count the languages he hears. Both east and west of the Park clutter a vast foreign population and at least a dozen languages are spoken in this vicinity. This is one of the most comospolitan spots in a cosmopolitan city. On warm nights the Park becomes a refuge for the homeless. Here, sandwiched between a blanket of stars, and less poetic, a discarded newspaper, one sees many a forgotten man; many a derelict is trodding the same ground cleared for him by industrious Dutch settlers.

On the one side of the Park are ferry boats which leave the Battery for Staten Island. When our family first moved to old Chelsea some years ago these ferry boats were a never ending source of pleasure for my brother, sister and me. When the West thirties were sweltering and the newspaper were replete with articles about "dog days" Mother would dress us and we would ride back and forth across the bay until we were so sleepy that heat didn't matter. In those days Manhattan's skyline was very different from the one we know today. The Woolworth Tower incited pride in every citizen, and there were no other buildings higher than it. One could see the Municipal Building and the old World Building. O. Henry had come and gone, furnishing later day writers with the model for the modern short story; Walt Whitman's poetry throbbing with the heart beats of a great city was still a topic for discussion as to its merits. Frank Ward O'Malley was the ace reporter, women were beginning to adapt their gait to the hobble skirts and I hadn't even started kindergarten. Yet, it is not so long ago, as measured the way time is today. We move at a rapid pace. What it once took years to accomplish can now be done in a matter of minutes.

The Battery Park as we know it today is a newer section of Manhattan since it is composed of filled in land. There are a few monuments adorning the Park, like the statue of John Ericsson near the Barge Office. There is the cannon known as the Oyster Pasty Cannon which excavotors exhumed when the building at No. 55 Broadway was under construction, also the Ft. George Monument erected in 1818. For many years this monument was missing until it was discovered during subway excavations. This perpetuates the site of the southwest bastion of the old fort. Then there is a statue of Verrazzano placed in the Park by the Italian residents of New York City to commemorate their compatriot's visit to New harbor in 1524.

Most of the shadows hovering around the Battery conceal themselves near the Battery wall erected around the water's edge. Here they are free to roam molested by naught save the lapping of the waves against the wooden piles of the ferry slips or the rays of light cast by Liberty's torch. Perhaps once in a while the rumble of trucks along the cobblestone, disturbs their revels, but otherwise they complacently wend their ways along their old Battery haunts.

It was here that sailing vessels, their holds heavily laden with rich produce from mysterious far-away lands, used to lay anchor whilst their cargoes were unloaded. It was here that the aristocracy were wont to prominade, lovers to stroll amongst the majestic trees which flourished in the Park. It was here that prominent visitors first set foot upon American soil, it was here that countless immigrants came to enrich the new land with their industry and toil.

The Battery has often been called the "Gateway of America." No other name could be so apt. Although the great transatlantic liners now dock further up the Hudson River, years ago their human cargoes were disgorged upon the Battery. This was the immigrant's first sight of these United States. Battery Park was their first vision of the "land of opportunity." There they landed many times fleeing persecution and famine, determined as all good fairy tales say "to seek their fortune."

In 1824 upon his return from Europe Lafayette was accorded a gala welcome in this Park. More than 6,000 people were assembled here to greet him. Castle Garden, or Fort Clinton when it was first constructed in 1807, was the scene of this occasion. This building, later the Aquarium, was designed by McComb, the same distinguished architect who was responsible for City Hall. In 1835 Morse demonstrated his telegraph here. In 1850 this became the site of Jenny Lind's memorable American debut. She had been brought here by the master showman, Barnum, and amply rewarded his good judgement by captivating everyone within hearing of her voice.

This was one of the operatic triumphs of the ages. Disappointed ticket purchasers swarmed the bay in boats, hoping thus to catch a few strains of the voice about which everyone was talking. And then it came—clear and resonant over the water—an epoch-making event in the annals of showmanship, for nothing Barnum ever arranged after succeeded in overshadowing the brilliance of this success. In Rosenberg's "Jenny Lind in America" speaking of the duet with Belletti he says, "She sang it deliciously, and the approbation of the audience broke out so vehemently that they were at length compelled to desist, and this from sheer exhaustion."[2]

Beginning 1855 and for more than thirty-five years thereafter this building was used as an immigrant landing station. It is not a long stretch of the imagination to say that some of the 8,000,000 immigrants who had been received here could return years later, victorious over the countless struggles, and financially successful enough to buy the ground upon which they first trod American soil. Then the glories that were Castle Garden found repose and a new dignity in the remodeled building which was converted into an Aquarium.

The Aquarium has since been transferred to another section of the city, but during the time when it was located in the Battery approximately 2,000,000 people a year visited. Once in a while, on a Sunday afternoon it was a very interesting trip to walk through the deserted financial canyons, letting one's imagination run amuck, then end up at the Aquarium. The exhibits one saw comprised specimens from all over the world, totaling between 3,000 and 7,000 fish. Under Battery Park there was a large reservoir into which fresh salt water was pumped from the sea. The exhibits upstairs may have been salamanders, turtles, electric eels, alligators, a species of "chameleon" fish, etc. [This historical building, reminiscent of much that transpired in this Manhattan of ours over a Century and a Quarter, still stands. There are rumors that the Federal Government would like to acquire the building as a national landmark but since the City of New York owns it, such a measure would require some preliminary arrangement between the State and the Federal Government.]

The Battery, rich in a monetary sense, is also wealthy in tradition for it represents the first settlement of New York by the white man. Though today very little remains of the early Dutch settlers of New Amsterdam, most evidence being consumed first by the great fire of 1776, later by that of 1835, many names of streets and squares still suggest the thrifty Dutchmen who first tilled the soil.

Broad Street was the principal street, probably because it was broad enough to construct a canal, thus reminding the Dutch of their homeland. It was called "Heere Gracht" or "Gentleman Canal."[3] Wall Street was once the location of a wall built around the city in 1653. Coenties Slip was named after the home-loving couple, Coen and Antye Ten Eyck, combining the syllables of their names and thus uniting in the memory of Manhattanites who trod that place those who had been so united in life.[4] William Street was first called "Smith's V'ly" or valley. The Battery was named after the battery in Fort George; Bowling Green because the inhabitants used to assemble on the Green for bowling; Whitehall Street, in memory of Peter Stuyvesant's white house, etc. In these and other names the old New Amsterdam is always recalled to modern "Big Towners."

One can picture the early Dutch traversing the irregular cow paths which led from the Battery to their farms, their Governors dispatching

7

petulant complaints to the mother country, recording the fact that cows and goats constantly invaded the Fort in their search for more succulent pasture. Or the irate colonists meeting in groups to denounce the British, or the crowd which gathered to watch "that crazy Fulton" sail his "Clermont" up the Hudson. (Robert Fulton later died at One State Street; Feb. 23, 1815). Yes, and the belles and beau brummels of the Eighteen Hundreds who used to prominade on the Battery walk. A little more than two generations ago the Battery was the finest residential neighborhood of the city, home of the Whitney's, the Rhinelander's, the Schermerhorn's and other of Father Knickerbocker's First Families.

In literary glamour the Battery ranks as one of the favored districts of writers. Indeed, many a tale owes its inspiration to the imaginations incited by Battery haunts. Bunner's famous hero in "The Story of a New York House" lived at the old house located at No. 7 State Street. This house, one of the mansions of a hundred years ago, still exists as a home for Irish immigrant girls. On the balcony overlooking the waterfront is a statue of the Holy Virgin, while inside one attends Mass in a room which saw many a ball a Century or so ago. Washington Irving's brother of "Salamagundi" fame lived at No. 17 State Street.

Some years back my husband's office used to be located in the building at that same address. Many a time I would arrange to meet him in the lobby so we could lunch together. While waiting I used to play a little game of wondering. I would wonder what these literary men of bygone days would discuss over a pipe of tobacco or a glass of fine old port. Right on this very spot! Politics, no doubt, Men always discuss politics. Perhaps maritime affairs, for they could look across the Park and view the activities of all the boats entering or leaving New York harbor. Maybe they may even have confided romantic secrets to each other. A real romanticist at heart, I like to think that they did. By that time Andy would be emerging from the elevator and we would be off to Fraunces' Tavern.

Old Fort George, originally Fort Amsterdam, was situated on the site of the present Custom House. In 1635 when it was completed, it occupied the space between Whitehall, Bridge and State Streets and the Bowling Green. In colonial days the Fort was used to guard the entrance to the harbor. It enclosed the barracks, Governor's House and a church. It was here that all business of the island was conducted, spiritual, political and social. In those days the water line came right up to the Fort, the land now occupied by Battery Park having been filled in during the year 1783.

The old Fort went under various names during the Century and a Half in which it guarded the entrance to Manhattan. Each time it was captured, and each time a new monarch mounted the English throne,

8

the Fort's name was changed. It was successively named Manhattan, 1623; Amsterdam, 1625; James, 1664; Willem Hendrick, 1673; James, 1674; the Fort in New York, 1689; William, 1689; William Henry, 1691; Anne, 1702; and George, 1714. It had been under the respective flags of Holland, Britain, Holland, Britain, American, Britain and finally America.[5]

Today presiding over this very spot stands the $7,000,000 Custom House. Here are located the offices of Collector of the Port, Surveyor of the Port, Internal Revenue Service, Bureau of Foreign and Domestic Commerce, Steamboat Inspection Service, Passport Agent and Secret Service and Radio Bureaus. Inside the Custom House there are two tablets, one commemorating the site of Fort Amsterdam, the other in memory of the ground upon which the first Mass was read in Manhattan, by the Rev. Thomas Harvey, in 1683. There are also ten paintings of colonial ports of the Seventeenth Century.

Directly in front of the Fort stood the Bowling Green, a spot forever familiar to history loving Manhattanites. It was truly the village green. Social festivities, dancing, children playing, soldiers parading, all these activities centered 'round the green. In 1641 Governor Kieft inaugurated the annual cattle fair and farmers brought their finest cattle and hogs to be exhibited for sale on the green.

This same Governor, history tells us, was the perpetrator of one of the most brutal Indian massacres in the history of New York. The wholesale slaughter of a tribe of Indians who had fled to New Amsterdam for protection against enemy tribes was the result of a whim of Governor Kieft. After the massacre the Governor's soldiers marched triumphantly, if such acts of violence could ever be considered a triumph, through the gates of the Fort, about where No. 4 Bowling Green now stands. Three times the soldiers repeated these attacks upon the Indians, returning through the gates each time with heads of murdered Indians dangling from their spears. The Dutch West India Company, advised of Kieft's cruelty, finally recalled him.[6]

The iron railing which fences in a little patch of anemic looking grass is all that is left of the old Bowling Green. If one looks closely at the fence he may see where the heads surmounting the posts were ripped off by a frenzied Revolutionary mob, while inside the railing stands a statue of Abraham de Peyster, Mayor of New York 1691-1695. During the Revolutionary period this fence used to surround an equestrian statue of George the Third, erected by England for the Colonists August 9, 1770. Though in the light of present day values the sum appears to be a very large appropriation for the purpose, £800 were provided by the Colonial Government to defray the cost of erecting this railing.[7] During the Revolution the main part of the statue was melted

9

into 42,000 lead bullets, ironically used as defense against the British. Somehow the tail and bridle of the horse escaped the melting pot as they turned up at a farm in Wilton, Conn. in 1878. These tarnished remnants of a once glorious statue which adorned the Bowling Green may be seen at the New York Historical Society.

To one side of the Fort was the famous Burn's Coffee House, formerly, some historians claim, the King's Arms Tavern. It stood on Broadway, opposite the Bowling Green, near what was formerly the private residence of the Van Cortlandts.[8] This served as the meeting place for merchants as well as the Sons of Liberty. October 31, 1765 some two hundred merchants met here and signed a resolution protesting against the Stamp Act. From here they proceeded to Bowling Green where effigies of Lt. Governor Colden were burned. At No. 115 Broadway there is a monument placed by the Holland Society to commemorate the site of this historic event.[9]

A picture of Bowling Green today presents a striking contrast to that place of yore. Standing on the steps of the Custom House and looking up one of the longest thoroughfares in the world, Broadway, one sees the tall buildings wherein are located most of the two hundred steamship companies whose boats grace our shores. It has been estimated that when shipping is good there have been as many as two hundred and fifty nine ships docked in the Port of New York in a single day!

Millions of dollars are invested in the buildings one sees. The site where Alexander Hamilton's house once stood now holds the Standard Oil Building, assessed at $12,250,000. The red fronted Produce Exchange Building at No. 6 is worth nearly $55,000,000. On the site of the old Stevens House at No. 25 is situated the $11,000,000 Cunard Building. No. 1 Broadway, long ago famous as containing the house from which Major André convicted himself by sending letters to Benedict Arnold is now the location of the International Mercantile Marine Company. If spectres of days gone by wander in this vicinity, they must certainly pause longer at this busy point where Broadway wearily disgorges its traffic into Bowling Green. At one time the property now known as No. 1 was owned by Abraham de Peyster who built several small houses on the land. Comm. Sir Peter Warren, so closely connected with Greenwich Village, was a resident there before he settled further uptown. The main glories of No. 1 seem to have been attained during the time Kennedy erected the Kennedy Mansion on the site for it figured historically as being the successive headquarters of Washington and Howe. Records also show that Nathaniel Prime, the wealthy merchant once resided here. In 1882 Cyrus W. Field bought the site and erected an office building.

Such a transition! Lofty office buildings, shooting forever skywards; people scurrying hither and yon, bent upon the various activities so vital to Manhattan. To the east a few tenement houses, perhaps housing some of the army of night workers who take charge of cleaning the thousands of offices; scattered about on side streets and in drug stores, the several lunch counters where "coffee and" is served to the busy toilers;—all this is the downtown Manhattan as we know it today; a kaleidoscopic view of the Battery and Bowling Green sections; there people move fast and think faster, where one sees an alert yet stereotyped Manhattanite, where everything—people, buildings, money and brains—are only a part of the "Big Town of Ours."

CHAPTER NOTES

1. "Correspondence of Aaron Burr and His Daughter Theodosia," letter of July 10, 1804, p. 170.
2. Rosenberg, C. G., "Jenny Lind in America," p. 23.
3. Moss, Frank, "The American Metropolis," Vol. I, p. 15.
4. Ibid., Vol. I, p. 44.
5. Gilder, Rodman, "The Battery," p. 113.
6. Booth, Mary L., "History of the City of New York," Vol. 1, p. 112.
7. Stevens, John August, "Progress of New York in a Century," an address delivered before the New York Historical Society, Dec. 7, 1875, p. 13.
8. Wilson, James Grant, "Memorial History of New York," Vol. II, p. 368.
9. Trask, Spencer, "Bowling Green," p. 13.

The Harbour of New York from the Battery

CHAPTER TWO

Wall Street: The Money Mart

"Just where the Treasury's marble front
  Looks over Wall Street's mingled nations,
Where Jews and Gentiles most are wont
  To throng for trade and last quotations;
Where hour, by hour, the rates of gold
  Outrival, in the ears of people,
The quarter-chimes, serenely tolled
  From Trinity's undaunted steeple."

"Pan in Wall Street" by E. C. Stedman.

ONCE upon a time, as our favorite childhood stories began, there was a street which started where Broadway is now and ran east to the river. This street was called "Wall Street" and today it has become famous the world over. So romantically woven is its history that any narration of events happening there appears to be like a fairy tale, yet a truer story, a more interesting story, could not be told.

Other districts of Manhattan may have undergone more transitions, but Wall Street has only experienced three. There was the Dutch period when all the land was in farms and one had to undergo untold hardships to reach the remote locality later known as Greenwhich Village. Then there was the glorious Revolutionary period when "the street" was considered a very fine residential section; when American history was in the making. Lastly, there came the time when aristocratic mansions gave way to banks and commercial houses, forming the nucleous of Wall Street as we know it today.

In the middle of the Seventeenth Century the forests surrounding Wall Street were inhabited by Indians who scalped anyone intrepid enough to venture into the woods. The woods also contained voracious wolves which preyed upon what little cattle the Dutch possessed. Finally, Governor Kieft ordered every man who wished to share in its protective privileges to help in the building of a fence. This was to keep the cattle from straying away as well as a defense against Indians. This fence or wall was built on the site where Wall Street is now, hence the derivation of the name. Later, in 1653 another fence was constructed under the leadership of Peter Stuyvesant. This was built in the same place as the first fence had been, but was an improvement on Gov. Kieft's crude barrier. So great was felt the need for protection, now not only against the Indians but the British as well, that the Dutch subscribed 5,000 guilders within two days to defray the cost of the wall.[1] This was removed in 1699 and the stones used to build the City Hall which stood on the site of the Sub-Treasury.[2]

Were one to take a stroll down Wall Street in the year 1710 a striking scene would present itself. Starting at Trinity Church, for there has always been a church on that spot since 1696, and looking down towards the river, he would see trees and domestic animals and perhaps a thrifty farmer's wife on her way to the "Fly Market"—in short—a real pastoral scene. If the casual observer were inquisitive enough to turn his head sideways he might even see a bear, as the Dutch are known to have indulged in bear hunts in the vicinity of Cedar Street and Maiden Lane.

At the other end of the street—about where Pearl Street is now—there existed a slave market. Captain Kidd who owned a house on Wall Street used to visit the mart regularly, until the desire for more lucrative enterprises overtook him. Due to popular demand the slave market was abolished and fine residences began to spring up, ushering in the Revolutionary period. Then, indeed, Wall Street was at the height of its social glory.

By the end of the Eighteenth Century Wall Street had become the center of fashion and great entertainments were tendered by those who lived in the vicinity. Secretary and Mrs. Jay gave one ceremonious dinner weekly to which the best society of the city came. Illustrious men of letters, diplomats, and distinguished foreign visitors could always be found at the Secretary's table. Secretary of War and Mrs. Knox also entertained lavishly. Sir John Temple, first British Consul General lived there with his popular American wife who was Miss Bowdoin of Massachusetts. The fact that Sir John tended to incline toward the American cause lost for him the Lt. Governorship of New Hampshire. But he was exceedingly popular as the British Consul General serving the city of that day in much the same capacity as Grover Whalen did in the Twenties, that is, as more or less of an official host to the city's distinguished visitors.

The Dutch Ambassador and his daughter, Miss Van Berckel, were also noted members of this coterie. Alexander Hamilton and Aaron Burr—all-round perennial rivals—were well known figures and no doubt their continual disagreements were the subject of many a drawing room conversation.

Today this street of such humble beginnings is considered by many to be the most important street in Manhatten, for two-thirds of the world's business is carried on here. It is a street of money—where commodities are money, stocks and bonds. It is a street where the term first employed by Washington Irving is aptly used, for here the "Almighty Dollar" is king! Only here, across the counters of the New York Stock Exchange could 297,446,059 shares of stock be transferred at a total value of $1,859,525,825.[3]

If again, with the activity which characterizes this Twentieth Century of ours, we stand at Trinity Church and look down the street, gone are the old buttonwood trees in front of Nos. 68 and 70 where the Colonial brokers used to gather to transact business. The people in silks and satins and laces prominade there no more. The great homes wherein sparkled Colonial hospitality have all disappeared, and in their stead one sees a veritable canyon of gloom, darkened by shadows of majestic skyscrapers which line "the street's" sides. The only relief from this gloomy impression is gained by the presence of the many people who throng the thoroughfare. Among these one may see mere slips of messenger boys whose daily work consists of carrying thousands of dollars worth of securities back and forth, as if the little leather brief cases contained nothing more important than the day's newspaper; or a financial Croesus brooding about affairs of international importance; or the young stenographer planning what dress to wear when she meets her best beau after Wall Street ceases to exist for the night. All strata of life are represented here from the sandwich man advertising the nearest passport photographer to the banker's daughter who dropped downtown for an advance installment on an allowance probably already too generous.

As one penetrates deeper he is impressed by the silence, a silence so unexpected in view of the crowds which throng the street; a silence and quietude which seemingly compels observance. Then one notices the facial expressions—tense and harassed. Seldom does one see people gay and laughing, like in a Broadway crowd or a Fifth Avenue crowd. Even in boom times or during the Christmas season when all New York is in a gay holiday mood, the passerby in Wall Street goes about his affairs very seriously, as though, like Atlas, he carried the weight of the world upon his shoulders. And perhaps many of these people do carry a great deal of weight upon themselves. Perhaps the preoccupied air one notices

14

is justified. Sometimes, just a smile from some of these people may mean the difference between rags and riches to others.

Wall Street, romantically as well as financially linked with the progress of this Manhattan of ours; Wall Street, where one may become wealthy or destitute overnight; Wall Street, where behind the yards of ticker tape which engulf one lies many a tragedy; what bits of history you recall to us! Here the United States Congress once met. At No. 33 Alexander Hamilton had his office while his rival, Aaron Burr, opened his office in nearby Cedar Street. No. 56 was once the home of Captain Kidd which came to him by virtue of his marrying the former Widow Cox. In 1689 William Cox bought the house situated on this lot for £60, after which he appears to have conveniently passed into the Great Beyond leaving his widow, Sarah, free to take as her second spouse one John Oort. This latter marriage did not long endure, however, for we learn that soon the romantic Sarah was left a widow for a second time and in May 1691 she gave her heart and hand to Captain William Kidd who later became the notorious pirate.[4] In 1839 this same lot which was originally £60 was sold for $100,000. The Title Guaranty and Trust Company are located on Widow Cox's former lot.

Embedded upon this street are not only the footprints of time, but those of many a famous personage as well. The great financiers, Hamilton and Gallatin, Aaron Burr, founder of the Manhattan Company, and in our own times the Rockefellers, the Morgans, the Bakers, etc. have all trod this path. Washington, Webster, Jay and other statesmen were very familiar with Wall Street vicinity. Famous poets and writers lived nearby or used to frequent the homes of their friends who resided in the street. Irving, forever immortalized by his "Life of Washington," (for whom he was named) was born in the house at No. 128 William Street. This renown writer spent many of his boyhood years at No. 131. His first meeting with George Washington is said to have taken place here, when as a baby, his nurse lifted him up to receive the President's blessing.

Imposing banks have developed within the shadows where the First President met the baby who was later destined to chronicle his life. They reach heavenward, their foundations firmly implanted upon Wall Street. Alexander Hamilton's bank of 1791 was the first one to be established on Wall Street. This he called the Bank of New York. It still does business in the same place, a tribute to the sagacity and foresight of its illustrious founder. Eight years after Hamilton's bank was incorporated, The Manhattan Company in which Aaron Burr was interested was established at No. 23 Wall Street. The year 1805 brought two more financial enterprises to Wall Street, The Merchants Bank at No. 25 and the United States Bank at No. 38. Two years later The Mechanics

Bank opened at No. 16, thus the beginning of Wall Street's present dominance in finance was initiated more than 150 years ago.

Wall Street's prominence in the financial world first began to be felt during the time of Jacob Little who was known as the "great bear of Wall Street." Since Jacob Little was the fore-runner of all modern manipulators, it might be well to dwell a moment, at this point, on the singular personality who lived only for the satisfaction he could derive from trading. Many more were to follow in the path of this "great bear of Wall Street" whose spectacular career brought him to bankruptcy four times. Little rallied from the combined attacks of his Wall Street colleagues three times, but the fourth time he did not recover and on December 5, 1856 he failed to the extent of $10,000,000.[5] This wizened looking man who taught Wall Street how to sell short was diametrically opposite to what the public had come to expect of the great financiers, who were then coming to the fore. Tall and lean, he gave one the impression of being perpetually hungry. He derived no pleasure from the social amenities to which his associates adhered. His entire existence centered around trading and to this end he devoted all his energy and most of his time, for it is alleged that Little would not leave the "Street" while anyone remained to trade.[6] Little built up a business to gigantic proportions, rising to be one of the foremost operators. He met his Waterloo with Erie when he sold short on that stock and was unable to maintain his position, on which occasion the pious Drew made his initial soaring into the realms of high finance.

The Wall Street of Little's day has changed physically; basically its method of operation remains only slightly altered, for the most part in such activities as come under legislative control. There are still "bears" and "lambs"—operators manipulate and unfortunately an occasional panic crops up to plague the country.

One of the unchanging features of the "Street" is the Sub-Treasury. Nestled in between lofty buildings, it is the most striking on the street because it is low and the tall surrounding structures form such a noted contrast. Rich in its Doric architecture, yet dignified and strong in appearance, with its many stone steps leading down to the Ward statue of Washington, one never passes without a momentary pause in retrospection. The Sub-Treasury started its historic life as the old City Hall, built in 1699 on land donated for the purpose by one of New Amsterdam's famous Knickerbockers, Abraham de Peyster. In front were the pillory and whipping post, where Dutch justice was meted out to the miscreants of the time.

After English occupation, the City Hall continued to serve the Colony much in the same manner as during the time of Dutch rule. It became the abode of the city's first library. This consisted of 1642

16

volumes representing a bequest of the Rev. M. Millington of England. The books were transported to the Colony and deposited in the City Hall, thus forming the first public library to be established in New York. This was in 1730. Later, other volumes were added and in 1772 King George III granted the library a charter under the name of the New York Society Library.[7]

In 1789 City Hall was remodeled and called Federal Hall. Its doors were formally swung open on March 4, 1789, the day appointed for the assembling of Congress. Due to poor transportation facilities, a quorum was not obtained until April 6, when the new Congress, finally assembled, was at last able to announce the names of the President and Vice President.[8] The work of planning the new Federal Hall by converting the old City Hall, was done by Major Pierre l'Enfant to whom also goes the credit of designing the City of Washington. The Major, however, never received any compensation for his labors, though the Common Council, in recognition of his work, did grant him the freedom of the city and ten acres of land situated in what is now Third Avenue and 68 Street. At the time, the land was so far out as to render it worthless, and Major l'Enfant declined to accept such poor remuneration for his work. He was then offered $750 which was also scorned, and so in the end he received nothing.[9]

The present building was constructed in 1812 for a Custom House. In 1862 it was remodeled. What that earth has seen is written in fire and blood; of financial panics—leaving calamity and despair in their wakes; of the great fires which swept the city; of soul stirring meetings and in our own times, of the mysterious Wall Street bombing which shocked the world in 1920, when the explosion killed 30 people. In 1735 the Zenger case for free speech was won here; in 1765 the Stamp Congress met here; twenty years later it became the meeting place of the Continental Congress, so this site is not only important to our municipal history but it is definitely a part of our national history, as well.

On this site Washington took oath as First President of the United States. Inside the Sub-Treasury is a plaque commemorating this event. On April 4 Congress, which was then convening in Federal Hall, gave Washington the entire 69 electoral votes for President. John Adams received 34 for Vice President. On the 16th of April the great General left his beloved Mount Vernon and journied through a series of triumphant welcomings to his Inauguration. He arrived in New York on April 23, 1789 and was inaugurated on April 30. A few moments before the ceremonies began it was discovered that there was no Bible in Federal Hall. And so a Bible was hastily borrowed from St. John's Lodge and the First President of the United States took the oath of office on an English Bible containing the portrait of George II. This historic volume is now in the possession of St. John's Lodge No. 1 in the Masonic Temple, New York City.[10]

Wall Street was a gay place during the week of festivities preceding the Inauguration. The Colonists had suffered great hardships and privations during the War of Independence, and many years were required to recuperate from these ill effects. But the Inauguration was the culmination of all their strivings for at last their great ideal of representative government was to be realized. It was no wonder that General Washington's arrival was heralded with great enthusiasm. He arrived at the Wall Street Wharf on the afternoon of April 23. The cheering spectators made the wharf front black with humanity, bells tolled the General's arrival and cannons boomed the welcome to the First President-elect. The festivities incidental to the Inauguration continued for six days. After the celebrations were over, and Washington had been sworn in as First President of the United States, Wall Street resumed its normal way of life and once again elegantly attired ladies and gentlemen of fashion were to be seen passing Federal Hall.

It is not possible to visit Wall Street without seeing the handsome Gothic Trinity Church located at the head, on Broadway. Curiously enough, Trinity (which signifies three) is the third church to be erected on this site, the present church being constructed over a hundred years ago. The English Church was the name under which Trinity was originally established. The first Divine Service was read there on Feb. 6, 1697. This edifice remained until 1776 when it was destroyed in the great conflagration which swept the lower city. It was not until 1788 that it was rebuilt. In 1841 during the process of inspecting a leaky roof it was found more expedient to build a new church than to try to repair the old one. Hence, for the third time a Trinity was erected on the same spot—a Trinity which is as familiar to most New Yorkers as it is to denizens of Wall Street. The cornerstone contains a lead box into which was placed among other articles a copy of Trinity's Charter, dated May 6, 1697, a Bible and a Book of Common Prayer. The lead box is still in the cornerstone, and presumably will stay there until a fourth Trinity is erected, for one may sentimentally suppose that there will always be a Trinity at the head of Wall Street.

This is perhaps the wealthiest church in the nation, not only because it stands on a most valuable tract of land, but also because it has an income of half a million dollars yearly. The entire tract of land between Fulton and Warren Streets from Broadway westward to the river was granted to "the English Church of New York." Trinity still retains most of this grant.

There has been great litigation over this grant and several law suits on the part of Mrs. Anneke Jans Bogardus' heirs to recover title. It appears that in 1670, upon the decease of this lady, a majority of her heirs conveyed the farm she left to Governor Lovelace. This personage subsequently lost his share which was confiscated for debt and later granted by Queen Ann to Trinity. Anneke Bogardus' farm at the time of her death consisted of approximately 62 acres from Warren to Duane Street on Broadway, thence northwesterly and north along the river. As the years went on this tract increased in value, just as the descendents who did not join in the transfer, increased in number. Sporadic law suits have been instigated by these descendents though the Trinity Church's claim has usually been upheld. In 1868 delegates representing more than 2,000 of these heirs met in Philadelphia. They came from five states issuing bonds to pay their expenses.[11]

Surrounding the church is an old graveyard where many an emminent person slumbers his last sleep. After Alexander Hamilton's brilliant career was extinguished by his duel with Aaron Burr, his remains were brought to rest in this cemetary. The impressive funeral cortege passed through Wall Street, prominent statesmen, diplomats and soldiers and students all following the coffin to its final destination in one of the saddest processions the street has ever witnessed. He was buried in one corner of the churchyard and one may see the monument which was erected there to perpetuate his memory.

Hamilton's wife and his son Philip, who was also killed in a duel, are buried in this churchyard. Reposing near Hamilton's remains is the body of Aaron Burr's great friend, Davis. Davis accompanied Burr to the fateful duel and remained loyal after other friends and relatives had deserted him, a friendship which was completed when Davis buried the erstwhile Vice President after his tragic life had run its course. Robert Livingston, to whom Milbourne uttered the awful curse, "Robert Livingston, I will implead thee at the bar of Heaven for this deed," lies in Trinity. Milbourne and his father-in-law, Leisler, were condemned to death for treason. The younger prisoner became so incenced at the part Livingston played in his trial that he pronounced the famous accusation against his accuser. Lady Cornbury, Queen Ann's cousin is also buried there. Philip Hone in his "Diary" under date of Dec. 10, 1839 describes how workmen who were removing the tower foundations of Trinity opened the vault of Lady Cornbury and there discovered a large plate perfectly legible though it had been interred 133 years. "The arms of this noble lady, who was sister of the Earl of Richmond and a viscountess in her own right, are engraven on the plate, with her pedigree, age, and time of death, etc., distinctly, but very crudely, written below."[12] Mr. Hone proposed that these relics be presented to the Historical Society, but the officials did not agree and so a new tomb was prepared and the relics reinterred.

19

William Bradford who set up the first printing press in the Colonies, Captain Albert Gallatin, and a host of nameless prisoners who died in the Sugar House Prison are all interred here. It is claimed that between eight and fifteen bodies from the Liberty Street Sugar House were buried daily during those difficult times.[13] Their uniformed bodies were placed in rows then covered with earth. No coffins or funerals were accorded these unknown heroes of the American Revolution, and their bones repose in Trinity today in unmarked, nameless graves.

Perhaps the most romantic grave in Trinity is that of the legendary Charlotte Temple. Even today, many a tear is shed over the plight of this hapless creature. The story of this beautiful girl is familiar to a great many New Yorkers. One generation after another has kept her grave moist with sympathetic tears dropped over the flat stone which is supposed to be her resting place. There are some who doubt that the grave actually contains her body, but the evidence supporting the fact that she really existed as Charlotte Stanley has never been doubted by her family, the Haswells. And though Trinity harbors the bones of great statesmen, philanthropists and heroes with imposing monuments to perpetuate their memory, no grave there incites more interest and speculation than that of the betrayed girl who was left alone to bear her child in shame, despair and poverty.

The fate of Montressor, who deserted her, has long been forgotten in the light of succeeding years, but Charlotte Temple's memory is poignantly kept alive and as vibrant with life as the sun whose rays have fallen upon her grave these hundred and fifty years. Very often visitors place floral offerings on her tomb. Many times I have seen bouquets placed there by sympathetic New Yorkers;—and this in a city and on a street which has often gained the epithet "inhuman." Perhaps the reason for this compassionate interest in Charlotte Temple's grave is because nothing so touches the human heartstrings like the story of a broken heart.

Conservative estimates place the number of souls reposing in Trinity as being more than 150,000. Some of the graves are thirty feet deep. Then hundreds are buried in vaults beneath the church. In 1852 a realtor of Greenwich Street headed a movement to have Albany Street extended across the graveyard. So great was the opposition to this plan that it had to be dropped.

In ground so hallowed by the heroic deeds of those who lie here, it has always shocked my sentimentality to observe the several office workers who on Spring days make picnic lunches in the cemetary. It almost seems sacriligious! Here, also unmindful of the historical sanctity of the place, may be seen lovers walking arm in arm, or business men taking an after lunch constitutional, or settling no one knows what

20

momentous affairs, while the sirens whistle from river traffic on the one side, and the muffled rumble of the subway emanates from the other.

But no matter how many skyscrapers are erected to glorify this era of "Big Business"—no matter how much Wall Street progresses—I hope I shall always see the spire of Trinity gracing its head. I hope I shall always be able to enter the church to find peace and quietude just a few steps away from the frenzied, hustling whorl of humanity which make up modern Wall Street. Once inside, I can reflect on life here as it used to be when there were no movies and the art of conversation was considered a worthwhile passtime.

In those days a great part of the social, political and business life centered about the coffee houses. Indeed, one cannot think of Wall Street of the past without referring to some of the coffee houses famous in Colonial days. As early as 1642 the Dutch had constructed what well might have been the first skyscraper in Mahattan. This was a combination coffee house and inn and was known as "Aunt Metje Wessell's Tavern." It was five stories high and was located at the corner of Pearl Street and Coenties' Slip, about where 75 Pearl Street now is. In 1653 it became the Stadt Huys or first City Hall. The gallows, ducking stool, stocks and pillory were also here. Today there is a tablet there to mark the site.

Then there was the Merchants' Coffee House which opened about 1738 in the neighborhood of the Meal Market. At first it was located on the northwest corner of Wall and Water Streets. Later, in 1772, now a famous gathering place, it moved diagonally across the street to the southeast corner. It is said that between the years 1744 and 1801 at least thirty-two prominent societies held meetings in rooms of the Merchants' Coffee House. It served its patrons as a stock exchange, Lloyds and a shipping agency where mariners came to buy and sell ships. As its name suggests, merchants from the nearby market also frequented the Coffee House. In 1914 the Lower Wall Street Business Men erected a tablet on number 91 stating the history of this famous landmark.

By 1971 the Merchants' Coffee House had become too small to accommodate its growing list of patrons so an association of merchants organized to construct a larger place. They accordingly purchased the first location of the Merchants' Coffee House on the northwest corner of Wall and Water Streets. The well known Tontine Building was constructed on the property and it was called Tontine because of the tontine form of inheritance. The stock exchange of New York was located here. As at Lloyds two sets of books were kept; one to record ships' arrivals, the other for their clearance. The Chamber of Commerce, probably the oldest commercial organization in America independent of government

21

support, used to meet here before they moved to more commodious quarters. The well known Tammany Society also convened here.

Thus time has wrought its changes upon the little street of such humble beginnings. Passing through the labyrinth of buildings which rise majestically skyward, one cannot help but recall the brilliant history of this thoroughfare. Merely a lane it is, yet since the first settler plod his path there, it has made history. It has always made history, only the history it writes is written in pages of international banking and financial conquests. But even though it is one of the best known streets in the world, synonomous with money and high finance, I like it best when it is deserted. On a late Sunday afternoon when a fading sun casts Trinity's shadow across the street, when it is empty and forlorn, like a giant monster from whom all inhabitants have fled, then I can breathe freely of the sheer romance of this Wall Street of ours!

CHAPTER NOTES

1. Villard, Oswald Garrison, "The Early History of Wall Street," p. 4.
2. Ibid., p. 16.
3. Federal Writers' Project, "New York City Guide," p. 53.
4. Hill, Frederick Trevor, "The Story of a Street," p. 25.
5. Warshow, Robert Irving, "The Story of Wall Street," p. 79.
6. Ibid., p. 64.
7. Villard, Oswald Garrison, "The Early History of Wall Street," p. 26.
8. Booth, Mary L., "History of the City of New York," Vol. II, p. 592.
9. Wilson, James Grant, "Memorial History of New York," Vol. III, p. 46.
10. Hill, Frederick Trevor, "The Story of A Street," p. 110.
11. Gerard, James W., "The Old Streets of New York Under the Dutch," p. 60, 61.
12. Hone, Philip, "The Diary of Philip Hone," edited by Allan Nevins, Dec. 10, 1839.
13. Moss, Frank, "The American Metropolis," Vol. II, p. 161.

WALL STREET towards Trinity Church, 1904, showing Stock Exchange and columns of the Sub-Treasury Building

CHAPTER THREE

Hallowed Soil: City Hall Park

Ah! never shall the land forget
How gushed the life blood of her brave—
Gushed, warm with hope and valor yet
Upon the soil they fought to save.

"The Battle-Field" by William Cullen Bryant

IF Manhattan were to be dissected and each section assigned some distinguishing feature, I believe all would agree that the earth of City Hall Park must be forever connected with liberty and thus hallowed within our hearts as the site where the first thoughts of freedom saw the light of day. It was a spark, feeble and weak to be sure, but as it went along on its way the little spark gathered momentum emerging victoriously as the conflagration which established these United States. The ground should be revered always for upon it were voiced the first protests of discontent with British rule. This was some years before the Declaration of Independence when indignant colonists had assembled there to complain against the tyranny of British officals.[1] The initial rumblings of dissatisfaction with existing government regulations echoed from within the very shadows of the present City Hall, which seems only suitable and quite natural.

What we now know as City Hall Park used to be called the "Fields" or "Commons." It was situated on the outskirts of the village of New Amsterdam in the Fourth Bowery.[2] As the Commons it became the peoples' meeting place and whenever there were matters requiring public discussion or whenever the wrath of the colonists gave vent to itself, it was to the Commons that these earlier Manhattanites convened. When there was rejoicing or dissatisfaction—it was to the Commons that the populace betook itself. Here their voices gave out in a

23

common cry; here they aired their grievances; here these early patriots daringly suggested a new nation, which, as Lincoln uttered nearly a century later should be "conceived in liberty" . . . Certainly the site is peopled by the sentiments of these Sons of Liberty, whose deeds are legendary and many of whom were later to perish under most cruel and inhuman circumstances.

In 1764 the Fields or Commons was the scene of a violent demonstration against the impressment of seamen from the Colonies. In those days it was the practice when a ship lacked a full crew, to kidnap or "shanghai" available men to fill in. This was called "impressment" and later such acts developed into one of the primary factors leading to the War of 1812. It so happened that in 1764 four colonists, fishermen, were carried aboard a tender from a man-of-war on the Halifax station. The following day, while the Captain of the tender was ashore, the boat was dragged to the Commons where it was burned. The Captain denied pressing the fishermen who thereupon were released.[3]

The next year the Sons of Liberty met at the Commons to protest against the Stamp Act. There is no doubt but what this demonstration was the beginning of the American Revolution which took ten years to come to a head. The actual contention was not the fact that the Colonists were forced to buy stamps which the mother country had imposed on many commodities. Objection arose from the fact that England was levying a tax against a people who had had no share in representation. "Taxation without representation" became the byword of the Sons of Liberty. When a British ship carrying the first consignment of stamps anchored off Fort George, that October day became one of gloom for the Colonies. Flags were flown at half-mast and the Sons of Liberty prepared to prevent distribution of the stamps.

Cadawallader Colden, then Lt. Governor in charge of the Fort, asserted that he was determined to have the stamps distributed; but he had reckoned without taking into consideration the temper prevailing amongst the Colonies for the people were equally resolved that the stamps should not be distributed. On November 1, 1765, which was a Friday, the day dawned ominously with the ringing of bells, the firing of guns and half-masted flags. Liberty was the subject of many talks. Everywhere there were gatherings of people who had left their daily tasks to meet and discuss "taxation without representation."

To the Commons they went, a veritable uprising, thence to the Fort where they demanded the stamps. Unsuccessful, they returned to the Commons and erected a gibbet from which Cadawallader Colden was hung in effigy. Thus emboldened, the mob—for by this time excitement was running high—daringly carried the scaffold and effigies to the Fort.

They threw stones at the soldiers thence repaired to the Bowling Green where the Governor's carriage was thrown into a huge bonfire which the Sons of Liberty had ignited.

Thus so closely linked with the fight for freedom, it seems only fitting that City Hall Park should play some part in the eventual attainment of liberty. And so it did—for when the die had finally been cast, the Declaration of Independence was read from the Commons. The crowd went wild with enthusiasm. There is a tablet on City Hall commemorating the reading of the Declaration of Independence.

When New York was still New Amsterdam the frugal Dutch would occasionally drive their cattle along a crude cow path past Chatham Street, now Park Row, and the hungry cattle grazed just about where the Commons later appeared. After the land had passed into British hands it was decreed that a public gallows be erected on this site. This decree was executed in July 1727, the gallows being built at the upper end of what we now know as City Hall Park.[4]

On the north side of the present Chambers Street, probably near Broadway, there existed a negro cemetary.[5] This grim reminder of New York's past was brought to the notice of present day Gothamites when excavations for the Municipal Building were commenced. Many historical relics have been unearthed during the city's ceaseless process of digging—to construct new subways (as long as I can remember there has always been a subway under construction on Manhattan)—to erect new skyscrapers and the many other reasons for which people are forever disemboweling Manhattan's crust. But this time the workmen engaged to excavate for the foundation of the Municipal Building came upon bones and skeletons which had been girded by heavy iron belts and chains, instead of the usual objects the workmen had been wont to uncover during the course of their operations.

Not that skeletons and bones have not been dug out of Manhattan's earth before, as often they have been uncovered in the vicinity of long forgotten burial grounds. In 1850 workmen who were excavating at the northwest corner of Morris Street and Broadway came across skulls. Though it was at first supposed that these skulls represented cruel evidences of murders committed by the English garrison during the Revolutionary War, actually the workmen had struck an old graveyard which had been transferred as far back as 1677.[6]

However, skeletons in chains . . . this was a novel occurrence in New York where strange and unusual things are daily events. Blasé New Yorkers who take most things in their stride began to wonder. History books were consulted and delving back into Manhattan's history a connection was found for the remains were believed by some to have been

25

the victims of the terrible Negro Plot of 1741.[7] It was a dark and shameful episode projecting itself out of the past.

When the last wintry blast was blowing in from the Battery, and the Colonists were preparing the welcome spring soon to arrive in all its ephemeral glory, the few thousand souls comprising Manhattan arose one morning to a terrible realization. Rumor spread like wildfire. The negor slaves, so it was said, were plotting to burn the city along with all white inhabitants and establish their own government with a black king. This was not a new idea as thirty years before the city was faced with a similar situation.

On February 28 of the year of which we now speak, 1741, a robbery was traced to Hughson's, a low tavern situated on the west side near the Hudson River, then popular as the rendevouz of negroes. It was thought at that time that many of the negro slaves who frequented Hughson's used to dispose of stolen goods on the premises. The following month, March 18, a fire was discovered in the Governor's house and it soon spread to some of the surrounding buildings. A few days later the Colonists were further alarmed by the mysterious burning of Captain Warren's house. Next to be fired were Van Zandts storehouse, then the Thompson house—all of which culminated in the discovery of live coals under John Murray's stable.[8]

The people's minds went back thirty years to the Negro Riot of 1712. Could this be a repetition of that terrible calamity which visited the settlement? The Island was inundated by a wave of horrible suspicion and gloom as the inhabitants prepared to evacuate and take shelter in the farms. It was thought that the negro slaves were conspiring to burn and capture the city.

Meanwhile, Mary Burton, who was Hughson's indentured servant, was held as a witness in the robbery which had been traced to Hughson's. When questioned about the plot she maintained a stubborn silence until her interrogators pointed out the alternative of jail, which seemed to bear such weight on the frightened negress that she proceded to spin a yarn of such magnitude as to astonish the Colonists. Mary, with the imagination and awe for the unnatural peculiar to her race, for though she was light the blood of primitive Africans surged through her veins, concocted a tale implicating Hughson, his wife and three blacks. She said the conspirators met at Hughson's where they outlined a gigantic plot to destroy all whites, set up Hughson as Governor and a negro king. Next she brought in Peggy, an Irish girl of many aliases, who was known to be a prostitute to the negroes and who was then mistress of a big black named Caesar. Fantastic tales were spun, each day the names of new plotters were added to the growing list; Mary was making the most of the notoriety she was receiving, and basking in the aura of astonishment created by those who gullibly accepted her story.

In normal times and under ordinary circumstances, Mary Burton's testimony would have gained little credence. The times, however, were not normal and the people were in a state bordering hysteria as each day Mary and the other witnesses who, to save their own necks, tightened the noose about someone else's, divulged new information increasing the magnitude of the plot. It was remembered that for long the slaves had been restive under their bondage and often they were heard to utter threats against their masters. Coupled with this there were still many left to tell of the dreadful experiences of thirty years previous, which, of course, always lurked in the backs of people's minds. The slaves at this time comprised one sixth of the 12,000 population.[9]

Mary Burton's accusations fell upon fertile ears. These early New Yorkers were psychologically prepared for just such a happening as this ignorant slave girl described the blacks to be plotting. Peggy also made a confession which she later retracted when she found that it did not secure her pardon.

There was a trial, to be sure . . . English jurisprudence guaranteed it to the accused. But according to the law of that time a slave could not testify against a white person, yet Mary Burton was permitted to testify against Peggy, which proves that the law was not carried out to the letter. The people were so aroused that judgment had, of necessity, to be partial. It was so biased, in fact, that there was not one lawyer in the Colony who would lift a finger in defense of the ignorant blacks, many of whom were falsely accused and could have had as much to do with the Nego Plot as they could with writing an artistic appreciation of Shakespearean heroines.

Executions began in May when two blacks paid the penalty. The executioners next turned their attention to the Hughsons and Peggy, all of whom were hanged. Believing mere hanging not sufficient punishment, Hughson's body was hung in chains to swing and decay amidst the April breezes blowing in from the Battery. A few days later a negroe's body was placed beside that of Hughson. This display of justice and punishment—depraved, revolting and cruel as it was—hung where all could see, the decomposed bodies giving off such foul orders to be dissipated by the gentle breezes blowing in from the bay. As the sun's rays changed in intensity—for it was then April and summer was well on its way—the bodies began to drip, Hughson's body finally bursting and filled the air with as vile a stench as the city has known.

Reason had fled. The city was activated by a wild terror and the strange panic of assusations which had sprung up. Suspicion reared its ugly head as the Colony was swept by a sudden overpowering fear, a panic which had been produced by the testimony brought out at the trial, this apparently changing daily in accordance with the attention given the witnesses. In the wake of this reign of terror 154 negroes were imprisoned, of whom 14 were burned at the stake, 18 hanged, 71 transported and the rest pardoned. There were 24 whites arrested, four of whom were executed, the Hughson couple, Peggy and a priest named Ury.[10]

Now, in the time of good Queen Ann the penalty of death was imposed for the commission of any one of forty crimes. If the criminal were a white man, the prescribed form of death was by hanging; if he were a negro the manner in which he paid the penalty was left to the judge.[11] Hence, it can be seen that the negroes implicated in the conspiracy were subjected to whatever penalty the judge imposed. Sentences were carried out on these unhappy creatures on a spot located at the old intersection of Pearl and Chatham Streets. Some were hung on an island which existed in the center of the Fresh Water Pond.[12] Some were executed on the Commons.

Many who perished thus were innocent victims of mob hysteria, prevailing in the city. No doubt those of the victims who were black were interred near to where their tortured bodies writhed in the torments of an agonizing death. Possibly their remains were buried in the Negro Cemetary previously mentioned. But Lewis avers, and his theory is a likely one, that after sentence was carried out on the Commons, the hapless negroes were burned at the stake, their bones were covered with earth and left on the spot where their cries of stress had wrent the still air.

And nearly two centuries later, when New York undertook to construct the Municipal Building, this evidence of cruelty was unearthed—this evidence of a dark spot on Colonial history—for one can condone misjudgment, one forgive a mistake, but one cannot pardon unspeakable tortures and cruelties which a wildly hysterical mob inflicted on the creatures implicated in the Negro Plot, many of whom were too ignorant to conceive of a plot of such magnitude as they were supposed to have thought out, and most of whom were, in a last analysis, scape goats, for in order to escape or to gain more time each victim accused others. Thus it went on, a continuous travesty upon Colonial justice. When it was over Mary Burton received the hundred pounds reward and the pardon promised her, and the city set apart Sept. 24 as a general day of thanksgiving for having been saved from destruction.

By 1809 the Commons was quite popular. The suggestive gallows had been removed and the burial ground was transferred to another section, thus eliminating long standing objections on the part of surrounding property owners. The Commons was coming into its own as Manhattan's village square. Its shaded footpaths attracted strollers who would prominade within its confines, but we learn from a record of that time, however, that the elite did not deign to confer their presence on the Commons, as, according to their complaint, it had become too much like its name. They favored Broadway where it was quite fashionable to prominade between the hours of 11 and 3.[13]

Be that as it may, however, some of the city's richest citizens lived around it and nearly all the merchants of New York resided below Chambers Street.[14] There were good hotels in the vicinity as well as the old Park Theatre, traditionally famous as having had General Washington as its honored spectator on more than one occasion.

The City Hall Park today is like an oasis. Emerging out of the canyons of lower Broadway one comes upon a spot of green, with benches conveniently placed, offering a brief respite and trees which invite one to enjoy the coolness of their shade. In winter of course, the Park's attire is different, but it is still an oasis in the sense that after trodding along byways hemmed in by huge skyscrapers one comes upon this irregular plot of ground where sparsley planted trees form a pleasant backdrop from which the City Hall gracefully emerges.

In 1812 or thereabouts the comparison would not have been so apparent. Coming up Broadway the stroller would have seen from afar the lovely City Hall which had been erected but two years previously. A fine blending of French Renaissance and American Colonial design it stood then, as it does now, in City Hall Park surrounded by elm, willow, poplar and catalpa trees. The City Hall is still reputed to be one of the finest examples of this particular style of architecture extant. Certain it is that even to one unfamiliar with its architectural beauties it presents a degnified yet restful appearance.

The Park is interlaced with cement walks along which benches are conveniently placed. It is a curious thing to note that seldom does one find the benches occupied by these business men and women of the neighborhood except perhaps during a lunch hour. At that time people employed in surrounding office buildings emerge for a breath of air. Sometimes they bring their lunch. One does find though that the benches are put to good use by the great number of hoboes who drift over from the Bowery. Aimless, homeless and shiftless—there they sit, watching people coming in and out of the subway kiosks or speculating on the fate which brought them there. They discuss all world problems and have a solution for nearly all the baffling enigmas confronting mankind. These discussions consume a large part of their time, for truth is, Trinity's melodious chimes, gently imparting the passage of time, registers not upon their carefree minds, except, perhaps, as a

29

reminder to seek a free meal or a free cot over on the nearby Bowery. These vagrants, for in reality they have neither homes nor the wherewithal to sustain themselves, follow a regular routine, traversing certain streets at a regular time, sooner or later taking in City Hall Park as part of their given course.

True it is that quite a few of these people are predisposed to inflict themselves on other parks of the city. Some prefer Madison Square Park and some will go as far uptown as Bryant Park, but one is always sure to find that they are well represented at City Hall Park. The old Commons serves as their parlor and office, a parlor and office which is probably the most inspiring in all Gotham to a liberty loving people.

The spirit of freedom still lives in this old Park. It manifests itself in the beautiful statue of the great patriot Nathan Hale, whose dying words, "I only regret that I have but one life to lose for my country" have lived on these many years. It is unfurled with the flag atop Liberty Pole, to the west of City Hall, for during the years between 1766 and 1776 the brave Sons of Liberty hoisted five successive poles before the English relinquished the Colonies.[15] It peers out of the words of the plaque on City Hall:

"Near this spot in the presence of General Washington the Declaration of Independence was read and published to the American Army, July 9, 1776."

It flies with the very pigeons which blithely flap their wings and bask in the sun's rays. It is reflected in the eyes of the shoe shine boys, who with their shine boxes slung carelessly over their shoulders, patrol the Park with their invitations of "Shine Mister?"

Certainly it is only proper that into the midst of this tradition of liberty and freedom, New York's beautiful City Hall should be situated. This edifice, gracing the north section of the Park, required slightly less than ten years to build. It embodies the combined efforts of a Frenchman, a Scotchman and then a second Frenchman. The design of the building has been credited to the French architect, Joseph F. Mangin, senior partner of the firm Mangin and McComb, which won the award for the best design submitted. Mangin was associated with John McComb but there seems to have been some disagreement between the two architects for Mangin's name does not appear in connection with subsequent matters relating to the building's construction. In fact, the Frenchman did not attend the ceremonies held in laying the cornerstone, and the new committee appointed John McComb to supervise the building's construction.

Nothing was spared to make this seat of New York City's government the finest in the country. Marble was brought from West Stockbridge at great trouble and expense for transporting the stones over the Berkshires was a trying task, and many times the architect had to supervise the building of roads and the strengthening of bridges in order to ship the marble to New York.[16] Copper for the roof was imported from England. When the building was completed at a cost of over half a million dollars, the City Hall was undisputedly one of the most beautiful buildings to be constructed in the United States. Curiously enough, though the front and two sides of City Hall were constructed of the whitest of marble, ordinary brownstone was used in building the rear. It was thought at the time that the city would never grow beyond the City Hall and the civil authorities deemed it wasteful to use marble in building the north side.

Though early engravings show the City Hall to have been white, today it is a dull weather beaten brown. The steps leading up to the main entrance have been worn thin by the constant tread of the many people passing under the portico. Facing the inside of the main entrance is the circular staircase which is a remarkable architectural feature, due to the fact that no support is visible. It is said that when the building was first opened, people were afraid to ascend the staircase and it was necessary to post two soldiers, one at each side to reassure the public.

At the top of the stairway facing the front of the building is the Governor's Room. Originally intended to serve as the Governor's office when he happened to be in New York City, it has been put to a variety of uses. The famous portrait of George Washington painted by Trumbull still hangs in this room.

As one leaves the Governor's Room, to the right is the City Council Room, a particularly interesting feature of which is a balcony, again constructed without any visible means of support. The room is richly panelled in mahogany and is decorated by one statue of Thomas Jefferson. In the center of the room are seats and desks for the 17 Councilmen, so arranged that 10, representing the majority, are on one side and 7, the minority, on the other.

At the opposite end of the hall is located the Board of Estimate Chamber where one may admire beautiful crystal chandeliers which seem to harmonize quite well with the white woodwork and panelling. Throughout all the halls and corridors are hung portraits of men who have distinguished themselves in government. The Mayor's Suite, the Aldermanic Rooms and various other portions of City Hall are all decorated with valuable paintings, antique furniture and delecate carvings making the building a veritable treasure house of art objects.

31

The City Hall is such a lovely building that one often wishes it were landscaped in a style befitting its elegance. As it is, though, considering the way in which the land seems to be swallowed up in Manhattan, one must be grateful for the few trees and walks which the city Fathers judiciously have seen fit to retain against onsloughts made by encroaching business buildings.

CHAPTER NOTES

1. Moss, Frank, "The American Metropolis," Vol. II, p. 247.
2. Wilson, James Grant, "Memorial History of New York," Vol. I, p. 190.
3. Ibid., Vol. II, p. 347.
4. Ibid., Vol. II, p. 165.
5. Ibid., Vol. II, P. 165.
6. Moss, Frank, "The American Metropolis," Vol. II, p. 137.
7. Lewis, Alfred Henry, "Nation-Famous New York Murders," p. 122.
8. Headley, J. T., "Pen and Pencil Sketches of the Great Riots," p. 29.
9. Hardie, James, "Description of the City of New York" p. 51.
10. Booth, Mary L., "History of the City of New York," Vol. I, p. 368.
11. Lewis, Alfred Henry, "Nation-Famous New York Murders," p. 123.
12. Ladies of the Mission, "The Old Brewery and the New Mission House," p. 16.
13. Lambert, John, "North America," p. 58.
14. Barrett, Walter, "The Old Merchants of New York City," Vol. I, p. 1.
15. Federal Writers' Project, "New York City Guide," p. 96.
16. Henderson, Helen Weston, "A Loiterer in New York," p. 137.

The Park and City Hall

CHAPTER FOUR

Newspaper Row

*To speak his thoughts is every
freeman's right,
In peace and war, in council
and fight.*

Homer, Illiad Bk. II

I T is difficult to calculate with any degree of accuracy the important effect which the printed word has on a people. The influence of newspapers on moulding the general shape of public opinion cannot be overestimated. Just as water—gently, almost imperceptibly seeping into the earth gives sustenance to plant life, so does the newspaper nourish the roots of common thought. Yet, such intellectual food was not always available through reading a newspaper, for time was then a newspaper would not dare to venture any manifestation of opinion. It supplied the news, unembellished, cut and dried as it was. The right to express a thought in print or to criticize public officers is our heritage only because our forefathers fought to make it so. And no where was this so true as in the vicinity of the little strip which New Yorkers have affectionately dubbed "Newspaper Row."

Newspaper Row is really a hypothetical term originated during the last decade of the last Century. It applied to the group of buildings overlooking Park Row because so many newspaper offices were located there. Though short in length, it has a history fascinatingly rich in tradition. It lies to one side of City Hall, representing the background of New York City's press—a background supplying both prestige and progress to a profession upon which we depend and so much depends. It was the Charles Anderson Danas, the Bryants, the Greeleys and those other early newspaper men who labored long and hard to raise the city's papers into the realm of journalistic enterprise. It was here, too, that the famous war correspondent, Richard Harding Davis, obtained his first job in New York. Davis was hired by Arthur Brisbane who was then managing editor of "The Evening Sun." He started at $30 a week.[1] Davis covered the news of six wars and when he was not reporting he wrote fiction and articles. When he started to work for "The Evening Sun" that journal had already become well established. Charles Anderson Dana had purchased it in 1868 and under his able guidance the paper increased its circulation.

At one time "The Evening Sun" was housed in the old Tammany building at Frankfort Street and Park Row, next door to the Tribune's building. During this time there was bitter litigation between owners of the two buildings which was caused by the projection across the line of the Sun building of a huge stone in the northern wall of the Tribune building. Even though this stone was set far below the street surface, it was the cause of a pitched legal action.[2]

Newspaper Row had of necessity to be situated in Lower Manhattan. First and foremost, the raw materials were readily available. Then there was the matter of transportation. Park Row and the City Hall area were easily accessible from many parts. Aside from this, Lower Manhattan was the first to be settled and it would neither be wise nor expedient to print a paper in a remote part and then travel through wilderness to accomplish distribution. But this does not mean that the Park Row section was selected for the express purpose of forming what we now know as Newspaper Row, for such was not the case. Newspaper Row was somewhat like Topsy in this respect: It just grew. It could have been anyplace in Lower Manhattan, but it just happened to be around Park Row.

The first newspaper published in Manhattan was the "New York Gazette" which William Bradford printed.[3] The second newspaper made its premier appearance to Colonial Manhattanites on Nov. 5, 1733. It was published by Peter Zenger who had been an apprentice of Bradford's. He called his paper "The New York Weekly Journal."[4] Though this second paper lasted only 19 years, it brought about enduring results. It was as a direct result of Zenger's trial for seditious libel that freedom of the press was established, a privilege still enjoyed by American newspapers.

At the time of the trial New York was a Crown Colony. The Dutch, who had first settled New Amsterdam were still here, but the stronger influence was that exerted by the British. English customs were very much in evidence and, of course, English jurisprudence was in operation. Col. William Cosby was Governor. He had started his career well enough, showing his good-will towards the Colony by remaining in

England six months longer than he had planned to prevent passage of a sugar bill which would have acted to the detriment of Colonial trade.[5] Later, the Governor began to evince signs that he was becoming contemptuous of the Colonies, an attitude that was manifested in various ways but which became particularly obnoxious during the Zenger trial.

Zenger was not in agreement with policies of the Government party and his paper carried caustic comments and articles of a satirical character directed against the different branches of government. He fearlessly attacked the corrupt and arbitrary administration of the tyranical Governor Cosby for which reason he was finally arrested and held for trial. Zenger discussed frankly all the grievances which he had against the government and which were shared by most of his readers. The Council ordered Nos. 7, 47, 48 and 49 of Zenger's paper to be burned as libelous and deditious, but the officials refused to obey. The sheriff then ordered one of his negroes to perform the duty which the others had refused. This order was carried out within a stone's throw of the present Park Row, taking place on the east side of what is now City Hall Park. The citizens showed their contempt for this decision by remaining away as the Park was empty of spectators when Zenger's paper was burned.[6]

Zenger was fortunate in retaining as his lawyer Andrew Hamilton who was then in his eightieth year. The venerable lawyer eloquently defended his client who was acquitted amidst triumphant exclamations of those who witnessed the trial. The verdict won unanimous approval throughout the city and the distinguished jurist, through whose logical presentation of the case the happy verdict came about, was voted the freedom of the city "for the remarkable service done to the inhabitants of this city and colony by his defense of the rights of mankind and the liberty of the press."[7]

Thus the first step towards emancipation of the New York press was inaugurated. Newspapers were not however, completely free to print whatever they wished due to the old English law of libel then vigorously enforced in the Colonies. It remained for another Hamilton, Alexander, this time, to unloosen the fetters binding free speech by working for modification of this libel law.[8] It will be seen from this that the establishment of freedom of the press in New York is a direct result of the efforts of two Hamiltons. To them we are indebeted for achieving this great service, so necessary if a free land is to remain free.

After the two Hamiltons had fought for this small guarantee of freedom of the press certain innovations made their appearance in New York newspapers. Editorials took on a new zest. Previously aspirants for political office used the pamphlet as a mode of expression, but in the early days of the Republic views of a political nature began to be embodied into editorials. To supplement these views and emphasize the editorials, cartoons were devised. The initial appearance of the cartoon is said to have been in Benjamin Franklin's "Pennsylvania Gazette" for May 9, 1754.[9]

The appearance of a Newspaper Row and its subsequent expansion ran parallel to the political and industrial development of the United States. During the hundred years following the signing of the Declaration of Independence the young nation was faced with grave and difficult problems—all of which were reflected in newspapers of the day. There were the important questions relating to the new Government and always in the background was the perennial slavery question, which seems to have been a problem sporadically breaking out into print. In addition, there still had to be settled the suffrage question. To baffle and bewilder these early public servants whose duty it was to weld into good Americans the heterogeneous masses entering the new nation, were numerous other problems of a less serious nature. All these conditions served to create doubts in people's minds with the result of a splitting of public opinion: Definite sides were taken. Newspapers did likewise, following the general trend of public opinion and it was not long before the press had developed fixed partisan characters. Simultaneous with the increase in the number of causes was growth in the number of newspapers. This was particularly true in New York. In 1776 four papers were published; in 1810 the number had increased to 66; in 1828 to 161; in 1840 to 245 and in 1850 there were 428 publications printed in New York.[10] In 1850 there were 50 daily, weekly, monthly and semi-monthly journals published in New York City.[11] By 1890 there were hundreds of papers published in New York, many of which were printed in the Newspaper Row vicinity.

Given a cause to fight for, unhampered by arbitrary rulings of corrupt officals and unrestrained by long outmoded statutes, papers were born, then nourished by legislative measures enacted to insure their continued freedom. Newspaper Row was at last free to develop—to start surmounting the obstacles leading to the zenith of that golden era of journalistic enterprise—the 1890's. It was then in truth that Newspaper Row had an opportunity to burst forth in bloom, exhibiting simultaneously its potentialities as a source of instruction and amusement as well as news. It began to mold itself into a positive shape, for by that time Newspaper Row was well on its established course.

At one time the "Row" was the location of all the principal New York dailies. The "Sun" and "Tribune" were next to each other, while further on the "Times" "World" and "Herald" were printed. The Morning and Evening Journal were published a little off Park Row on William Street. The "Evening Post" was published in a building at

Broadway and Fulton Street. All these papers had their individual histories, fraught with bitter and antagonistic duels: Their editors fought not only with caustic words but oft times their differences were accentuated by occasional flashing of arms. Though each was established with the embodiment of different principles, collectively they represented various manifestations of the growing metropolis. Each paper had its own ideas: Each advocated the practice of those ideas.

The oldest paper now published in New York is "The Evening Post" (now called "The Post"). This publication originated as the official organ of the Federalist Party, under direction of Alexander Hamilton. The first issue appeared for sale Nov. 16, 1801. It was edited by William Coleman who seems to have been kept busy warring off attacks from Chettham in "The American Journal" and Duane in "The Aurora," both Republican sheets.[12] William Cullen Bryant took over the editorship in 1829. Under Bryant "the Evening Post" rose to be one of the most important organs of the Democratic Party, though towards the Civil War it tended to assume a Republican attitude. While political matters were commonly discussed in all papers, the bearded poet did not neglect the literary side of "The Evening Post." Contributions were printed from such leading writers as Cooper, Irving, Halleck and other literary lights of the day. It was an expansive era for English and American literature; some of the best material of the day found its way into the columns of "The Evening Post."

Bryant, who could raise his voice in rich melodious description or point out the countless wonders of nature, when the occasion demanded could also pen the scathing epithets which sometimes appeared in "The Evening Post." On the death of President Harrison every newspaper in New York went into mourning: that is, every newspaper except "The Evening Post." Bryant said he regretted the death of Gen. Harrison only because he did not live long enough to prove his incapacity for the office of President.[13] Again, when Nicholas Biddle the financier, passed on Bryant reported that ". . . After bringing thousands to utter poverty, by the frauds and extravagances of his bank, he passed the close of his life in an elegant leisure at his country seat on the Delaware. If he had met with his deserts, he would have passed it in the penitentiary."[14] This led Philip Hone to remark, "How such a black hearted misanthrope as Bryant should possess an imagination teeming with beautiful poetical images astonishes me; one would as soon expect to extract drops of honey from the fangs of a rattlesnake."[15]

Be that as it may, however, one cannot lose sight of the fact that Bryant was a personality of many admirable phases. He was like a highly cut diamond, so to speak, each faucet representing an activity, yet each scintillating with the same degree of intensity as its neighbor.

He was not only a rare and gifted poet, who could evoke visions of strange beauty and loveliness through his manipulation of words, but he was a journalist of the first order. Aside from these abilities, he was a silver-tongued orator and was often called upon to preside at public functions. Bryant's "Evening Post" was located at 41 Nassau Street, near Liberty Street.

"The New York Morning Herald" another daily of those days, was projected and edited by James Gordon Bennett who with his son is acclaimed as one of the most remarkable editors this country has produced.[16] The first issue was released on May 6, 1835 from a cellar at 20 Wall Street.[17] Though it started as a "yellow journal" the "yellowness" soon faded and the paper became one of the nation's foremost newspapers. Bennett sent Stanley to Africa to look for Livingston. He also originated the interview. He is said to have employed 63 additional correspondents to report the Civil War at a cost of $525,000 during the four years. All in all, he had originality and a keen sense of selecting items appropriate for an all-round paper. He was forever adding new features and specialties to the paper. At the time of his death he had built up the most important and valuable newspaper in the country, due as much to his business acumen as to his discrimination as to what should go into a good paper.

The Tribune was established April 10, 1841 by Horace Greeley, growing out of the earlier Whig "Log Cabin." During the time when Newspaper Row was an actuality, for it has since practically disappeared, the Tribune Building was on Spruce and Nassau Streets. Greeley had strong prejudices against women suffrage, lax divorce laws and theatres but he was also an anti-slavery leader and he exercised great influence in the movement for the abolition of slavery.[18] Greeley's attitude in this respect provoked caustic criticism from the South and made bitter enemies for him in the North. Among the latter was Bennet, who usually took issue with Greeley on any subject that Greeley supported.

Such able publishers as Greeley and Bennett did much to elevate the levels of news reporting in spite of the fact that their respective editorships were tinged with personal antagonism sometimes finding vent in the most acrimonious charges. Though both were capable journalists, giving a tremendous impetus to the newspaper profession, they also devoted much time, energy and space to their own feud. At one time Bennett, whose facile pen lent itself with equal enthusiasm to vitriolic attacks or editorials of glowing praise, printed an editorial suggesting that Horace Greeley be tried for murder for bringing about the Battle of Bull Run.[19] It was an era of vituperative journalism. Editors called each other such names as today would win the victim a libel suit. It was no wonder that newspaper men of the time frequently had recourse to duels.

Greeley was nominated for Vice President in 1872 but the Republicans won by a landslide. This embittered the editor who died soon after. A few days before his death he said, "I was an abolitionist for years, when to be one was as much as one's life was worth even here in New York,—and the egroes have all voted against me. Whatever of talents or energy I have possessed, I have freely contributed all my life to protection, to the cause of our manufacturers; and the manufacturers have expended millions to defeat me. I even made myself ridiculous in the opinion of many whose good wishes I desired, by showing fair play and giving a fair field in the "Tribune" to Women's Rights; and the women have all gone against me."[20]

On November 29, 1872 Greeley passed away, disappointed and recoiling under the sting of frustrated hopes. Disappointed though he may have been, he exerted a strong influence upon Newspaper Row as years later editors were still emulating the principles which he introduced.

Even "The New York Herald" lamented Greeley's passing for when news of the editor's death reached that paper, the next editions appeared with the following: "As the happy suggestions of the Thanksgiving season are in every heart, the philosopher and philanthropist, who helped probably more than any contemporaneous American to secure the blessings for which thanks are given, has yielded up his mortal spirit and quietly and peacefully gilded out with the tide. The world was better and nobler for his being in it, and yet he died of a broken heart. . . ."[21]

It is a curious coincidence that though the founders of these two papers wrangled interminably, in after years the two publications were merged and the papers founded by Bennett and Greeley are now combined and known as "The New York Herald Tribune."

Across the Park Row from City Hall Park the Pulitizer Building rears its mass of brownstone. This is now serving as an office building but in the good old days of Newspaper Row, it was the place from which "The New York World" was published. This paper started as a religious publication, bringing out its first issue on June 1, 1860.[22] Joseph Pulitzer—the Horatio Alger of the newspaper world—bought "The World" from Jay Gould on May 9, 1883 at a cost reputed to have been $346,000.[23] When Pulitzer bought the paper it had an anemic circulation of less than 12,000 copies a day which at the end of four years had reached the robust circulation of 200,000 copies per day.[24]

Pulitzer may be said to have taken over the reigns of newspaper editing where others left off. Bryant, Bennett and Greeley had penned their last word. The spurt of activity occasioned by the slavery question, thence the Civil War and reconstruction, had spent itself out. Editorials lacked fire and enthusiasm previously displayed. It was an opportune time for Joseph Pulitzer to display his talents. He came, he saw and he conquered the Row as it had never been conquered before.

Newspaper Row has disappeared as curiously as it appeared. The only paper printed in the old Row is "The Sun." All the others have moved from the locality. Perhaps someday the papers will congregate at another point and form another Newspaper Row. Who knows? One knows only that all is changing; that what was here yesterday has disappeared by the morrow. What was a certainty one day is only "water under the bridge" the following. This is what we have experienced in this city of ours; this is what we have come to expect; a constant face-lifting.

CHAPTER NOTES

1. Downey, Fairfax, "Richard Harding Davis; His Day," p. 55.
2. Moss, Frank, "The American Metropolis," Vol. I, p. 198.
3. Mayes, Martin, "The Development of the Press in the United States," p. 30.
4. Lee, James Melvin, "History of American Journalism," p. 38.
5. Wilson, James Grant, "Memorial History of New York," Vol. II, p. 209.
6. Ibid., Vol. II, p. 238.
7. Ibid., Vol. IV, p. 135.
8. Ibid., Vol. IV, p. 136.
9. Lee, James Melvin, "History of American Journalism," p. 78.
10. Payne, George Henry, "History of Journalism in the United States," p. 393.
11. Booth, Mary L., "History of the City of New York," Vol. II, p. 734.
12. Lee, James Melvin, "History of American Journalism," p. 137.
13. Hone, Philip, "Diary of Philip Hone," edited by Allan Nevins, entry dated April 6, 1841, p. 556.
14. "The New York Evening Post," for Feb. 28, 1844, p. 2 col. 1.
15. Hone, Philip, "Diary of Philip Hone," edited by Allan Nevins, entry dated Feb. 28, 1844, p. 686.
16. Villard, Oswald Garrison, "Some Newspapers and Newspaper-Men," p. 274.
17. Hudson, Frederic, "Journalism in the United States," p. 429.

18. Parton, James, "The Life of Horace Greeley," Chapter XVI, p. 200-217.
19. Payne, George Henry, "History of Journalism in the United States," p. 314.
20. Ibid., p. 332.
21. "The New York Herald," for Nov. 30, 1872, p. 3 col. 1.
22. Lee, James Melvin, "History of American Journalism," p. 269.
23. Seitz, Don C., "Joseph Pulitzer: His Life and Letters," p. 129.
24. Ireland, Alleyne, "Joseph Pulitzer; Reminiscences of a Secretary," p. 44.

Park Row and Bridge Entrance

CHAPTER FIVE

Chinatown

"Oh, East is East, and West is
West, and never the twain
shall meet,
Till Earth and Sky stand presently
at God's great Judgment Seat;

Rudyard Kipling

WHAT a medley of thoughts are summoned to mind at the mention of Chinatown! Reminiscent of the sweet smell imparted by burning sandlewood, it is a place of legendary mysticism; a place where, as the old China gradually releases its hold to the new and modern China—absorbing more and more occidental habits and customs—east becomes partly west and the twain do meet.

The vice and unlawful enterprises which flourished in Chinatown thirty years ago—conditions which found themselves depicted in many police and welfare reports—have dwindled into something one reads about in mystery stories. The physical aspects, however, have undergone very little change. The streets are still slightly more than crooked alleys, wending their complicated yet aimless ways past a curio shop here or a grocery store there, until they finally desist and in the sheer futility of it all, come to an abrupt halt.

The district known as "Chinatown" consists of Pell, Mott and Doyers Streets. Picturesque restaurants and shops line both sides of these streets with once in a while an overhanging balcony protruding from a building. At night these balconies are illuminated by colorful lanterns which diffuse lights of various shades. Sometimes there is a banner or a flag draped over the balcony railing. Chinatown certainly does not lack in what is known as "atmosphere" and what it may lack, the sight seeing guides are sure to invent.

In the early part of the Nineteenth Century Chinatown was mainly settled by Germans with a scattering of Irish families. These people were quite home-loving people living in respectable harmony with their neighbors. It was the time when sceptics were astounded by the opening of the Erie Canal; illuminating gas saw its way into many buildings, Edwin Forrest, the great American actor was scoring phenominal success in "Othello" and for the second time in the history of these United States, an Adams was president. In short, it was the year 1825.

There were no Chinamen in Chinatown. In fact, if local historians are correct, the first Chinese did not appear in Mott Street until 1858.[1] Fourteen years later there were 12 and by the time the year 1880 rolled around 700 souls of oriental blood had settled in the little region of New York's Chinatown. Soon this number increased to between an estimated 10,000 and 15,000. In later years many of these have emigrated to outlying districts until today, though Chinatown is headquarters for 18,000 Chinese, the actual population of Chinatown is only around 4,000.[2]

My first impressions of Chinatown were gained at the age of seven, for that is how old I was when I first viewed the wonders of this place so foreign to what I had ever seen before. Sensations received then still remain with me, though they seem to be less vivid as the years go by. What simple things impress the fertile brain of a child! The beautiful colors of an embroidered robe; the way a shaft of light strikes a plate glass window; the sing-song cadense of the Chinese language! No matter how many years intervene, fragments of that first impression of Chinatown are always hovering about in my mind. Earlier impressions loom high upon the vision of my horizon, interminably mingling themselves with later day conceptions. I still see the venerable Chinaman, queue hanging down his back, pitter-pattering along Pell, Mott or Doyers Streets; I still shudder with apprehension when I remember with what qualms I trod the narrow angular little Doyers Street, for I had been led to expect that any minute there would be an exchange of hatchets between warring tongs.

These tongs were certainly a problem to those bulwarks of the law whose duty it was to maintain order. They originated as benevolent societies but in the early part of the century a degeneration transformed the tongs into the Chinese counterpart of American gangs.[3] Usually they fought for control of the gambling and opium rackets, much as the Chicago gangsters used to fight over the large revenue derived from sale of illegal liquor. However, their weapons were different, for whereas the American gangster liquidated his opponents by shooting, the Chinaman was prone to use a hatchet, the blade of which was so sharp that it would very nearly decapitate its victim.

The two most prominent tongs were the Hip Sings and the On Leongs, though less significant ones sprung up as time went on and profits from gambling and opium increased. Tongs, however, are typically American and were not introduced from China as many people believe. Though Chinese in character, they are fundamentally as American as apple pie. They were an outgrowth of the Chinaman's attempt to acclimatize himself to occidental civilization. Be that as it may, the tongs received a very lucrative income from the tributes they imposed upon gambling and opium smoking. In fact, when one considers that at one time the three small streets of Chinatown harbored as many as 200 gambling games and nearly a like number of opium dens it can readily be seen that there was money to be made in this base business.[4]

At the turn of the century Tom Lee, oft called Mayor of Chinatown, was leader of the On Leongs. Mock Duck was the Hip Sing leader. There was rivalry between these two men as well as between individual members of the tongs they controlled. When a member of one tong felt that he had been injured by a member of the other tong, the flag of the highbinder would be hoisted. That would be the signal for hatchet men to fling their hatchets at the first member of the rival tong they encountered. Many of these affrays took place in a little crook of Doyers Street which has come to be known as "Bloody Angle." The New York Police claim that more men have been murdered here than any other place of a like area in the world.

Tom Lee, the crafty old leader of the On Leongs, was an old acquaintance of my father's back in the year 1900. Lee had a curio store on Mott Street with his living quarters above. But to know more about Tom Lee you must first hear the story of our sugar bowl. It was of a white background with delicate scenes painted in red and representing rural scenes of China. Typical of the Chinese style in art, the design apparently sprang from nowhere and went off into the infinite leaving in its wake trees, bridges, flowers, etc. My mother was always very careful to take specially good care of this sugar bowl for she prized it as the first engagement present she received. My father took her to see Tom Lee to whom he introduced her as his future wife. When the visit was over Tom Lee handed her the sugar bowl with the cryptic statement that "Jelly—(my father's name is "Jerry")—had velly many lady flends." Seemingly, Tom Lee had a sense of humor.

Tom Lee lived an eventful life. Rich and powerful, he had to be on constant guard against attacks from the Hip Sing hatchet men. Once, Judge Warren W. Foster mediated and induced the On Leongs and the Hip Sings to sign a treaty of peace, however, the doves of peace scarcely had time to spread their wings when war between the tongs broke out anew and hatchets went flying around the "Bloody Angle." The Chinese Government cooperated in effecting another truce which lasted until 1909, culminating in one of the most disastrous wars in the tong's history. There followed sporadic outbreaks of wars until 1924 until which time it was often necessary to request official collaboration from the Chinese Government in quelling the blood shed. Nothing has been heard from them in years, and it would seem that tong wars are a thing of the past in Chinatown.

Chinatown abounds in restaurants. The city health authorities will tell you that these Chinese restaurants maintain the cleanest kitchens in the city. Everything is spotless and what is more inducive to a good appetite, some of the native dishes are a symphony in culinary art. This, of course, excludes such American concoctions as chop suey and chow mein which the skilled Chinese cook could not have dreamed of even during an unguarded moment. The Chinese disclaim all credit for these dubious dishes and rightfully so. But there are many Chinese plates over which a gourmet could go into ecstasies.

As I am more or less food minded, a visit to the Chinese grocery stores always intrigues me. The fresh vegetables such as Chinese cabbage, bean sprouts and tender pea pods are usually displayed in the window. There is one store in Chinatown which displays its dried foodstuffs in the window, too. There are dried shrimps and oysters and dried sea horses which are used medicinally. There are also many things such as sea slugs and shark and octopus fins which I am sure few will recognize. Sometimes the store contains a section where meat and poultry are sold. There are a few wholesale grocery stores supplying Chinese products to the many Chinese restaurants scattered through out New York and outlying districts.

Aside from the restaurants, the other shops of Chinatown are, for the most part, curio and souvenir stores. They sell delicate Chinaware, ornaments such as artificial flowers and vases, rings, necklaces and jewelry. Once my mother bought us beautiful feather fans. Mine had an ivory frame from which orange colored feathers emerged. When the fan was opened there appeared dainty painted flowers of the most delicate hues. Gladys' fan was blue. How lovely they were! I have not seen these fans on sale for many years. Perhaps they do not make them anymore. Perhaps they have been relegated to the era of smelling salts, hobble skirts, hug-me-tights and suffragettes.

Another thing that has vanished from these shops are the omnipresent bowls of lychee nuts from which the amiable Chinese store keeper always invited his customer to partake. In the olden days, we never made a purchase but that we did not leave with a few lychee nuts. Even when we called for laundry we were invited to help ourselves from the bowl of lychees which was always on the counter. Its disappearance is a sign of these changing times from which no mortal nor place can escape.

Chinatown has gone modern on us. True, the fable still persists that there is buried treasure in Doyers Street. The story goes that one of the Doyer family (for whom the street was named) concealed a fortune in the walls of his house. Every once in a while, as when they had that fire some years ago, the story is revived. But no one ever finds a trace. Possibly it is just another myth like so many others associated with this place.

Loquacious guides still horrify sightseers with tales of violence and vice connected with the old Chinese Theatre, now converted into a mission of the New York Rescue Society. Legend had it that many victims of tong wars were buried in the basement, but no evidence has ever been found to cooroborate such a rumor. Be that as it may, however, when The Rescue Society took over the Theatre they walled up many underground passages leading from the Theatre and ripped the opium bunks from the walls. The hooks still remain and Elmer from Elmira and Prunella from Paducah gaze in wide eyed horror as Chinatown guides deliver their "spiel" with special concentration directed towards these hooks. This to the accompaniment of strains of "Rock of Ages" while meetings of The Rescue Society take place upstairs.

But, as stated before, Chinatown has gone modern on us and what little remaining atmosphere there is is no doubt maintained for the benefit of the tourist trade. Though the children go to college and have learned to pronounce the English letter "r," they are still taught the culture of their forefathers. There is a Chinese school at Sixty-four Mott Street where the younger generation become proficient in reading and writing Chinese characters. There are three Chinese daily newspapers published which have a very good circulation.

A curious left-over from old Chinatown is the wall newspaper in Mott Street. Most of the space of this paper used to be devoted to the activities of the tongs, but during the last war readers avidly followed the progress of China's relentless military operations against Japan. Today, subscribers to Chinatown's wall newspaper eagerly scan the wall for news concerning China's internal strife. Modern Chinese are intensely conscious of the hapless plight of their Mother country. All over the district one finds reference to the suffering and deprivations endured by their unfortunate countrymen in China. Though of late years Chinatown has been assimilated into the great melting pot of Manhattan, and the kimonoed Chinaman, queue hanging down his back, is a thing of the past, the American Chinese maintain a sympathetic interest in Chinese affairs. One senses this in Chinatown, even though the ma-

46

jority of its residents are rapidly learning to pronounce the English "r" and the younger generation speak, think and act like other children all over the city.

CHAPTER NOTES

1. Asbury, Herbert, "The Gangs of New York," p. 300.
2. Federal Writers' Project, "New York City Guide," p. 104.
3. Federal Writers' Project, "New York Panorama," p. 119.
4. Asbury, Herbert, "The Gangs of New York," p. 302.

CHINATOWN, Mott Street, ca. 1900

CHAPTER SIX

The Tombs

"Give us, in mercy, better homes when we're a-lying in our cradles; give us better food we're a-working for our lives; give us kinder laws to bring us back when we're a-going wrong; and don't set Jail, Jail afore us, everywhere we turn."

Charles Dickens, "The Chimes, Third Quarter"

A SIDE from the beauty of line which they convey, buildings in themselves are not interesting, except to an architect or to those to whom they may have some special significance. But buildings in connection with people who have lived in them take on a glow which piques one's curiosity. They acquire a new meaning. An edifice like The Tombs, for example—now abandoned and in the process of demolishment—viewed disinterestedly, fails to awaken any spark of interest within us. But considered in the light of its prisoners, following their fate to a finality, the gloomy building on Centre Street, its very bleakness now accentuated by the fact that it lies vacant and uninhabited, arouses a latent curiosity, which pursued along its natural course, unfolds many situations and conditions no less than startling in their revelation.

By a curious quirk of fate, The Tombs emerges within the shadows of the once notorious Five Points from whence came a goodly portion of its inmates. It was connected to the Criminal Courts Building by the well known Bridge of Sighs over which many prisoners were led from their cells to the Court for trial and ultimate pronouncement of

48

sentence. Now The Tombs stands alone—isolated and forlorn—awaiting the wrecking crew which, judging from its present appearance, will soon take over.

The present Tombs is the second such to occupy this site. In 1839 an earlier Tombs stood upon the same ground, but when it became outmoded and inadequate to meet the needs of the growing city it was demolished to make way for the present Tombs. This was opened in 1901 though it was not completely occupied by the City until January 6, 1903 when appropriate ceremonies to commemorate its opening were presided over by Mayor Seth Low and Commissioner Thomas W. Hynes.

The entire structure always appeared dismal, likened often to a medeival castle. Cone shaped turrets emerged from the roof while a high stone fence surrounds the lower story. One almost expects to see the fair features of a Scott heroine peering from a tower window, or a drawbridge rise from the entrance! Instead, there is an arched doorway, now closed against the tread of human footsteps whilst the fortress awaits its final fate.

Spanning the intervening years is a bridge under which (as is true of many places in this Manhattan of ours) much water has passed. In the days of the Dutch, little thought was given to caring for prisoners and no thought at all to crime prevention, for when it was suggested in 1789 that the City buy this ground for a Park, the idea met with ridicule and was the subject of many jests.[1] Had people more foresight, they would have seen that a pleasure ground in a locality which showed every indication of becoming congested, would have had far reaching effects upon crime prevention. But the little attention devoted to social conditions is readily understandable when one realizes that the important task of supplying enough food for the settlement and of warding off attacks of Indians was a full time job leaving of little opportunity to devote to miscreants. Everyone had a job to do and there was neither time nor patience to waste on wrong-doers.

In our early history delinquents were accommodated in a place set aside for them in Fort Amsterdam. After the Stadt Huys was built offenders against the settlement were thrown into the compartment reserved as a jail. It must be remembered that at the time the Dutch occupied New Amsterdam, the Stadt Huys served as a combination City Hall, tavern, court and a jail; and in 1652 a class was assembled there for the purpose of receiving the first public instruction, under the tutelage of Jan de la Montague.[2] This Stadt Huys was built in 1642 under Governor Kieft's orders, being erected at Pearl Street and Coenties' Slip. The Stadt Huys continued to serve as a jail even after the English captured New Amsterdam, but in 1699 it was declared to be unsound

49

and the prisoners removed to the new City Hall on the site of the present U.S. Sub-Treasury Building.

This arrangement of confining prisoners within the premises of the City Hall was, at best, neither practical nor prudent. Escapes were common and accomplished with ease. The disadvantage of carrying on the municipal government and, at the same time, trying to keep a weather eye out for the prisoners, soon became apparent. After numerous complaints raised because of the facility with which inmates escaped, an Act of Assembly provided for erection of a new jail.

The next record we have of a place of confinement for transgressors is Manhattan's establishment of a real jail in 1756. This was called the New Gaol and later, by common consent, it was called the Debtor's Prison. It stood in The Fields, now known as City Hall Park.

Thus it is evident that more than one hundred years had elapsed from the time of Manhattan's settlement to the erection of a jail separate and apart from other administrative departments. This absence of the need for a jail was due no doubt to the severity of punishments meted out to wrong doers of that day. Certainly it can never be claimed that the punishment suited the crime.

In comparison with practices employed in modern penal institutions, punishments were severe and oft times cruel. This does not imply that the judiciary branch of the Colonial Government was given to gratifying barbaric urges to inflict torture, though very often in examining the old records of the time this may appear to be so. The Dutch and the Colonials whose duty it was to enforce the law were not sadists; they merely executed the forms of punishment which were in use in their mother countries, Holland and England. Thus we find the record of an offender who was scourged, gashed on the cheek, and banished for 25 years for having noisily demanded wine in a private house.[3]

An intricate system of torture existed and stipulated punishments were decreed for specific offences. The whipping post appeared in all American Colonies and as late as 1873 it was still in use in the State of Delaware.[4] Other modes of punishment were subjection to the tread mill and the ducking stool. Capital punishment was decreed for some crimes we now classify as misdemeanors. Specifically, we find that in 1784 six men and one woman were hanged; two for murder, three for "highway robbery;" and one for "housebreaking;" and one for "burglary." The following year there were six of which three were executed for "burglary;" two for "forgery;" and one for "highway robbery."[5]

Imprisonment for debt was common, though how the debtor was expected to repay his obligations once he had been clapped into prison did not seem to occur to earlier officials. Happily, we learn that the public were usually generously disposed to those sentenced for debt. The custom arose for the prisoner to suspend a shoe or a bag from his prison window into which the charitably inclined passerby would drop coins. Later, as people became more enlightened, a more rational attempt was made to have the punishment fit the crime and such drastic measures were found to be impracticable and were abandoned in favor of more feasible judicial treatment.

Some of the Dutch laws provided that "no person shall strip the fences of posts or rails under penalty, for the first offence, of being whipped and branded, and, for the second, of punishment with the cord until death ensures." Thankful to relate, in view of more humane feelings which we now display towards offenders, there does not exist a record of anyone having paid the death penalty for this offence.[6]

Inane as some of these early laws of New Amsterdam may appear to be, it must be conceded that the Dutch were unusually liberal and tolerant as regards punishment to wrong doers. While New England was seething and burning alive hundreds of innocent men and women on the hysterical pretext of witchcraftery, these unhappy persecuted creatures were often able to find refuge within the more enlightened confines of New Amsterdam. Mrs. Anne Hutchinson fled from her persecutors to a safe haven in New Amsterdam, as did Roger Williams when he was driven from Massachusetts, for while the common law of England recognized witchcraft as an offence and Queen Elizabeth, who was reputed to have been one of the most enlightened women of her time, believed it, there has never been discovered any law against witchcraftery among the Statute Laws of New Nederland, or New York, as it later was called.[7]

By 1830 the penological situation in New York had reached a deplorable state. The city's principal prison was the Bridewell which had been constructed before the Revolution—in 1775. It was outmoded and insufficient to cope with the growing needs of the young city. Population had increased to over 200,000 and along with this addition there was also a proportional increase in criminals. The citizens agitation for a new prison was eventually taken up by the Common Council which august body took constructive action towards remedying the situation. Consequently it was decided to accede to public demand and erect a new prison. The location selected was the old Collect Pond upon which the present Tombs stands its last.

At this point it may be wise to delve back a little into the days when Manhattan was valued at $24.00, for the topography of the Island was very different from what it is today. With this idea in mind it should not be difficult to visualize this Collect Pond, bounded by White and Walker streets on the north, Pearl Street on the south, Mulberry Street on the east and Elm Street on the west. This pond drained into the North River, the stream thus made passing in a northwesterly direction across Broadway at Canal Street, thence flowing on its lonely way through Lispenard's meadows into the North River. The Pond had various names during its reign, the English calling it "Fresh Water Pond" while the Dutch named it "Kalchook" from the decomposed shells which were deposited on the western shore. This name was later abbreviated into "Kalch," "Callech," "Colleck," from whence it is supposed that "Collect" was derived.[8]

Early chroniclers of "Manahatta" tell us that the Collect was a limpid pool of fresh water as deep as 50 feet in some parts. The adjacent terrain was hilly and it must have been a pleasing sight to stand on one of the overlooking hills and look down the peaceful quietude of the Collect and the surrounding valley. It was a favorite spot of the Indians who were later displaced by the early Dutch settlers. Fish were abundant in the Collect Pond. They bit the bait without any trouble, wriggling and squirming as the settler pulled in his line. For those living near it was never a problem to provide the means for a tasty meal. And in the winter time, when old Jack Frost had cast his mighty spell over the Island, the Collect froze over into a delightful skating pond to which the settlers came from all around. It was even used for experimental purposes for when John Fitch required a body of water upon which to try out the first screw-ball propeller craft, he chose the Collect.

"The pond, meanwhile, remained the same deep, clear and sparkling—a miniature sea in the heart of the city. Its waters still furnished food for the angler, and rumors were rife of strange sea monsters which had been seen therein, one of which carried off a Hession trooper in the days of the Revolution. It was a man-trap, too, for the unwary traveller, and, from time to time, a citizen, who had mistaken his way in the darkness or had drank too deeply, fell from its banks and was drowned where now is solid ground. The possibility of such a transformation had not yet occured to the busy speculators; but schemes were projected to convert the beautiful lake into a means of ornament and profit. One company proposed to buy up the lands about it, and, preserving the lake in its primitive condition, to lay out a portion of the grounds as a public park, and realize their expected profit from the enhanced value of the remainder.[9]

This lovely body of water upon which the Indians used to paddle all the way over to the North River and where the Dutch enjoyed the fishing and the celebrated skating—passed through a variety of vicissitudes, until finally the surrounding hills no longer were able to look upon their reflections mirrored in the translucent pool. Mr. Charles Sutton, one time Warden of the Tombs, informs us that though as early as "1787 the pond was reported as in a filthy condition, owing to the practice of throwing refuse into it."[10] It was not until 1808 that anything was done to remedy this condition. At that time the City Fathers voted to remove the encircling hills and use the earth to fill up the Collect. This was accomplished, streets were laid out, Centre Street running directly through what used to be the Collect Pond, and thus the lovely Collect became only a memory.

It was this site upon which the eyes of the Common Council fell when it was decided to build a new prison. Ground was broken in 1835, on what was formerly the old Collect and in 1838 The Tombs Prison reared its impressive Egyptian walls, ready to house the criminal population of New York. That same year, 1835, the Bridewell was demolished and some of the stones incorporated into the construction of the new Tombs prison.

The correct name of this singularly gloomy building was the Halls of Justice but by public agreement, it became known as The Tombs, a name which was handed down to the second prison on that site. This was due to the fact that the style of its architecture was reminiscent of an Egyptian tomb. The building is said to have been one of the best examples of Coptic architecture.

George Wilkes was incarcerated in The Tombs for libel in 1844. While he was interned he wrote a diary from which we are able to glean a more or less general description of this first Tombs. Wilkes relates, among other items of interest, that all cooking operations were carried out by means of steam. The section where male prisoners were housed consisted of a long corridor of four tiers. The Tombs was so planned that a man at the desk and another at the 4th tier could watch every part of the building. Due to its having been constructed over filled in ground, The Tombs was very damp, so damp that at times water oozed from the walls.[11]

When Charles Dickens visited America, he too described The Tombs . . . "A long narrow lofty building, stove-heated as usual, with four galleries, one above the other, giving round it, and communicating by stairs. Between the two sides of each gallery, and in its centre, a bridge, for greater convenience of crossing. On each of these bridges sits a man: dozing or reading, or talking to an idle companion. On each tier are two opposite rows of small doors. They look like furnace doors but are cold and black, as though the fires within had all gone out. Some two or three are open, and women, with drooping heads bent down, are talking to the inmates. The whole is lighted by a skylight, but it is fast closed; and from the roof of there dangle, limp and drooping, two useless windsails."[12]

53

This earlier Tombs was connected to a building at Franklin and Centre Street known as "Bummers' Hall." It was quite a large room used principally to confine drunks picked up throughout the city. It accommodated about 200 people and was usually filled to capacity over the week-end. Apparently, then, as now, people were more prone to give vent to their feelings the last of the week. The reasons for the popularity of "Bummers' Hall" over the week-end were varied, but the main reason was due to the fact that receiving their pay on a Saturday and having the following day free to recuperate, many took advantage to go on a good spree. This usually ended up in "Bummers' Hall." Times have not changed very much for week-ends in New York are still just as hectic and any officer in the Police Department will tell you that the weekends are their busiest times.

The first Tombs has been razed but the tales of its prisoners still linger and many a story surrounds the diverse personalities who were confined behind the grim walls of this old bastion. These prisoners, like in all prisons, were a diverse lot. They differed in the sense of relative position and education as well as in the crimes for which they were committed to the damp doleful cells of The Tombs. Some were from lowly classes of the dreaded Five Points while others came from good families of refinement and education. To this latter class belonged John C. Colt whose case has been handed down as one of the most curious in Tomb's annals.

Colt was a professional man; one for whom there might have been a counter-part in any college town. He was a brother of the inventor of the revolver, coming from a wealthy and respected family.[18] The Colt home was on Broadway near Duane Street which was then the fashionable part of Manhattan. The younger Colt, impetuous, stubborn and determined, lived under the parental roof for a time or until family differences sent him flying bag and baggage to a furnished room which he rented for himself. The cause of his differences with his family is said to have been Colt's attraction for a Miss Caroline Henshaw, of whom he became enamoured and failing to receive his family's consent to a marriage, took to himself as his common-law-wife.

Thus established, Colt set himself to literary work in which venture he fared ill as publishers were none too eager to accept his material. His real forte developed in the realm of accounting. He prepared a text book on the science of bookkeeping which was being published by Samuel Adams who kept a printing shop on William Street.

One day in September, 1841, when the city enshrouded itself in one of those dreary cold days, a coldness which presaged the advent of winter, printer Adams disappeared. Little alarm was evinced at Adams' failure to appear at his usual haunts as he was known to have been an admirer of the opposite sex and it was thought that possibly some comely damsel was the reason for his disappearance. And so those of his friends who were the logical ones to press an official investigation into the printer's failure to appear at his regular abodes, winked slyly and assumed a "laissez faire"attitude towards the matter. Nothing was thought of poor Adams until some days later the city was horrified to learn of the discovery of his dismembered body which had been stuffed into a packing case consigned to "John Benoiste" in St. Louis, Mo. Then the finger of suspicion pointed to Colt who was known to have seen the murdered man on the day he disappeared. Colt confessed, was convicted and sentenced to die. The prominence of Colt's family coupled with the brutality of his crime attracted much publicity to the case. The prisoner had influential friends among whom was Payne, writer of "Home, Sweet Home." These friends did their utmost to have Colt's sentence revoked, but all to no avail.

On the day set for his execution, Colt was married to his mistress who had remained loyal and faithful during his difficulties. On this same day a fire broke out in the cupola which was built over the main entrance. Preparations for the execution were interrupted to extinguish the fire which was quickly brought under control. As though the old Tombs had not seen enough excitement for one day, when the keeper came to lead the condemned man to his execution, it was found that the prisoner had cheated the gallows by committing suicide. November 18, 1842, the day all these events took place, was a busy day for the old Tombs.

The inmates of the first Tombs were a motley crew. Politicians, gamblers, murderers and confidence men—all were confined in the Tombs. Tweed knew what the inside of the Tombs looked like, and so did old Croker who was remanded there after the shooting of John McKenna on November 3, 1874. Stokes also spent some months in the Tombs at the same time that John Scannell was awaiting trial for murdering the man who had sent his brother into Eternity. Fernando Wood who was accused of stealing $2,000,000 was another distinguished inmate.

Between the years of 1851 and 1886, thirty executions took place in the Tombs courtyard.[14] The first execution was that of a negro named Edward Coleman who forfeited his life on January 12, 1839 for killing his pretty mulatto wife who used to sell hot corn around Printing House Square.[15]

This is not a large number considering the situation into which the city was plunged immediately preceding and following the Civil War. New York was a wicked city in those days, "the modern Gomorrah" according to the Rev. T. De Witt Talmadge. Some of us who are prone to shout "crime wave" and extend a rigid forefinger directed at present conditions, would do well to delve back into circumstances as they existed in New York between the years 1850 to 1900. Crime ran rampant throughout the city, manifesting itself in varied forms of robbery, swindling, gambling, blackmailing, pickpocketing, etc. Running parallel with the different crimes, were all the evils and vices accruing from immoral practices. The notorious Five Points was reeking with evil of every kind and description. Centering around Paradise Square this crime situation possessed long tentacles which infected cankerous sores of infamy upon other sections of the city. This was especially true in those years of reconstruction following the close of the Civil War.

In those hectic days the confidence men gained lucrative profits, gold bricks found their way into the possession of several gullible purchasers and imposters and swindlers thrived on the proceeds gained from their various callings. In addition, there existed a large number of people who derived their incomes from bagnios, houses of assignation and from the earnings of prostitutes and street-walkers. From the latter group there emerged several well organized ways in which to extract money from the unwary, the panel house system perhaps being the most widely known.

This combined prostitution with robbery. Profits were received from both sources. On general principle, the victims of the panel house were usually selected by the girl in the case who cruised the neighborhood in search of prosperous looking men to whom a scandal would be distasteful. She would invite him to her room where a confederate usually lay waiting behind a false wall containing the secret panel. In the dim light of the room the potential victim would not be aware that anything was amiss. While his attention was engaged the girl's confederate would quietly slip the panel back, remove the money from the victim's clothing and make his exit. The man was sure the girl could not have robbed him, but due to the circumstances attached to the incident, he could not call in the police for fear of creating a scandal.

The greatest problem of the day seems to have been the social evil and other vices which grew out of it. This was due to a number of reasons. First the prostitutes had followed the soldiers and at the close of hostilities, when the army was disbanded, they threw themselves upon the city. The police were cognizant of the situation but, as in many instances, they, too, or the politicians who controlled them were sharing in the profits and nothing was done about it. In addition, for many years very little publicity was given to prostitution and its attendant vices. It was therefore only to be expected that, unchecked and unmolested, this problem became one of the major concerns of the city.

In 1866 Bishop Simpson of the Methodist Church confounded an audience at Cooper Institute by declaring that the prostitutes of New York City were as numerous as the Methodists. This statement focused public attention upon the situation and brought forth a reply from John A. Kennedy who was then the Superintendent of Police of the Metropolitan area. Kennedy's rejoinder is worthy of note in that he produced the following statistics as a rebuttal to the Bishop:

747 "waiter girls" employed in concert and drinking saloons
621 houses of prostitution
2,670 public prostitutes
99 houses of assignation

were the numbers of people and places engaged in disorderly practices, as recorded in New York Police records.[16] The population of New York City at that time was approximately 1,000,000.

Considering that vice and crime were allowed to flourish, the wonder is that there were so few murderers housed in The Tombs. Murders there were, but only thirty convicted murderers paid the penalty in the old Tombs courtyard.

The present vacant structure and its predecessor has known nearly every type of criminal extant, but the eddying current of Manhattanites, perpetually in a hurry, pass to and fro along Center Street, seemingly quickening their pace as they walk briskly by The Tombs. And who is there who can blame them?

Once the empty building succumbs to the wrecking crew, there will be few tears shed over its demolishment. It holds no pleasant memories. Inside damp, due to the fact that it rests on filled in ground; outside forbidding and dreary, it will not be missed. Pity it is that civilized society has need of such buildings, but one supposes that human nature being largely imperfect, there will always be the necessity for such corrective institutions. We are advancing, however. Criminals and those who break the law have never enjoyed such humane treatment as in this day. Yet, there is much to be done and all modern sociologists are in accord that it must start with the child. Children must never be reared in such rookeries as the Old Brewery in the Five Points. The city, in order to progress must provide its children with all the means at its command to ensure a happy childhood. Only thus will the use of such prisons as The Tombs become unnecessary.

CHAPTER NOTES

1. Hewitt, Edward Ringwood and Mary Ashley, "The Bowery," p. 16.
2. Earle, Alice Morse, "The Stadt Huys of New Amsterdam," p. 21.
3. Lewis, Elizabeth Dike, "Old Prisons and Punishments," p. 10.
4. Sutton, Charles, "The New York Tombs; Its Secrets and Its Mysteries," p. 39.
5. Ibid., p. 152, 153.
6. Earle, Alice Morse, "The Stadt Huys of New Amsterdam," p. 17.
7. Gerard, James W., "The Old Stadt Huys of New Amsterdam," p. 47.
8. Sutton, Charles, "The New York Tombs; Its Secrets and Its Mysteries," p. 44.
9. Booth, Mary L., "History of the City of New York," Vol. II, p. 579.
10. Sutton, Charles, "The New York Tombs; Its Secrets and Its Mysteries," p. 46.
11. Wilkes, George, "The Mysteries of The Tombs," p. 12.
12. Dickens, Charles, "American Notes," p. 46.
13. Trumble, Alfred, "Secrets of The Tombs," p. 11.
14. Byrnes, Thomas, "Professional Criminals in America," p. 368.
15. Trumble, Alfred, "Secrets of The Tombs," p. 8.
16. McCabe, James Dabney, "Secrets of the City," p. 283, 284.

Tombs Prison, Spring, 1873

CHAPTER SEVEN

The Old Brewery and the Ill-Famed
Five Points

God knows it's time thy walls were going!
Through every stone
Life-blood, as through a heart, is flowing;
Murmurs a smother'd groan.
    "The Old Brewery" by Rev. T.F.R. Mercein

RECLAMATION of New York's notorious Five Points was actually initiated in 1852. Previous to that, and in fact for many years after, it was impossible for the police to cope with the problem of patroling this bed of crime. Murders were committed at the rate of one nightly for fifteen years. Often no trace of the victim was ever discovered; he just disappeared. Crime, disorder and debauchery were the accepted requisites for tenants of the Five Points area. Anyone not fulfilling these lawless requirements behaved in accordance with two alternatives: either they moved to more respectable environs, or they comported themselves in the manner expected of the Five Pointers.

It was in 1852 when the section was at the height of its debauched existence, that the Missionary Society bought the Old Brewery, thus beginning the first step in rehabilitation of the notorious region. This step, viewed in the light of events transpiring during the following fifty years proved a slow and laborious process for grabbing the bull by the horns in no manner tamed the ferocity of the beast. Workmen were commissioned to tear down the odious rookery, during the operations of which several sacks full of human bones were retrieved from between the walls where murderous hands had concealed the evidence of their heinous crimes.[1]

When it was announced that the Old Brewery was to be demolished, legends and stories of buried treasure ran rampant in the city. It was commonly believed possible that the ruffians and robbers who had made their headquarters in the famous "Den of Thieves" had cached some of their loot in the Old Brewery. And well they may have, for did not this building, reeking in crime, hide secrets of a more sinister hue? At any rate, during the first stages of its razing, the Old Brewery was the scene of many a treasure hunt. As far as can be ascertained nothing of value was ever discovered, although periodic attempts to unearth hidden treasure gave rise to much speculation and served to consume many columns of the newspapers. Many stories made their way into print, some fabulous, some having sound justification, yet the treasure which was supposed to have been concealed in the Old Brewery remained as elusive as Ponce de Leon's "Fountain of Youth."

The Old Brewery was the center of such infamy as New York has seldom seen. The building, erected in 1792 was transformed into a dwelling in 1837. Rats—both of the human and rodent species—inhabited the rookery, the cellars of which were divided into twenty rooms used in former days to house the plant's machinery, but now converted into human rat holes. Asbury states that the building contained 75 rooms in addition to its cellars and that it was known to have housed at least a thousand people. Many times these tenants, who lived under the worst possible conditions, accepting miscegenation, incest and sexual promiscuity as ordinary, never ventured outside their rooms for weeks at a time.[2]

Although well neigh a century has passed since this den of vice and evil spread its ugly tentacles out to contaminate the rest of the Five Points, its notorious reputation still exists. It is not possible to consider the Five Points without some allusion to this abominable nest from whence sprung many of the denizens of the early Five Points. These people fought with outsiders as well as with each other. They organized themselves into gangs upon which they bestowed such titles of high-sounding ferocity as "Plug Uglies," "Dead Rabbits," "Roach Guard," etc. They knew no order, respected no authority and were quite content to live not only in filth and squalor, but in a condition of lawlessness and evil, as well. This aura of complete badness embraced their physical as well as their spiritual being, and it is not surprising to learn that many of the city's epidemics gained a foothold in this region. On May 14, 1849 the first case of cholera for that year appeared in the Five Points. By the time the epidemic had subsided, there was an estimated death toll of 3,000 lives which the plague had cost the city.[3]

A hundred years ago this was the breeding place of crime, misery and every conceivable form of human wretchedness. Particularly was this an evil spot for children. They were born in over-crowded tenements, many times never glimpsing the sunlight until they themselves were able to walk or crawl to the pavement. These children never went to school for the reason that they had no clothes to wear and even if clothes were supplied, they were so infected with vermin as to impair the health of the other children. It has been estimated that in 1868 40,000 children were roaming the Five Points—destitute and exhibiting every indication of becoming prospective vagrants.[4] Some of the children of delicate age were addicted to drink; many were confirmed alcoholics. There was a case of a five year old Italian girl, Lucie Zucherichi, who was taken from a Mulberry Street tenement to Presbyterian Hospital, dying of cirrhosis of the liver which had been produced by continuous drinking.[5]

Not so long age, my father and I, bent upon discovering vestiges of "Old New York" set out upon a pilgrimage of what in former years had been known as the "bad Five Points." We traversed the irregular streets, saw the spot where the Old Brewery stood, later to be replaced by the Five Points Mission, and still later giving way to a tavern which now occupies the site—we observed the people, clean, energetic, healthful mothers proudly perambulating their robust offspring in Columbus Park—we sought in vain for some scene reminiscent of the Five Points of old.

But nary a trace of this former iniquitous rat hole of vice remains. In fact, as is so often true in this city of everlasting changes, even the name Five Points is rapidly being consigned to the past. The original Five Points was formed by the intersection of Cross, Anthony, Little Water, Orange and Mulberry Streets. During the course of the city's growth and the successive municipal improvements some have been renamed. Anthony became North Street, Orange was transformed into Baxter and Cross became Park Street. Little Water Street disappeared. Paradise Square was incorporated into Mulberry Park and the name changed to Columbus Park. It can readily be seen from these changes that identifying the Five Points of old was a task rendered difficult by the alterations wrought in the topography as well as the renaming of the Streets. Today the Five Points is actually three points formed by the converging of Park, Worth and Baxter Streets.

The "Cradle of the Gangs," as Herbert Asbury calls it, is now not very different from many other sections of Manhattan. Quite a few public buildings—municipal, state and federal—have been built in the region northeast of City Hall Park. In fact, the vicinity around Foley Square, which lies slightly southwest of the old Five Point intersection, is dotted with governmental office buildings. The Supreme Court Building, U.S. Court House, State Office Building, Court Square

Building and Hall of Records all form a part of this neighborhood. Still further south is the Municipal Building, which, though adequate to house the many city offices in 1913 when it was built, does not pretend now to house all the offices required to keep the city government in operation.

All in all, standing upon the former infamous Five Points and taking in the present surroundings, it does not look very menacing. No qualms of fear engulf one as he casually loiters over the spot which was so dreaded in former years. Nothing could be further from reality than Dickens' description of this place as he found it when he visited the Five Points in 1841. The breeding place of vice and crime has been taken over by the graceful buildings from which the affairs of many branches of government are directed.

On the day of the visit previously alluded to, it was a Saturday afternoon and so quiet and lonesome as to be nearly deserted. My father caught sight of two elderly women sitting on the steps of the New York State Office Building—cleaners or charwomen, they were, who had finished their work for the day and were now relaxing on the steps of the building wherein they performed their labors. As they appeared to be residents of the neighborhood, we engaged them in conversation which lasted nearly an hour and proved to be a most valuable font of information.

Our first surmise was correct, as both had been living in the Five Points section for 60 years. One had moved to Brooklyn, she confided, but growing homesick for her birthplace, she moved back to the Five Points after a few months. They knew everyone in the vicinity—did these two old charwomen. They told us many interesting tales about the prominent people who came up from the Five Points area. The eldest of these two old cronies offered the information that in her youth there were stories of a tunnel running from Mott Street to Mulberry Street, through which Tong hatchet men used to escape after having dispatched their victims. Subsequent investigation has revealed no trace of its existence so whether or not there was such a tunnel is a matter for future investigators.

Night was approaching and with the first shadows cast by a fading sun, the Five Points began to display apparent signs of life. Visitors on their way to Saturday night supper in Chinatown passed us on their way up the slight hill of Park Street. An aged Jewish woman, stooped from the weight of many winters and the burden of a basket of "Bagles" she was carrying, approached us. The women knew her: Rosie they called this modern Five Pointer. She had been a resident of the neighborhood for forty years, yet the only English Rosie knew were the two significant words "penny" and "nickel." My father handed Rosie a ten cent piece and she must have translated this into its Yiddish equivalent, for she wandered off, the wrinkles of her careworn face forming themselves into a broad grin. We left the two old ladies with their tales of the bad old Five Points, while we wandered around the reclaimed section as it is today.

The population consists of Chinese, Italian and Hebrews, each nationality more or less segregated into its own section. Although the Jews have their own community in lower Manhattan, occupying quarters further north around Grand, Delancey and Essex Streets, they are also in the Five Points. On Elizabeth and Bayard Streets they operate a unique market known as the "Second Hand Clothing" market. Always commercially inclined, the operators of these stores do not wait for the customer to make his appearance. They stand in front of their shops and solicit business from the sidewalk. Do you want to buy an old pair of shoes? Are you looking for a suit that "may have seen better days?" Walk along Elizabeth Street, near Bayard. It is safe to say that no less than a dozen enterprising salesmen will call your attention to his wares. Where do they acquire these hand-me-downs? Perhaps they come from estates—their former owners having no earthly use for the garments—they are sold to liquidate the estate. Maybe they once graced a gifted artist whose great talents, unrecognized and unacclaimed, brought him naught but proverty. Perhaps they are clothes altruistically donated a Bowery habitué who promises to reform, but whose taste for "smoke" induces him to part with the gifts so hopefully given by the many missions in the neighborhood. If each article displayed in these vendor's shops could talk, what a wealth of material we should have to spin yarns, for this raiment which one sees so carelessly displayed in the "Second Hand Clothing" market, comes from all over the city.

The Italians have congregated around Mulberry Street which is part of "Mulberry Bend" the oldest Italian settlement in Manhattan. Mulberry Bend was between Bayard and Park Streets and along with the rest of the Five Points it enjoyed a very unsavory reputation. When, after lengthy agitation, Columbus Park came into being, Mulberry Bend disappeared and along with it went many slums with which it had become associated. The Italians, however, did not relinquish this part of Manhattan upon which they had taken hold, for the neighborhood still boasts a large Italian population. This is particular visible on religious holidays when processions wend their way through streets gayly decorated with colored lights and vari-colored banners.

Some of the Italians have left their original homes in Mulberry Street and have established other distinctly Italian neighborhoods in different sections of Manhattan. Further uptown in the East One Hundreds, there is a large Italian settlement, however, Mulberry Bend still remains one of the first footholds taken by the Italians in Manhattan.

The Chinese have settled a little east of the Five Points. Chinatown comprises Doyers, Mott, and Pell Streets and parts of Chatham Square. It is a little village which was until a few years ago completely oriental in character. Within later years Chinatown has absorbed many of the ways of its occidental neighbors and today it is a sad blending of modern American and ancient Chinese, for it cannot be considered as wholly Chinese, nor yet is it entirely American. This, however, is true of many neighborhoods of Manhattan which have been subjected to foreign infiltration.

During the twenty-five years preceeding the Civil War, New York harbor became a huge receptacle into which thousands of immigrants blithely set their weary feet. The masses of people who had fled Europe for political, social or economic reasons literally swarmed to these shores. Some travelled inland and were absorbed in the great settlement of the west. Others, though, never left New York. Among the latter there came a large number of Irish who settled in the Five Points area, thus at the outbreak of the Civil War the pugnacious, witty Irishman and his family were the predominant nationality in that locale. There were negroes, too, many of whom were the descendents of freed slaves from Revolutionary times.

Perhaps the most obnoxious place of the Five Points of that time, paralleling in evil and crime even the Old Brewery, was "Cow-Bay" or Little Water Street. This was a cul de sac about thirty feet wide at the mouth which narrowed down to a point about one hundred feet at the entrance. It was a small bay in the Collect where farmers drove their cattle for water. Later, that is in the halcyon days of the Five Points, it became an alley lined with dilapidated tenements on both sides while its center was filled with filth above the shoe tops.[6]

This was a fertile field for the ministrations of social workers as nearly every room in the wretched neighborhood contained people who needed help. And very often it was as much as his life was worth for anyone to venture into Cow-Bay to tend these creatures. A missionary describes one of his sick calls which he and his assistant made to a woman who lived in Cow-Bay. He tells of calling upon this woman who was in excruciating agony as a result of excesses. She was lying on the floor, as devoid of clothing as when she came into the world, covered only by a quilt which was so dirty as to be indistinguishable from the floor upon which her emaciated body writhed in pain. As though this sight were not revolting enough, the missionary goes on to tell that this miserable room in which he found the wretched creature also harbored the decomposing body of a white woman who had been beaten to death some days previous by the negro with whom she was cohabiting.

Such scenes as this were not uncommon in this section of Manhattan.[7] One surmises that if the records of charitable organizations and the daily news items of the time were consulted, many such happenings would come to light.

Another incident tells of the murder of a child who was careless enough to display a penny which she had received begging. Her body remained in the room—a room which was incidentally shared by 26 people, though it was only 15 feet square—for five days, after which she was finally buried in a grave which her mother dug in the floor of the same room.[8]

When such conditions were permitted to exist, as well as to spread, one must not be surprised at the results. There was an utter and complete disregard of law which manifested itself in violating not only rules and regulations written into man-made statutes, but extended, as well, to the very laws upon which so many religions are based.

It is interesting to note that the first sign the Five Points evinced of developing into a crime center was when Rosanna Peers opened a green grocery in Center Street. In reality, and to use modern parlance, this was nothing more than a "speakeasy" where liquor could be bought at lower prices than elsewhere. Thieves and criminals and murderers flocked to Rosanna's and soon this waxing establishment was doing so well on the proceeds extracted from its dubious clientele that other green groceries began to open in the neighborhood. They were a tough and hard lot, these habitues of the Five Points, and toughest and hardest of them all were the butchers whom Asbury calls the aristocrats of the Points.

When Center Market opened the butchers decided to celebrate the occasion with a great ball and supper which auspicious event took place, according to the announcement, "in the spacious rooms over said market." The ball was a magnificent affair, graced by the presence of His Honor, the Mayor, and one thousand others. The ladies were handsomely gowned, the decorations were lavish. Nothing was spared to make the Butchers' Ball and Supper one of Gotham's outstanding events for that year.[9]

The papers for the following day carried glowing accounts of the festivities. "The Sun" for January 19, 1839 said, "everybody present entered con amore into the festivities of the occasion. The supper, prepared by Mr. & Mrs. Niblo, was worthy of Lucillus—'earth, air and ocean rifled of their sweets.' "

These butchers were often leaders of the different gangs which controlled the surrounding territory. Usually they met in such grocery stores as Rosanna Peers operated. In time, therefore, these green groceries gained a very unsavory reputation for they were nothing more than dens of iniquity and infamy. By 1865 the Points and Paradise Square area boasted 270 saloons and many times that number of green groceries, dance halls and houses of prostitution.[10]

The butchers were strong men and hearty eaters and drinkers. Their principal sport was "bull baiting." Civilized Manhattanites may shudder at bull fighting, yet they would do well to hearken back some years to when Mr. Winship who was one of the old Fly Market butchers, managed an arena which could accommodate 2,000 people. The arena was constructed on the remains of a Revolutionary fort where the great patriots of the American Revolution heroically defended the city against General Howe and his British troops. The site was called Bunker Hill and was on the property of the Bayard family. The hill was later levelled off and the Bayard dead, resting in the family vaults on the southeasterly side, removed to other burial grounds.

It was upon this site that Butcher Winship erected the bull-baiting arena. This sport must have been very popular to necessitate an arena with a seating capacity of 2,000. The diversion, for such it was, consisted in chaining a live bull to a swivel ring and then releasing dogs to torment the brute. The spectators would place wagers as to the number of dogs the frenzied bull would gore.

Some years later the Five Points idea of what constituted a sport had not changed very much. Kit Burns was operating his Rat and Dog Pit at 273 Water Street. This "sport" consisted of throwing live rats into a pit and releasing dogs to kill them. Bets were made as to the number and the time a dog would take to kill the rats. Dog fights were also staged in Kit Burns's pit.[11]

But for the most part what these earlier Five Pointers relished most was dancing. The terpsichorean art or "tripping the light fantastic" was one of the principal diversions of the times. There were several dance houses in the vicinity of Paradise Square. While the blue bloods oft congregated around the Battery for their prominades, the red blooded citizenry were wont to patronize the Five Points and often as not, as a result of their lawless revelry much of their red blood flowed in the surrounding streets—streets which today echo the footsteps of busy civil employees, in days gone by giving forth unto such abandoned revelry as to precipitate from the pen of Dickens: "This is the place: these narrow ways, diverging to the right and left, and reeking everywhere with dirt and filth. Such lives as are led here, bear the same fruits here as elsewhere. The coarse and bloated faces at the doors, have counterparts at home, and all the wide world over. Debauchery had made the very houses prematurely old."[12]

Thus we progress and forge ahead—trying along the way to incorporate that which is good and worth preserving into a place deserving of this magnificent isle. We legislate, we embark upon vast slum clearance projects—projects which other cities would hesitate to undertake—we plan, we demolish, we construct, but in the end well may we feel the thrill of accomplishment.

CHAPTER NOTES

1. Asbury, Herbert, "The Gangs of New York," p. 19.
2. Ibid., p. 14.
3. Wilson, James Grant, "Memorial History of New York," Vol. III, p. 435.
4. McCabe, James Dabney, "Secrets of the Great City," p. 191.
5 Moss, Frank, "An American Metropolis," Vol. III, p. 53.
6. Asbury, Herbert, "The Gangs of New York," p. 12.
7. Ladies of The Mission, "The Old Brewery & The New Mission House," p. 199.
8. Asbury, Herbert, "The Gangs of New York," p. 14.
9. Moss, Frank, "An American Metropolis," Vol. III, p. 39.
10. Asbury, Herbert, "The Gangs of New York," p. 10.
11. McCabe, James Dabney, "Secrets of the Great City," p. 388-392.
12. Dickens, Charles, "American Notes," p. 48.

FIVE POINTS, Worth Baxter and Park Sts., 1859

CHAPTER EIGHT

The Notorious Bowery

"The Bowery, the Bowery!
They say such things and they do strang things
On the Bow'ry, the Bow'ry!
I'll never go there anymore!"

U NLIKE the peaceful suggestion of its name, a corruption of the old Dutch farm word, "bouwerie," the Bowery today is one of the saddest streets of forgotten men. The famous words of the old favorite, "The Bowery, the Bowery, I'll never go there anymore," apply more now than they ever did in the days of old. Indeed, when Charlie Hoyt wrote these words which Harry Conor made popular in the hit of 1892, "A Trip to Chinatown," they were intended to convey the thought that life on the Bowery was so hectic, so overflowing with riotous living, that it was best not to return. Now the street is so dismal with the numerous "flop-houses" missions and dingy shops synonomous with it, that one has no desire to return.

The Bouwerie Lane was for many years the only thoroughfare leading to Fort Amsterdam. It ran through old Peter Stuyvesant's farm, a lonely road, flanked on both sides by uncleared wilderness, but with the advent of settlers, the little lane began to assume larger proportions. The Dutch West India Company was the indirect influence behind this growth for it was this agency which promoted settlement of the colony. Realizing that the New World offered lucrative profits in fur trading, the Dutch Company also concluded that if they were to derive any dividends from this business, it would be necessary to bring settlers to work the land. Accordingly, substantial inducements were offered to farmers willing to surmount the many difficulties and hardships attached to settling the new land.

68

There were little or no altruistic motives behind this offer. The venture was purely one of expediency on both sides. Here was a case where the Dutch West India Company could realize a fortune by commercializing the fur industry, but the only inhabitants on Manhattan Island were Indians whose tendencies were so ferocious and hostile as to prevent exploitation of the valuable industry. So the Company hit upon the scheme of transporting farmers and their families to the New World, mostly for the purpose of establishing permanent contact. Upon their arrival they were granted a partly cleared tract of land. The farmers, on the other hand, saw in this offer an opportunity to better themselves. Thus colonization began and the first white settlers were introduced to the Bowery vicinity.

It was not long before the thrifty and industrious Dutchman had wrested a sizeable clearing of habitable land from the "forest primeval." Soon the ground between Wall and Fourteenth Streets had been divided into 6 "bouweries." Now, it must be remembered that at that particular time Manhattan was the home of the Indian. The Dutch were appropriating lands wherein the Indian had been free to roam long before the advent of the white man. In fact, the Bouwerie Lane was originally an Indian trail named Weck-quaes-geek Path. The Indians were not in accord with this usurpation of their land. Then, as though pouring oil upon a smoldering fire, the Dutch West India Company sent a Governor to rule the colony who, by his cruelty and acts of violence against them, fanned the embers of the Indian's resentment.

This Governor must have been the Dutch colonial counter-part of our modern racketeers. Governor Kieft's conception of levying tribute (which he employed freely against the Indians) had much in common with illicit practices of our own day. In order to protect them against their enemies—enemies which they never had until the white man set foot upon their shores—Kieft ordained that the Indians pay a tribute in furs and corn. This tax aggravated the Indians who realized fully well that they received no protection at all from Kieft and that this was merely a pretext to take their products.[1] This was one of the reasons which led to continuous outbreaks of war between the Indians and the Dutch.

Occasionally the "bouweries" fell prey to the onslaughts of the Indians. The more Governor Kieft did to quell the red man's fury, the more their feelings became incensed. The Dutchmen, in their own turn, and under orders from their Governor, perpetrated such outrages on the Indians—at times massacring entire villages—as has seldom been known in the annuals of warfare. At one time a group of Dutchmen on their way to South River stopped off at Staten Island and stole some hogs belonging to De Vries. The Raritans, a tribe of Indians which then

69

inhabitated the western bank of the Hudson, were blamed for this theft. Upon hearing this news, Kieft who was always ready to wreak his cruel thrusts against any tribe hapless enough to warrant his attention, commissioned Koopman Van Tienhoven and 70 men to go forth and demand reparations from the Raritans. Though Van Tienhoven tried in vain to control the blood-thirsty men under his command, it was no go. The soldiers fell upon the unlucky Raritans only ceasing their murderous rampage after ten Indian warriors lay slain at their feet.[2]

The real success of the settlement of New Amsterdam dates from the time of office of Peter Stuyvesant whose name looms in capital letters in the chronicles of Manhattan's early history, notably that associated with the Bowery. Stuyvesant, though stubborn and choleric, was at the same time a good fighter and a just one. He had been Governor of the Dutch West India Company's colony at Curacao during which time he lost a leg while fighting the Portuguese. When he arrived in New Amsterdam conditions were so that only an energetic and determined executive would retrieve the lost fortunes and honor which New Amsterdam had suffered as a result of Kieft's rash treatment of the Indians. The Indians had retaliated against the colonists, and the colonists who saw their hard labor wasted, blamed Kieft for all the misfortunes which befell them. Kieft was recalled and subsequently lost at sea on the way home. Old Petrus Stuyvesant had a sorry task before him for he not only had to cope with the dissatisfaction of the colonists, but he also had to maintain peaceful relations with the Indians.

He improved the city streets and under his leadership the colony grew and prospered. Even after he surrendered New Amsterdam to the British in 1664, he continued to reside in the land of his adoption, enjoying the respect and admiration of his friends and enemies too, for he was every inch a man. When Stuyvesant died he was buried in St. Mark's-in-the-Bowery, Second Avenue and 11 Street. His final resting place is marked:

"late Captain General and Commander-in-Chief of Amsterdam in New Netherland now called New York and the Dutch West India Islands, died in August A.D. 1682 aged 80 years."

For many years after his passing lower Manhattan had living memory of old Petrus Stuyvesant as until 1867 there was a pear tree growing at the northeast corner of Third Avenue and 13th Street which had been planted by the irascible old Captain General.

As the streets laid out under Stuyvesant's direction grew longer and the town grew into a city, houses were built closer together. Pavements were constructed and other improvements made until by the middle of the Nineteenth Century the Bowery had become "the street" in Manhattan.

Simultaneously with the growth of the district was the development of it as a theatrical center. The Bowery was probably Manhattan's first "Great White Way" holding forth in this capacity for nearly fifty years. In the heyday of vaudeville if an actor played the "Palace" on Broadway, his success had been assured and he was a star. By the same token, between 1800 and 1850 the leading lights of the theatrical profession played on the Bowery. The theatres were the best in New York and offered the finest talent of the day.

Among the many theatres which flourished in the neighborhood was the ill fated Park Theatre. It was opened in 1798 north of Ann Street on Park Row. When General Washington died the theatre went into mourning and was closed on December 14, 1799. One of the rules of the Park was that no lady was to be admitted to the first and second tiers unless accompanied by a gentleman. John Jacob Astor and Beekman were the owners. When this theatre went up in flames a new Park was built on the same site in 1821. Here was the scene of many a thespian triumph. Edmund Keen, the Wallacks, Junius Brutus Booth, Charlotte Cushman, Ellen Tree and Fanny Kemble are a few of the galaxy of stars who twinkled there. Payne, later to achieve fame as the writer of "Home, Sweet Home," trod the boards of the Park at the tender age of sixteen. On Dec. 16, 1848 a second fire destroyed the theatre. Although it was not rebuilt, it continues to live in the history of the New York stage. The narrow passage between Beekman and Ann Streets which led to the stage entrance still exists. It is called "Theatre Alley."

Another theatre famous in its day was the Bowery Theatre. It was opened in 1826 on the site of the Bull's Head Tavern which had been purchased from Henry Astor. The Bowery was a good sized theatre having a seating capacity of 3000. According to some, it had the distinction of being the first theatre to be lighted with gas, although, in his book "Old Bowery Days" Alvin F. Harlow disagrees with this, leaning more to the idea that the Chatham Garden Theatre was the first to lay claim to this improvement. Mr. Harlow advances the possibility that the old Bowery was the first to be equipped with gas footlights.[8]

In 1828 the theatre was demolished by fire. It was rebuilt only to be twice consumed by flames within the next ten years. On May 6, 1839 it was reopened for the fourth time and for the fourth time it went up in flames. (April 25, 1845) It was promptly rebuilt. Christy's Ministrels made their premier performance in New York at the old Bowery. In 1879 the Bowery Theatre was renamed the "Thalia" and in 1893 it was given over to the performance of Hebrew plays. Some time after 1830 the old theatre was torn down and the site is now occupied by the Arcade Building.

Other theatres of the district were the Chatham, the New Bowery and the Peoples' Theatre. The Chatham opened in 1839 on the east side of Chatham Square between Roosevelt and James Streets. Edwin Forrest graced the procenium with his famous characterization of "Othello" on May 6, 1842. It was torn down in October, 1862.

It was about this time that the Bowery began to emerge from a fashionable neighborhood and build up the questionable reputation which is later assumed. Gangs were in the embryo stage of development, but unlike the later day gangster whose prototype they were, these earlier gangs fought for principles and not for money. And fight they did! As the saying goes, they would fight at the "drop of a hat." They were composed mainly of Irish, numbering amongst them some of the best brawlers in the city. It must not be supposed from this, however, that these men were shiftless or lazy. They earned their daily bread by the sweat of their brows, so usually their jobs were manual labor. If there was fighting to be done, they did it, entering into a fracas with all the energy they possessed, but they worked hard, too.

Many of the gangs were volunteer fireman, working without pay—dashing hither and yon—wherever and whenever the fire claxon sounded. In 1865 the volunteers numbered an approximate 4,000. The present system was created on May 2, 1865 in compliance with legislative action. From July to November of 1864, 3,810 volunteers were replaced by city firemen.[4] The volunteers were grouped into companies, each company trying to outdo and outrival the other. All the gang members of that time, and the political leaders, too, claimed allegiance to some company. Many times a fire burned itself out whilst rival companies disputed for the honor of extinguishing it.

The Bowery Boys or "Bhoys" were masters of the Bowery while the Dead Rabbits held sway over at the Five Points—the most lawless and dreaded section of the city. It took in the section around Mott, Mulberry, Baxter, Bayard and Elizabeth Streets. The Dead Rabbits were originally a faction of the Roach Guards. When a serious difference arose they broke into two parts. During a stormy session of the rebel faction someone threw a dead rabbit amidst them—hence the decision to assume that name.[5]

Members of both gangs were intolerant, critical and absolutely devoid of any sense of law or order. They were ferocious and would fight with any available weapon, using their teeth or fists when it became necessary. Yet, during their infancy these gangs rarely fought for money. They wrangled intermittently over politics or some princi-

72

ple, culminating their arguments with periodic violence. Many times the battles lasted two or three days without any respite.

The feud between the Bowery Boys and the Dead Rabbits raged bitter and violent, and during Fernando Wood's administration as Mayor it was aggravated by differences over politics. The most famous fight between the "Bhoys" and the "Rabbits" took place onJuly 4, 1857. According to newspaper accounts for that day the fight is supposed to have been brewing for some days prior to Independence Day when matters were brought to a nasty head.

To determine the causes for this bloody outbreak one must cast the spotlight upon political activities of the period. In the year 1854 there was great corruption in the municipal government which lasted some years. The Board of Aldermen was dubbed "The Forty Thieves." William Tweed was a member of this body though he had not yet succumbed to the depths of corruptive practices into which he was later to descend. He went to Congress, representing the Fifth District. This was in 1853 when Tweed was just 30 years old.

In 1855 the Mayor of New York, Fernando Wood, was ardently supported by the Dead Rabbits. The elections were so dishonest that Wood is said to have received 400 more votes from the Sixth Ward than there were voters in the district.[6] To understand such a situation one must realize that New York was a fast growing metropolis. Between the years 1840 and 1850 the population of the city had grown more than at any time in its previous history. Immigrants could not reach Ellis Island quickly enough, and when gold was discovered in California they swarmed into the port of New York. Most of the immigrants were Irish and their predisposition towards political activity is common knowledge. Wood capitalized on this tendency by catering to these new citizens. As a result of courting their votes, Wood was elected to the Office of Mayor by a plurality of 17,366. This was November 9, 1854. He was re-elected in 1856. He ran again in 1858 but was defeated, however in 1860 he was elected Mayor for the third time.

Wood's administration had so corrupted the city government, especially the police force, that the legislature intervened. They created a police force to be controlled by a Board of Commissions, appointed by the Governor. Fernando Wood resented this lessening of his power. This resentment was shared by the Dead Rabbits who were his staunch supporters. The new force took over amidst the grumblings of Wood's discontented partisans. On July 4, a day when liquor flowed freely on the Bowery, rowdies of the Dead Rabbit gang attacked two of the new policemen. The policemen fled taking refuge in a saloon at Nos. 40 and 42 Bowery which was also a meeting place for the "Bhoys." One of their assailants had the temerity to follow the policemen into the building which was the initiation of the fracas.[7] While the Dead Rabbits supported Wood, the Bowery Boys were adherants of the Native American Party which claimed that Wood favored the Irish and other foreign elements. The incentive for a "muss" as they called it, existed, so when the Dead Rabbit entered the Bowery Boys' domain, he was promptly dispatched in a manner befitting the Bhoys—whereupon the Dead Rabbits retaliated by storming the building.

Thus the great battle of July 4, 1857 started. Barricades were thrown up—the Bowery Boys defending theirs at Elizabeth Street while the Dead Rabbits had one across Bayard Street. The affray had taken on battle proportions. When it was over 7 men had been killed and 39 wounded. Probably the casualties were greater as after the fracas many whose names were not listed as dead had disappeared from their old Bowery haunts, causing much speculation as to the actual number killed that fateful day.

During the next thirty years the Bowery went along at a rapid pace. Racial communities were springing up. The neighborhood which the Dutch had wrested from the Indians only to lose it some years later to the Germans and Irish, was now a veritable melting pot. In 1885 Irish families were still predominant but Italians were moving in west of the Bowery building up a large Italian settlement which still exists around Mulberry Street. The Jews were opening shops; clothing, pawnbroking and dry goods, and auctioneering houses, too, all along the Bowery. Then there were the Chinese over in Mott, Pell and Doyers Streets. A motley gathering if ever there was one, each contributing to the Bowery the characteristics of his race; the pugnaciousness of the Irish, the tenacity of the German, the commercial acumen of the Jew, the exotic culture of the chinaman; all were blended into the cocktail of frenzied living called "The Bowery."

The early nineties found the Bowery in the most vigorous days of its existence. It was a hotbed of immorality and crime. One thought twice before he ventured out alone at night. For that matter, petty robberies and holdups were perpetrated in broad daylight. Leading occupations of the district were robbery, prostitution, swindling, graft and professional beggary. Untold dangers stalked the pavements and scenes of such lawlessness took place as to shock the entire city. It is almost incomprehensible how so much vice could be crammed within the short mile from Cooper Union to Chatham Square where the Bowery begins, yet patrolling this distance was a real problem to the Police Department. In 1898 there were over 99 places of amusement on the Bowery of which only 14 bore the extra listing of "respectable."[8]

These conditions were so common that they were even set to verse and music. Gone were the days when honest settlers tilled the soil of their "bouweries" and industriously set up a form of government in New Amsterdam. Gone were the days when high society frequented the Bowery theatres; gone were the decent families whose main object had been to raise honest children. In truth, the Bowery was given over to a style of living reminiscent of Hogarth's depiction of "The Harlot's Progress" or "The Rake's Progress."

Those were the days when a glass of beer, so large it had to be held in both hands, cost only five cents, a whiskey three cents. A relative of my father's who owned a bakery and restaurant there at that time used to serve a five course dinner for fifteen cents. He also found it necessary to have two loaded clubs which he kept in a convenient location. These, though used with a great deal of discrimination, were, nevertheless, in frequent service as the patrons were not always too eager to pay their checks.

Notorious "Suicide Hall" was located at 295 Bowery. McGurk, the owner was very successful as manager of the most disreputable saloon and sporting house the city has ever known. It was not an uncommon event for the entertainers to drug and rob unsuspecting patrons, and many a country lad left "Suicide Hall" a sadder but wiser fellow. This infamous "dive" as they were called in those days, drew its nefarious revenue for seven years. During only one of these years five women and one man committed suicide on the premises, hence the reason for the macabre appellation applied to McGurk's.[9]

Almost all the neighborhood barber shops specialized in removing black eyes. They always had raw beef on hand for this purpose. It was a common practice with them and no untoward interest was attached to the affair. Needless to say, the income derived from this source must have been a neat one. However, this custom, like that of tatooing, has gradually fallen into disuse although I am informed that there still exists one barber shop on the Bowery where one may take his "indiscretion" and emerge a respectable fellow, with never a trace of a recent brawl.

Tatooing was another fad of the day and nowhere in the city was the art more assiduously practiced than down on the Bowery. One could have any design he wished tatooed upon his flesh. Many women of the district adopted this fad, later exhibiting themselves in side shows of the day, but it was usually a sign of manliness to have several figures ornamenting one's arms and chest. Prof. O'Reilly, "World's Champion Tatooer," was the artist responsible for a great many of these designs. Indeed, many a grandfather today can display lasting monuments of O'Reilly's skill.

One cannot recall the "Bowery" of the "Gay Nineties" without remembering some of its famous characters. Everyone knew Chuck

Connors and Steve Brodie. Their names are synonomous with the Bowery of that period. Chuck Conners is said to have received his nickname because he used to broil chuck steaks over campfires in the streets. He was unofficial guide to the numerous sightseers who used to flock to the Bowery to ascertain if it really was as unsavory as its reputation. When he escorted his guests around they were as safe as they would be walking the sunny streets of Corntown on a Sunday afternoon. His word was law. He was as much loved by the many people he had helped as he was feared and respected by gangdom of that day.

Visiting royalty, famous stars of stage and opera, all saw the Bowery and Chinatown with Chuck Connors. Once he danced with Anna Held in a sketch called "From Broadway to the Bowery." Often he appeared in vaudeville skits, touring the country dressed in his "mouse grey" derby and the numerous pearl buttons he affected. However, he was most unsuccessful as a trouper because he had a habit of introducing impromptu lines and speeches into the dialogue. He would also call out to acquaintances in the audience, thus disrupting the performance. When his manager remonstrated with him about this practice he is said to have replied in his best Bowery dialect, "Youse guys is a lot of cuckoos, sayin' de same t'ings and doing' de same t'ings all de time."[10]

Steve Brodie, a contemporary of Chuck's, owned the saloon at 114 Bowery. This was the mecca of the sporting world and slumming parties of the day. Steve is supposed to have jumped off the Brooklyn Bridge on a dare, but the mystery surrounding this jump has never been satisfactorily cleared up. On the strength of this feat he obtained enough money to set up the saloon where he did a good business running it to Bowery standards then in vogue.

In the "Gay Nineties" the Bowery abounded in dime museums. The exhibits were novel—wild animals—freaks—venomous snakes—not to mention any personality of the day who had received wide publicity as a result of some exceptional or unusual feat. When Steve Brodie jumped, or announced that he had jumped off the Brooklyn Bridge, he was contracted to appear at one of these dime museums—Alexander's at 317 Bowery. Brodie, who had lived all his life around the "Five Points," knew the value of a dollar and was not averse to capitalizing upon the curiosity which his daring deed had inspired. Later, he found a brewery willing to set him up in business at 114 Bowery. Steve was never one to shun publicity; he craved it and lost no opportunity in having his name in the papers. His saloon paid well but when he saw a chance to make more money he did so. Like Chuck Connors, Steve was also given to acting. He appeared in a play, significantly called "On the Bowery" in which he enacted his leap from Brooklyn Bridge. The Irish lad then crowned his histrionic abilities with his own rendition of "My Pearl is a Bowery Girl."

Steve never seems to have done anything without seeing to it that publicity—and plenty of it—accompanied his actions. When the play opened at Peoples' Theatre on October 22, 1894, the Bowery was appropriately decorated. Political bigwigs sent floral offerings and the Bowery was bedecked in gay holiday attire in honor of its son. Brodie was received like a conqueror, as witness the following: "The Peoples' Theatre has seldom held a larger or more enthusiastic audience than that which greeted Mr. Steve Brodie last night in "On the Bowery." It was that famous actor's first appearance on his native heath. Flowers galore were handed over the footlights, including a miniature Brooklyn Bridge in posies. Pat Divver also sent a floral tribute. The blushing star made a speech. It was a great night for Steve."[11]

Brodie had a pleasing personality and knew how to make friends. Whether or not he jumped off the Brooklyn Bridge makes little or no difference. He and Chuck Connors lent color and atmosphere to a Bowery which otherwise would have been drab and dull. Their fabulous personalities decorated the "Bouwerie Lane." They were pointed out to visitors, most of whom thought they hadn't seen the Bowery unless they also saw Steve and Chuck.

The best known museums of Brodie's day were Worth's at 99 Bowery, the Globe at 298 Bowery and the New York Museum at 210 Bowery. The latter museum once carried as its feature attraction the Ford Brothers whose claim to fame lay in the fact that they had just put an end to the notorious career of Jesse James.

Going back some forty years ago you might have found the Brothers Yoelson (later known as Harry and Al Jolson) embarking upon their careers as "buskers." This was the term applied to those free lance singers who toured the saloons of the Bowery singing and entertaining patrons. They depended upon the generosity of the audience for whatever remuneration they received. Sons of a Jewish cantor, singing came easy to the Yoelson boys, for mere boys they were—not over fifteen. The boys left their home in Washington to seek their fortune on the New York stage. Like many others their first start to success came via the Bowery route.

Izzy Baline was another "busker" who started in the Bowery. His repertoire consisted mostly of the "tear jerkers"—a cross between a ballad and a torch song, which was the type of song then in vogue. Later, Izzy gave up singing for a living and started to write music. Tin Pan Alley was glad to discover this young composer. He wrote "Alex-

77

ander's Ragtime Band" which has since been succeeded by numerous other successful songs for it seems that almost all Irving Berlin's songs are famous.

Eddie Cantor and Weber and Fields were others whose rising star first appeared in the Bowery. The latter team were only around 12 years old when they first appeared in Worth's Museum. Later they came to the Grand Opera House on West 23 Street where my father used to take me when I was a little girl. I can still remember their comic routines.

But, that was the Bowery when the Century was young. Like Chuck Connors, McGurk and Steve Brodie, that era is fast becoming only a legend. A far different place is the one we visit today. We traverse the street with all its glamor of the past, with all the turmoil and notoriousness of a generation ago, to see only the broken down remnants of has beens. It is the haunt of the derelict, the ultimate refuge of men who have sunk so low that there is little hope of their ever being rehabilitated. Though in 1909 it was estimated that 25,000 men roamed the Bowery nightly, between Park Place and the Bowery,[12] this number has been decreased due to the man-power shortage. Still, the present number of homeless men wandering around this section is higher than any large city should comport. In a city like New York, where hundreds of dollars worth of spoiled produce is dumped into the Hudson River daily, there are thousands of men roaming the Bowery, hungry, not only in body, but their very souls calling out for sustenance. They walk the Bowery broken in spirit and health, little caring what becomes of them. Their only refuge is contained in a colorless liquid which they call "smoke" and which has so desensitized their feelings that they have no desire to lead normal lives anymore. For them death dogs their very footsteps, and everytime they fall into a drunken stupor may be the sleep from which there is no awakening. For these men there is no hope except the inevitable slab in the morgue which is their eventual destination. Many times these bodies are unclaimed in which case final disposition of the remains is made in Potter's Field where New York buries its unknown dead. . . . But out of this army of human wreckage, out of this undulating wave of living flotsam which rises and ebbs with the tide of social conditions, there are many who are worthy of help. Many are on the Bowery through no fault of their own and it is to help these few that the many missions have been established. It is to the everlasting credit of these missions that many of the men who otherwise would join the permanent "coterie" of Boweryites, are restored to their homes to become useful members of society.

And some of these men through their resumption of a better life do justify all the help dispensed by the religious organizations on the Bowery. A notable example was the late Tom Noonan. Noonan was converted in Sing Sing at about the age of eighteen years. Mrs. Maude Ballington Booth of the Volunteers of America took an interest in him and when he was released from prison he became connected with a group of Christian workers known as The Rescue Society.

During the many years of his affiliation with this organization, an organization in which he rose to be Superintendent, Mr.Noonan converted the homeless men who wandered into the mission, restored drifters to their families, and started many on the arduous journey back to society. His radio broadcasts were a source of interest and inspiration to the many of us whose pleasure it was to hear him speak. His death some years ago deprived the people of the Bowery of a real friend.

Another mission performing excellent services is The Bowery Mission at 227 Bowery. Every Sunday they broadcast giving those who are down on their luck an opportunity to appeal over the air for jobs and clothing. Most of the appeals are heeded. The Bowery Mission serves an average of 117,307 meals a year and provides sleeping quarters for hundreds of men. Their last report shows that 8,206 pieces of clothing were distributed, men received 24,025 shaves and 19,944 baths. A very important service rendered by The Bowery Mission is the "de-lousing" or fumigating of the men which Dr. St. John says the men call "dynamiting." The report of 1946 says that 8,100 men were fumigated during that year.

A short stroll along the Bowery of 1947 brings to view the many "flop houses" which make this street the haven of the homeless. Here, for as little as ten cents one may obtain a night's lodging, although the ten cent fee may not entitle one to sole occupancy of the cot. There are many missions on both sides of the street as well as the many breadlines which form in front of each, for even during times of plenty the Bowery always has its breadlines. Dingy shops and vulgar theatres have replaced the former gaiety that the Bowery used to know. One feels only sadness here as expressions of hopelessness and a sense of carefree despair accost one at every step.

Chatham Square, where the Bowery begins, seems to epitomize the very street itself. Though today the intricate maze of elevated structures shut out even a vestige of sunshine, I like to imagine Chatham Square as it must have been long ago. It was not always dark and gloomy with roaring trains passing above and the heavy automobile trucks rumbling over the cobblestones below. It was not always the parade ground of a never ending column of homeless men. There was a time when there were trees and the twittering and chirping of birds to grace the spot. Tradition has it that Charolotte Temple died in a house situated at the corner of Chatham Square and Pell Street.

But even now, as the Bowery metamorphosed from a notoriously gay section to a place of last refuge for the downtrodden, one notes that it shows subtle signs of undergoing another change. Here and there one sees business houses springing up and interspersed with the passing faces of those who care not whither they are going are the alert faces of business men eager to arrive at their destination. Indeed, though every city must have its slums, one ventures to predict that soon the Bowery as we know it today will be a place of the past, just as the glamorously wicked Bowery our fathers knew is a place of the past to them.

CHAPTER NOTES

1. Booth, Mary L., "History of the City of New York," Vol. I, p. 103.
2. Ibid., Vol. I, p. 105.
3. Harlow, Alvin F., "Old Bowery Days," p. 236.
4. Wilson, James Grant, "Memorial History of New York," Vol. III, p. 529.
5. Asbury, Herbert, "The Gangs of New York," p. 22.
6. Werner, Morris Robert, "Tammany Hall," p. 74.
7. Harlow, Alvin, "Old Bowery Days," p. 308.
8. Asbury, Herbert, "The Gangs of New York," p. 26.
9. Harlow, Alvin, "Old Bowery Days," p. 499.
10. Ibid., p. 434.
11. "The World" for October 23, 1894, p. 5, c. 6.
12. Harlow, Alvin, "Old Bowery Days," p. 524.
13. Figures supplied by "The Bowery Mission" as of September 30, 1946.

A Typical Scene on the Bowery, 1899, just above Houston Street on the west side of Bowery

CHAPTER NINE

Greenwich Village

*"Who so would be a man, must be a
Non-conformist."*

Emerson, Essays, First Series:
Self-Reliance.

O NE part of New York which I particularly like is Greenwich Village. It is one of the most delightful regions in this giant metropolis as year after year it steadfastly retains its old spirit of independence and tolerance. In Greenwich one feels free to do as he pleases without the conventional restrictions imposed in other places. Even the streets seem to begin and end wherever fancy dictates, conforming to no plan or design, just meandering in all directions and even crossing themselves like Waverly Place. And can you conceive of Fourth Street crossing Tenth, Eleventh and Twelfth Streets at right angles? Here, one finds the unexpected everywhere.

This is considered to be the oldest habitation of man on Manhattan Island, for an Indian village was already situated at the foot of West Gansevoort Street when Henry Hudson sailed the "Half Moon" up the river named after him. The Indians called the village "Sappokanican" which means "farm in the woods." It must have been a veritable paradise. We are told that wild turkey, deer and elk were abundant in the surrounding woods. Enormous lobsters, shrimp and tortoise were plentiful. Fertile soil produced all sorts of wild fruits and berries. Indeed, the exigencies of primitive living were reduced to a minimum. The Dutch used to catch large trout in the stream flowing through this land. In fact, much of the fertility was due to the many water courses located in the vicinity.

Between Charlton and West Houston Streets was a great patch of swampy ground through which Minetta Brook, or as the Dutch called it, "Bestavaar's Kill," flowed to the Hudson. The course of this old stream is very well located by George E. Waring Jr. and George Everett Hill in their pamphlet, "Old Wells and Water Courses." Thus, ". . . two rivulets united to form the stream. The western one rose near the intersection of Sixth Avenue and Seventeenth Street and flowed practically in a straight line, to the middle of the block bounded by Fifth and Sixth Avenues and Eleventh and Twelfth Streets, where it was joined by the eastern branch. The latter had its origin in a spring east of Fifth Avenue and above Twentieth Street, and ran, parallel with the other, to the southwest corner of Union Square; thence it curved to the west and followed an irregular course to the junction, receiving tiny tributaries on its way. From this point the brook flowed, in a southerly direction, to Fifth Avenue below Clinton Place. Then curving towards the west, it crossed Washington Square, ran parallel with and just south of Minetta and Downing Streets, across West Houston Street, to the little swamp already mentioned."[1]

In a section where nature provided most of the elements conducive to an easy living, it is very surprising that Greenwich was so long in becoming settled. However, it was very remote and communication with settlers on the southern tip of Manhattan was difficult. Then, too, the Indians had not yet been driven away from the vicinity, and while they were apparently friendly, the Dutch never knew when they would don their war paint. It was not until after the epidemics that Greenwich began to grow. In 1799 even the banks moved uptown in their panic to flee the scourge which was decimating lower Manhattan. They opened in small houses on a street beginning at what we now know as Sheridan Square. The street was called Bank Street, a name which it retains until this day. People flocked to the Village and when the epidemic had run its course, they remained permanently to enjoy the salubrious climate.

The Village today is the home of a heterogenous group of people. Though the Village no longer boasts as being the abode of large numbers of artists, it still harbors a few "pseudo" artists as well as many whose genuine artistic ability cannot be disputed. These, together with some white collar workers and a large industrial class make the Village sector their home. In the turbulent days of World War I Greenwich sheltered a bizarre crowd of altruistic souls each striving for success in some artistic pursuit. In addition, there were their bohemian friends who though incapable of expression in any artistic form, liked to be found in association with the genuine artists of the Village. There were also the sponsors of diverse movements and ideas and their main object was to hold gatherings for discussion of their theories. It must not be supposed however, that this latter assortment of progressives tried to impose their beliefs upon others for in no place in New York could one find a more tolerant or a more liberal class of people. All opinions were respected. If one had an "ism" which he wished to try out, there was no better place to launch it than Greenwich. The Village stood ready—a fertile ground upon which to sow the seeds of new thought. One attended these meetings and one tendered due consideration to the other's opinion. If one agreed—he joined the movement; if not, he was free to lend his ear elsewhere, or to introduce his own theories upon the liberal Villagers.

There were many such groups in the Village of those days. They were constructive and progressive, even though one did not agree with all they said and did. Upon just deliberation, though, one must concede that these gatherings constituted a socializing force the strength of which was felt in far distant parts. The tendency to compare ideas lent itself well to the environment as everything appeared conducive to a progressive succession of "movements." Some of these movements perished under the very momentum exerted by their overeager sponsors, but some took hold of public imagination and lived to fare better days. The Theatre Guild was one of the latter ventures, for it still thrives, a stimulating influence on Manhattan's theatrical life. The Theatre Guild grew out of a group of Villagers calling themselves "The Washington Square Players." It was the Liberal Club which gave these players their start. The club originated as an organization where people spoke on given topics with the ultimate aim of improving the mental attitude of the masses. The members consisted of a heterogenous group of intellectuals bent upon raising to a higher level the existing thoughts and opinions. The club allowed the "Washington Square Players" to give performances in the club rooms at MacDougal Street, which was a converted barn located at No. 133. Later, the "Players" moved to other quarters under the name "The Theatre Guild."[2]

The Village at this time was also the home of quite a few "faddists." Irene Castle had started the fashion of bobbed hair, a mode quickly adopted by female Villagers. Nearly all the girl members of the Liberal Club, then in its ascendency in Village life, cut their hair short. And so while women went in for short hair and men's trousers (the term "slacks" not yet having been devised to designate this article of attire) the male population of the Village grew their hair long and wore large flowing ties.

I remember the first time I saw a woman daring enough to walk in the street without stockings. We were living near Perry Street and this venturesome female of quite a few winters lived next to us. She derived her living from the sale of handsome pieces of batique which she used to dye and sell. She was a mild mannered, unprepossessing creature, not the sort at all that one would associate with what was then considered a very brazen feat. Walking along Perry Street, her black bobbed hair flying in the breeze, her unclad biceps created no stir in the Village. But let her go beyond Fourteenth Street and our neighbor would have been the cynosure of all eyes. Today it is quite an ordinary practice for ladies to go without stockings—and one very practical, too—so that our lady of the batiques was far ahead of her more restrained sisters.

In the Village individualism inspires respect. And from this there has sprouted the root of a great misunderstanding which has developed into many unjust criticisms of the Village. People said that it was wicked, that it was peopled by a cynical coterie whose only thought was sex and pleasure. The claim was made that there was a large group masquerading under the name "individualists"—a group which was said to repudiate nearly all social traditions. Greenwich Village became publicized from Paducah to Paris as a kind of Manhattan Montmartre, where money was scorned, sex experimentation a natural factor of everyday life, and riotous studio parties a common occurence.

This idea concerning the Village was quite common in the 1920's and 1930's when the unfavorable comments hurled at the artist's colony of Manhattan reached its apex. To anyone who knows and loves this wistful little section of New York, a false notion of existing conditions could not have been conceived.

The blatant truth was that because the Villagers were tolerant and unconventional as compared with inhabitants of more conservative parts—the fact is that because they were tolerent enough to permit the other fellow to live according to his own judgement—neither condemning nor condoning his errors—Paducah and Paris took it to mean that the Village was morally corrupt.

If some residents choose to pattern their mode of life after low concepts, very often they were not the Villagers, but outsiders who came there to do things and otherwise behave in a manner which they would not venture to follow in other sections of New York. Against these the Villager, that is, the genuine Villager, issued no complaint, because he was too tolerant to do so. The real Villager worked very hard and at times far into the night. It was not unusual during the time when Greenwich was subject to so much adverse publicity, to wend one's way through the intricate pattern of Village streets and find people burning the midnight oil well into the wee hours; for while the rest of United States was censuring and criticizing, Villagers were producing some of the finest pieces of artistic work accomplished in America.

Perhaps of the various criticisms hurled at the Village, the only one having any foundation was that which applied to money. As a group they were totally devoid of any sense of money values. While other communities in United States were placing undue importance on the Almighty Dollar, the Villagers forged ahead with a view to perfecting cultural values. The "Get-Rich-Quick-Wallingfords" were definitely discouraged from putting in an appearance upon the Village scene. There was a very well defined tendency to relegate money to the background which was, after all, merely a reactionary movement against the superiority accorded money in other parts of the United States. It was a time when everything was measured in terms of dollars and cents. And who could blame these people if, bored with the ascendency which money was reaching, they congregated in this region of Manhattan to work in accordance with values which they themselves had established?

The average Villager of those days was happy-go-lucky. It meant nothing to share his dollar in the hope that the morrow would bring better prospects. They were a genial crowd, helping and encouraging each other. If they were hungry, as many times they were, oft time the following day brought a feast. This mode of life attracted foreign artists as well as people from all over the United States who gravitated to the Village in the hope of achieving fame through the pursuit of one of the muses. Some were successful; others eked out a tragic existence until a merciful providence terminated their unhappy lives.

This was the case of a young Brazilian artist who appeared on the Village scene around two decades ago, which was just about the time that my own nomadic way of living brought me to the Washington Square sector. He was a graduate lawyer, who had received his degree from law school in Bahia, but feeling the urge to paint he abandoned that career in favor of the more alluring but less lucrative one of painting. Santos always had visions of becoming a noted landscapist. But in order to live he accepted commissions to do murals or to paint scenes of wooden medalions which he used to sell for three dollars each. For as little as fifty dollars Santos would undertake the decoration of a baby grand piano. It was very much the style at that time to have all-over designs painted on pianos and while some of these were monstrosities, the style did serve its purpose, for it supplied work to many artists who otherwise would not have had a market for their talents.

Meanwhile, Santos had become a real Villager. If he had to skip a meal he did, and if he met someone with less than his poor self, he shared what little he had. He made friends among the other people of the Village and with them attended the various gatherings which were always an integral part of Village life.

One bleak, cold February day of the Thirties, I met Santos on West Eighth Street. His overcoat was conspicuously missing and it is no exaggeration to say that he was actually shivering. "But Santos," I remonstrated, "you should never come out on a day like this without a coat. Why, you will catch your death of cold!" Then he told me that he had an overcoat but that he had loaned it to a tenor friend who was going to be auditioned for a job. That's the way things went with Santos, and with hundreds of his prototype who were to be found in the Village.

Seven or eight years later I again chanced to meet Santos. This time it was at the Automat on 14th Street and Irving Place. He looked pale and emaciated and generally worn out. His eyes alone were reminiscent of the old Santos for they still vibrated with a determination to succeed. I suggested that he ought to return to Brazil—to his people—and forget about art. I could not have made a worse suggestion! It was unthinkable to him that he cease the pursuit to which the elusive siren of painting was beckoning and leading him on with all the wiles of a Lorelei singing her enticing song. It did not matter that he had no money; the fact that many times he went without food meant nothing; it was of no consequence that often he was cold, for he was then living in a cold water flat over on Third Avenue; he was determined that one day he really would paint something worthwhile and all his sufferings were endured with that in mind.

The next time I saw Santos was at Bellevue Hospital where he had been taken in a very bad condition. Years of malnutrition and self deprivation had taken their toll from his wasted body. Lorelei had succeeded. It was only after he realized that there was no hope that he consented to be sent back to Brazil. It was then that his eyes lost that determined hopeful gleam which had been his dominant feature during the fifteen years I had known him. I knew then that Santos was already dead. He died two days before his boat reach Bahia.

Santos, though he came from afar typified the genuine Villager of that time. There were many others whose lives parallelled his; people who could have made decent livings in other walks of life, but who chose to eke out miserable existences in order to follow the Muses.

Incurably romantic? I should say so! If one had money, they all had money. Help was always forthcoming in a sort of irresponsible communal way. Not a very guaranteed sort of life you might say, but what is one sure of in this life aside from death? Nothing is certain, and so the blithe Villager pursues his course.

What force led a man like Santos to give up the profession he had studied and in which he could possibly have made a fairly good living, to take up painting? Santos had never had an art lesson in his life. All his work was unrestrained and uninhibited by any previous teachings. Even a lay art critic could see that his paintings were not the work of a genious. They were beautiful, to be sure, but they lacked an intangible quality which in the absence of a better name some people call depth. By that I mean that if he painted a running brook, one never imagined that he could hear the ripple which is caused by water running over pebbles. One could only see the scene, one never could hear it, as in some paintings. But Santos did show signs of promise and as the years went on his work did improve. It was on this fact that he banked his future and for which he was willing to suffer untold hardships. He always hoped that he would paint something really good, and when he was without money, food or fuel, it was this hope which kept him going.

Santos was exemplified in almost every Village street—people who forgot the past, accepted whatever the present had to offer, and looked forward to a successful future. In the meantime, a beneficient providence kept the wolf away from the door, or, if he had already crossed the threshold forced him to retreat and wait his next opportunity. Thus life went on—Villagers wrote their prose and poetry, painted their would-be masterpieces and molded their statues of Aphrodite or the American cow-boy, or rehearsed their crowning performance. However, through it all, the hardships and heartbreaks, they never lost that gay spirit of comradery which pervades the very atmosphere around Washington Square.

That is as true today, when many Villagers have moved away, as it was fifteen years ago. The residents have changed but the atmosphere has not. People are still childishly unconventional in work and habits—but wicked or bad—never.

Perhaps the hub of the Village may be said to be the Square. Personally, I do not believe there is any other section of Manhattan where such a noted and striking contrast is so apparent. On one side of the Square reside stolid influential Knickerbockers living in comparative opulence while on the other side lives a vast foreign population retaining habits and customs of other years and other countries. And residents from both sections pass each other under Washington Arch, each dreaming his own dreams, each intent upon a different activity. Some undoubtedly are planning what they will do when fame embraces them, for all true Villagers envision hopes of ultimate success. While those fortunate successful ones are perhaps recalling how years before they plodded these same paths maybe discouraged, maybe hungry. And they all have passed or some day will pass under the Arch, the magnificent Arch designed by Stanford White which marks the center of the Square.

Just as the Arch marks the center of the Square, the Square sets off the eastern extremity of the Village. Radiating from this pivotal point are all the activities which go to make this section one of the most interesting of all New York. North, south, and west one finds contrasts, each having to be analyzed separately, yet put together forming a fascinating conglomeration of ideals and people and places that are Greenwich Village.

Starting at the Square itself and observing the many people boarding Fifth Avenue buses, seeing University students changing classes, gazing at the Park with its apparently serene demeanor, one is almost led to forget the unsavory past of this spot. When a yellow fever epidemic swept the city, the ground was acquired as a Potter's Field to inter victims of the scourge. Between the years 1797 and 1823 it is estimated that 100,000 bodies were buried here.[3] In 1819 it was used as a public gallows where the hanging of Rose Butler took place. It was not until 1827 that the Square was converted into a Park. In 1833 there was a pump in the Square where surrounding residents used to send for water. The water was reputed to have been very soft, a quality which rendered it useful for laundry purposes.[4]

This, then is the eastern extremity of the Village and while the section can be described as a whole, if the visitor really wants to see what is sometimes erroneously called the "Monmartre of Manhattan" he must first visit its component parts, that is, north, south and west of the Square.

If it does not sound too didactical, suppose, for example, we start walking north towards Fifth Avenue. What do we see but a row of charming red brick houses whose inviting portals have inspired many a novelist to first rate production. Houses numbers 1 to 13, east of Fifth Avenue, are owned by Sailors' Snug Harbor, and this in itself lends a romantic aura to them for even though we must deviate from our course, how Sailors' Snug Harbor acquired this ground is a story in itself. Going back to those hectic post-revolutionary days, a large parcel of land adjacent to the Brevoort estate belonged to Andrew Elliot. When land belonging to British sympathizers was being confiscated Elliot somehow transferred his holding. Later, it was sold to Captain Robert Randall, freebooting commander of the privateering ship "Fox." And here it must be pointed out that in a fair description of the Village one cannot pass lightly over the people who have lived here. Just as history is made by events, events usually owe their occurrence to some human manipulation. And what could be more interesting than the history of a place written in tears and laughter, yes and in the life blood, too, of the people who have lived there?

So, my patient friend, come with me on board the "Fox" and meet one of the bravest privateers of his time, Captain Robert Randall. Captain Randall in life as well as in death was first a man of the sea, and so his will, drawn up by Alexander Hamilton, provided that almost the entire estate should be devoted to the establishment of a home for aged sailors. The property comprised about twenty acres bounded by Fourth and Fifth Avenues and Sixth and Tenth Streets. Even the name was provided for in this well known will. Thus, today, all the property is known as Sailors' Snug Harbor Estates. The home for seamen is maintained on Staten Island, on a beautiful site overlooking the Kill von Hull, but the large income used to maintain the home is derived mainly from holdings around Washington Square.[5]

And perhaps the most famous of all the property are the houses from One to Thirteen Washington Square, houses now a score over one hundred years old. One cannot think of the Square without this charming landmark of red brick dwellings. They represent scenes of struggle and hope to many a well known personage. However, land values in this vicinity are so high that it is only a question of time when the old row will yield to advances made by the omnipresent apartment skyscrapers climbing up in this neighborhood. In fact, about a year or so ago there were threats of demolishing these old homes but the rumor brought forth no end of protest, until the project was temporarily abandoned.

West of the Avenue there is another row of houses. They are mostly of brown stone with wide stone steps leading up to a spacious doorway. Many of these houses are vacant, a perplexing problem when one considers the present housing shortage. Years ago all this property was owned by the Rhinelander family. The first Rhinelander country home stands on the north corner of Fifth Avenue and Washington Square. It is a quaint red brick house with a row of smaller cottages behind it. The large house is separated from the cottages by a garden. It is a lovely sight, indeed, to pass on a summer day and catch a glimpse of green trees and flowers blossoming in what well might be the most valuable garden in all New York, a garden at the beginning of the world's most famous Avenue.

Across the Avenue are the Lafayette and Brevoort Hotels, two of the most venerable in the city. The Brevoort is more than a hundred years old. Historians will tell you that Eleventh Street was never cut through because old Burgher Brevoort conclusively argued the city surveyors away with a blunderbuss. Brevoort's son later presented his father's famous blunderbuss to Irving. Incidentally, it was this son, Henry, to whom Irving owed much of his success for in those days it was necessary for writers to have a patron. Henry Brevoort had strong literary tastes. When Irving wrote his history, Henry Brevoort took it upon himself to send copies to the great men of letters, Sir Walter Scott being one recipient. The Brevoort family owned much of the land in this vicinity, so that when the Hotel was opened in 1835 it took the family name.

The Lafayette, or the Old Martin, as old timers still call it, was opened in 1883. It flourished under various names, Hotel de Panama, Hotel Martin and later Hotel Lafayette.

Mark Twain's house stands at the corner of Eleventh Street and Fifth Avenue. James Fenimore Cooper once occupied this house also. The house overlooks Grace Church which was designed by Henry Brevoort's only son-in-law, James Renwick.

From this point on we must cease an orderly description of the Village and just gather up odd bits from here and there. An intriguing feature of this district, as we mentioned before, is its non-conformity. One discovers the unexpected just around the corner. Who would think of finding a garden on Fifth Avenue or a row of stables fitted up as studios, or streets of less than a city block ending up in little Cul de Sacs? The Village is dotted by Squares, Courts and Places: Jackson Square, Abingdon Square, Sheridan Square, Grove and Clinton Courts, Minetta and Patchin Places, etc. This brings us to the neighborhood of the land owned by Captain Peter Warren, later Sir Peter Warren. Sir Peter settled this region about 1744. He owned 300 acres. It is a curious fact that both the Warren estates and the Randall estates were built upon the proceeds obtained from government protected buccaneering.

Like Captain Randall, Peter Warren was a stout hearted man of the sea. Irish English by birth, he combined the Englishman's love of the sea with the Irishmen's love for a fight to found a fortune which he promptly used in gay entertainments and lavish spending. Peter Warren was only twenty-four years old when he commanded the squadron on the Leeward Islands station. During this time Post Captain Warren captured twenty-four prizes, one alone being a cargo of two hundred and fifty thousand pounds in plate.[6] The wary Captain was not entirely of an adventurous nature, however, for part of his prize money he used to establish himself as Squire of a large sylvan tract located in Greenwich.

On this site he built himself a home worthy of his achievements. Sir Peter's country seat was located in the center of the block now bounded by Bleeker, Fourth, Charles and Perry Streets. His home overlooked the river and one supposes that the site owed much of its attractiveness to this fact. It must have been a never-ending source of pleasure for this hearty man of the sea to be able to have his home on land from which he could have an excellent view of the majestic Hudson. The house stood through various vicissitudes until 1865 when it gave way to the onrush of the city's growth.

Sir Peter's three daughters all made distinguished marriages, and had streets named after their families. Charlotte married the Earl of

Abingdon. Abingdon Road, more familiarly known by the suggestive name of Love Lane was named after them. Ann married Charles Fitzroy, Baron Southampton, and Fitzroy Road was named in their honor. Susannah married Colonel Skinner. Our present Christopher Street was once called Skinner Road. Today, of all the land owned by the gallant Sir Peter, only Abingdon Square retains a name reminding modern New Yorkers of this family.[7]

Sir Peter did not end his days in Greenwich, as one would expect. Early in life he had married into the Delancey family. His wife, Susannah was a famous belle of the time and was a well known hostess both in England and the Colonies. Sir Peter was Admiral of the British Navy and the hero of Louisburg. He represented the City of Westminster at Parliament and upon his death was laid to rest in Westminster Abbey, where England does final honor to her distinguished sons. Today, if you ever have the opportunity to visit the Abbey, you will find Sir Peter Warren's tomb with the epitaph written by Dr. Samuel Johnson.

When Sir Peter died the Warren House passed to his daughter, Charlotte who had married the Earl of Abingdon. The house and surrounding lots then went to the hands of Abijah Hammond who sold it in 1802 to Whitehead Fish. This latter resided in Warren House until his death, whereupon, in 1819, it was sold to Abraham Van Nest.

Inasmuch as at this time the house was considered to be two miles beyond the city limits, the Van Nests used it as a summer residence. The journey to and from their city home in William Street was a long and arduous trip accomplished by stage. The Warren House rendered many years of service, finally giving way to the wrecker's hammer. It was demolished, the lovely old trees on the property were felled and the rapidly growing village of Greenwich was permitted to absorb the land.

Another distinguished resident of the section was the immortal creator of "The Age of Reason," Thomas Paine. In an era when the world was slow to recognize individual greatness, he was scorned and ostracized as an infidel. Even though it was he who drew thousands to the cause for American freedom by his concise book "Common Sense"—even though many people believed it was he who drafted the Declaration of Independence—even though it was he who induced the French King to donate $6,000,000 to the fight for American Independence—even though this English Quaker was the most ardent patriot of all Americans, his true value to the cause for liberty was never admitted. He was imprisoned in France, outlawed in the land of his birth and ostracized in the land of his adoption. The country to which he devoted his brillant pen and much of his money it earned for him, disfranchised him, even going so far as to prohibit him from riding in public coaches. Alas and alack! Why is it that so often great men, men who by their very deeds and benefactions should feel the warm glow of a thankful world, receive, instead, the scorn and ungratefulness of their fellow-men?

According to many historians Tom Paine was the most unjustly treated figure in the American fight for Independence. If this had been the fate of any other person of that time, the sting of ignominy would not have been so sharp, but to be denounced by the very people whose gratitude should have been beyond limits, was bitter, indeed. People forgot that it was Paine's cry of "These are the times that try men's souls!" which called the weary and disheartened soldiers at Trenton. They heard and were inspired with renewed courage and a hope reborn. Though it is a historical fact that "many of the soldiers were shoeless and left bloody footprints on the snow-covered line of march," Paine's words buoyed up their spirits, and the Battle of Trenton was won.[8] But, if the soldiers heard, Paine's immortal words were soon forgotten, and their author permitted to languish midst the scorn heaped by an ungrateful America. They said he was a drunkard, they called him an atheist and zealously attacked his personal habits. Yet, in his last will and testament Paine bequeathed all his possessions to Mme. de Bonneville, who had befriended him during the trying days of his final illness. The property, whatever little he had, was left to her for her children, that she, "might bring them well up, give them a good and useful learning and instruct them in their duty to God and the practice of morality."[9] And this from a man of whom Theodore Roosevelt applied the epithet, "Filthy little atheist."[10]

The next time you pass Bleeker Street try to picture Thomas Paine who, though he lived in the Village for only a short time, has come to be regarded as its greatest resident. Citizen of the world, as he was, he lived his life very much in the same manner as Greenwich does; a liberal, a romanticist, unwilling to conform to accepted notions and conventions, unless they be guided by reason, for in his own words, "The most formidable weapon against errors of every kind is Reason."[11]

It is not surprising that he selected this section as his home, as even in its early history there was something about the area around the Square which had a "kind of established repose which is not of frequent occurence in other quarters of the long, shrill city; it has a riper, richer, more honorable look than any of the upper ramifications of the great longitudinal thoroughfare—the look of something of social history."[12]

Try then to displace the present buildings in Bleeker Street and in their stead you will see a few frame houses surrounded by tracts of empty land. Here is where Paine lived and died—a far different scene from that which we see today. There was no Barrow Street as this was not opened until after Paine's death. At the time it was opened this street was called Reason Street, in honor of Paine's "Age of Reason." It seemed, however, that even this small honor was to be denied the noted Villager for soon the name was corrupted to Raison Street. In 1828 it took the name Barrow Street, thus obliterating even this small compliment.[18]

But enough! I told you one could not describe the Village without a glance at the people who lived there—bold visionaries, deep thinkers, creative writers and artists, as well as every day run of the mill people. Here we have gone to sea with Captain Randall, fought with Sir Peter, and been jailed and shunned with Thomas Paine. We have seen old man Brevoort admiring his trees on Fifth Avenue, and modern artists seeking inspiration in remodeled stables. We have seen the Village of prohibition days and we have pictured the serene and peaceful spot it was a century or so ago. We have followed the vicissitudes of the Square from the hanging of Rose Butler to the serious University student's discussion of Darwin's Theory with the honking of Fifth Avenue buses and the cry of the peanut man to furnish background sound effects. Yet, we have not seen all of Greenwich.

On the south side of the Square is another row of remodeled houses where we should pause again at one of them. It would be unseemly to talk of these houses without a word about the late proprietor of one of them, Mme. Branchard who presided over No. 61 Washington Square South. For fifty years, until her death in 1937, Mme. Branchard operated the most famous rooming house in the city. The voice of Adelina Patti once resounded through the house and even today echos of typewriters clicking out a famous story is not an unfamiliar one in those rooms. Frank Norris wrote "The Pit" in one of the front rooms. "The Sea" by James Oppenheim was another story born in Mme. Branchard's house. Noted roomers include John dos Passos, Rollo Peters, Theodore Dreiser, Willa Cather and many others. Even O'Henry lived at one time at Mme. Branchard's, for what locale of New York was unfamiliar to the poet who sang its song? Willy Pogany was another roomer until he moved to Patchin Place. One could almost say that Mme. Branchard's was an unofficial Academy of Arts and Letters.

Radiating in fan shaped directions from here is a vast foreign population. The Italians comprise one half of the residents. Years ago this part of the Village used to be taken up by the Irish but they steadily, though unwillingly, pushed westward to make room for the influx of Italians. At first the Irish objected in the pugnacious manner in which the "sons of Erin" are famous and many a fight ensued. Today, though, there is little or no friction between the two nationalities, as the Irish have gradually moved uptown and those few who remain are located west of the Square.

Though very dissimilar as to racial characteristics and backgrounds these two foreign elements can readily be distributed into one class. Both nationalities can be grouped into the laboring class of Villagers. They unload the giant liners docked at the Hudson piers and perform most of the labor for the public utilities. While many of the Italian residents go in for shopkeeping and factory work, the Irish have developed a dominant voice in local government.

Walking down Thompson Street one may as well be in the heart of Italy. In the eyes of those who pass one can see the vapor capped clouds of Vesuvious or traces of glimmering waves which once caressed the immortal Shelley's "Ariel" or armies of gladiators marching into the arena; centuries of history written in eyes which shine in the shadow of the Square.

It is wise, at this point, to call attention to the very obvious tendency of foreigners to form settlements where their own customs and habits are maintained. Thus, in Manhattan, we have Armenians, Puerto Ricans, Syrians, Irish, Germans, Poles, Czechs, etc. all congregating in one section making little cities within a city. The Italians have carried this process a step further for we have Northern Italians settling one region while their swarthy countrymen from the south establish themselves in another part of the Island. By far the great mass of Italian immigrants in New York came from Southern Italy. They settled first in Mulberry Bend and when that region became too crowded they overflowed into Little Italy or Italian Harlem.

The Italian settlement of the Greenwich area was accomplished by numbers of Northern Italians who, as soon as they landed, darted from Ellis Island to the streets adjacent to the Square. With the help of relatives or friends who already "knew the ropes" they established themselves as waiters or servants in the city's restaurants and hotels. Many of these immigrants later became owners of their own restaurants. They occupied Bleeker, MacDougal and Sullivan Streets and then absorbed adjacent streets of the neighborhood until the section became, as it still is, predominantly Italian.

Although there may be a radio in every tenement on both sides of the street, American customs are slow to be assimilated in this part of Manhattan. Whereas other foreigners learn the language as soon as they arrive, Italians are slow to take up the study of English. They cling to their own customs and language. Many times they are here for a good many years after which their only progress is an indifferent knowledge of the language. Italian immigration having been curtailed by the Immigration Act of 1921, this situation is not so common today, but previous to enactment of the Act, it was especially true.

At the turn of the century this condition caused much exploitation of the laboring class of Italians who were then entering the United States. When Italian immigration was at its peak and "padrones" were inducing credulous Italians to mortgage and sell their belongings in order to sail to the United States—where "money grew on trees"—the fact that the Italian did not learn English was a hindrance to his progress. He worked hard, performing such labors as required back breaking toil, and had very little to show for it. Not knowing the language, he was compelled to have recourse to a middle man who hired him out to a contractor. Oft times the middleman saw to it that the laborer was fired so that he could hire him out to another firm. Sometimes the "padrone" who had made his commission of the passage and the middle man who also exploited the unsuspecting laborer, was the same person. Thus the credulous Italian fell an easy prey to the mechanations of his unscrupulous countrymen upon whom he had to depend in the new country because only to him could he speak in his native tongue.

Though this system has long been relegated to the dear dead past, it has not made any difference to the Italian with respect to his learning English. In comparison with other foreigners who come to America, he is still slow to acquire a workable knowledge of the language. One must concede, however, that many times it is not necessary for him to learn English, for should he find himself located in this part of Greenwich, he can live tolerably well speaking and reading his native language. All the neighborhood stores are run by Italian shopkeepers. The signs outside are written in Italian and many of the products sold are imported from the home country.

Sprinkled throughout the neighborhood are grocery stores from which emanate the combined odors of olive oils, various cheeses and the pungent aroma of herbs, and bakeries where shining windows reveal luscious Italian pastries. There are paper stores where side by side with New York dailies are to be found "Il Progresso Italo-Americano" or "Couriere d'America" which are the two better known of a number of Italian publications. There are restaurants where one may order popular dishes from most of the Italian provinces, for they are nearly all represented.

Italy being almost exclusively a Roman Catholic country, her sons and daughters who have come to the new country naturally profess this faith, which in turn, is passed on to their sons and daughters. Native habits and feast days are meticulously observed, just as they were in sunny Italy; people from different provinces paying homage to special

Saints. Thus the Neopolitans glorify St. Januarius, the Sicilians from around Palermo pay homage to Santa Rossilia while those from the east coast of Sicily honor Catania's Sant' Agata. Other Saints highly honored are San Rocco and Our Lady of Mount Carmel.[14] It is not unusual to witness religious processions wending their way along the Italian streets of the Village. During such times the Italian Villager outdoes himself in decorating the streets through which the procession shall pass. Flags and banners are flown from windows and strung across the streets; flowers decorate the line of the procession; street shrines are erected and vari-colored arches extend from sidewalk to sidewalk.

Passing through this colorful district reminiscent of sunny Italy, it is difficult to image that at Charlton and Varick and MacDougal Streets once stood the glorious Richmond Hill made famous as the residence of the Adamses, and later as the home of the Dashing Burr, and his beautiful, ill-fated Theodosia. While a steady stream of traffic wends its way towards the Holland tunnel, few of the pedestrians whose business takes them past the spot are aware of the significance of Richmond Hill. It is difficult to visualize the lavish entertainments leisurely tendered by these hospitable colonials for all around are tall buildings and multitudes of people constantly rushing by. Here and there is a green spot showing out like an oasis in a desert of fire-escapes and tenements, but this is only a vacant lot which will soon be seized as the base for some gigantic building.

When Richmond Hill was in its heyday, there was much green, not like the few blades of anemic looking grass we find today. Tall trees surrounded Richmond Hill, stately in their winter bareness and lovely in their summer fullness. To this green spot—verdant and charming as it must have been in days of long ago—came Aaron Burr, imprudent, ambitious to the point of being rash, but withal a gentleman and a scholar and tremendously fond of the opposite sex.

We must pause again at the mention of Burr, for here again, we have a personality of the Village entirely different from any of the other residents. Though history looks askance at him and his wild dreams of a Southern Empire, though he was bitterly censured and socially ostracized following his duel with Hamilton, one cannot help but feel qualms of sympathy for this personable colonial gentleman and scholar who spent the happiest years of his life at Richmond Hill. One knows that he was a scoundrel, but one feels sorry for him just the same. Can you picture him sauntering up to the famous entrance gateway of Richmond Hill at what is now MacDougal and Spring Streets? Can you see him as genial host gathering round him leading personalities of the day? Even Alexander Hamilton is said to have been his guest at various times when Burr, with his lovely daughter as hostess, dispensed the honors as the master of such a country seat as Richmond Hill should. Burr in later life married the widow Jumel but the marriage was unsuccessful, and one is led to suppose that the once dashing financier often looked back upon pleasant times spent at Richmond Hill.[16]

With such antecedents as Greenwhich boasts, it is inconceivable that this quaint little Village—this independent colony should lose its identity. Some places live only in the light of the past and then sink sadly into present obscurity, but Greenwich Village does not conform. It is a far cry from Sapponikan or Sir Peter's country home, or tree shaded lanes leading up to Richmond Hill, yet the section is still charmingly quaint. In a district so unlike the rest of Manhattan, with twisting streets and here and there an unexpected alley to intrigue one's imagination, or a group of romantic old houses to carry one back through the years, it is not unnatural that artists should seek its atmosphere. Edna St. Vincent Millay, Theodore Dresier, the Norrisses, all sought local color in Greenwich Village. And before them, there were others. The tragic Edgar Allen Poe used to live on Waverly Place near Sixth Avenue. Walt Whitman was a Village resident at one time. John Masefield, the great English poet once portered in Luke Connors saloon over where Sixth Avenue, Christopher Street, West Eighth Street and Greenwich Avenue converges. Lafcadio Hearn lived at 149 West 10 Street.

For long the Village has provided inspiration and a haven to the artists and poets of the city. As success came, some moved to other parts, but one is almost sure that the Village harbors uncountable happy memories for many who are now famous in the fields of arts and letters. It has served its purpose and served it well.

One of the interesting features of living in New York City, I always contend, is that every ten years or so there is a decided change in the city's appearance. Though not so readily discernible as in other parts, this also is somewhat true of the Village area. The Village was one of the first sections of New York to adopt the sidewalk café, and in no other neighborhood do they lend such charm. In fact, this is where the fad really gained momentum. In the "good old summer time" if one looks south from Eleventh Street and Fifth Avenue as far as the Square, the Village landscape is enhanced by at least four "drink and squatteries" as one New York reporter so aptly put it. Here, on a summer's afternoon, while the Fifth Avenue buses pass to and fro, one may sit and leisurely sip refreshments shaded by colorful umbrellas. And what could be more pleasant in a city of hustle and bustle and constant change, than to pause in retrospection in this picturesque part of Manhattan where the past is so finely blended with the present as to be almost undistinguishable?

CHAPTER NOTES

1. Hill, George Everett and Waring, George E. Jr., "Old Wells and Water Courses of the Island of Manhattan," Part II, p. 2.
2. Federal Writers' Project, "New York City Guide," p. 129.
3. Rider, Arthur Fremond, "Rider's New York City," p. 237.
4. De Forest, Emily Johnston, "John Johnston of New York; Merchant," p. 149.
5. Bisland, Elizabeth, "Old Greenwich," p. 24.
6. "Old Buildings of New York City," p. 76.
7. Janvier, Thomas A., "In Old New York," p. 113.
8. Wilcox, Ella Wheeler, "Lest We Forget," p. 10.
9. Chapin, Anna Alice, "Greenwich Village," p. 170.
10. Berthold, S. M., "Thomas Paine, America's First Liberal," p. 171.
11. Paine, Thomas, "Age of Reason," Forward.
12. James, Henry, "Washington Square," p. 23, 24.
13. Janvier, Thomas A., "In Old New York," p. 137.
14. Federal Writers' Project, "The Italians of New York," p. 87, 88.
15. Bisland, Elizabeth, "Old Greenwich," p. 14.

259-263 Bleecker St.

CHAPTER TEN

In Chelsea

"Twas the night before Christmas
When all through the house
Not a creature was stirring, not
even a mouse."

"A Visit from St. Nicholas"
by Clement C. Moore.

O VER on the west side between the 'teens and the Thirties lies the most wistful and pathetic section of New York; poor forgotten Chelsea. When one passes the rows upon rows of three story brick houses now converted into the inevitable furnished rooms, which all houses in New York seem to pass through as a stage in their decline, one feels instinctively that fifty years or so ago these homes must have been the pride of the neighborhood. Some of them still retain proud vestiges of their former glory. Carved doorways, through which many a Chelsea beau may have passed in times long ago, revive romances which have slept these three score years. Brass door knockers which are charmingly simple in design still grace a few front doors of some homes, but for the most part, Chelsea today presents a sad reminder of the Chelsea Village that used to be.

The oldest house in Chelsea is Number Five Chelsea Square. It was built over a hundred years ago. Now it is used as a home for the bursar of the General Theological Seminary of the Protestant Episcopal Church. The Seminary is built in the surrounding grounds, standing there firmly impressive as a part of the Chelsea that was. It is a typical English building with grey stone walls along which creeping ivy entwines itself, here leaving place for a window, here for an arched doorway. On the Twentieth Street side there is a very inviting lawn

99

presided over by a few friendly trees. Here, on warm spring days one may see the theological students passing from classes in cap and gown, suggesting, for all the world, a real English college in the heart of Manhattan.

The entire block between Twentieth and Twenty-first Streets and Ninth and Tenth Avenues was given for the construction of the Seminary by a well beloved Chelseaite, Clement C. Moore. Whenever our thoughts turn to Christmas, they must inadvertently turn also to Clement Moore and to Chelsea. It was here in his home which had been his mother's and his grandmother's that he wrote "T'was the Night Before Christmas" which has endeared him to children all over the world, and which must always do so, as long as there is a Santa Claus to gladden the heart of childhood. In the ultra modern garden of London Terrace there is a monument to commemorate the former site of Chelsea House, where the poem was written in 1822. Every Christmas Eve it has become a custom for the children of the Church of The Intercession to visit their poet's grave in Trinity Cemetary at 155th Street.

Though remembered mostly as a poet, Clement Moore was also a very learned scholar. He was professor of Greek and Hebrew at Columbia College and a brilliant writer. He compiled the first Hebrew and Greek lexicon to be published in the United States. In 1823 he started cutting streets through his property to conform with the City Plan of 1811. However, although it was Clement Clarke Moore who established Chelsea Village on the ground which he had inherited from his father, and to which he had added during his life time, it was the poet's grandfather who first gave that locale the name of Chelsea. Captain Clarke named Chelsea after the Old Soldiers' Home in England, which had been founded by Charles II upon the suggestion of Nell Gwynne. As the original Chelsea was to be the home of the soldier after his battling days were over, so was Captain Clarke's estate to be the home where he would spend the rest of his days. But, the sentimental old soldier had reckoned without allowing for the pranks of Fate. The home which he had built with such fervent hopes in 1750 was burned to the ground. The Captain passed away in a neighbor's farmhouse to which he had been carried from the flaming structure during his last illness.

Later, the Captain's widow rebuilt the house and it stood until 1852. Like so many other homes of its time, it was a square building with two stories from which a flight of steps descended into the spacious garden below. Resting upon a slight promontory so that it overlooked the noble Hudson, it must have been a fine location for a home. It must be remembered that in those days the Hudson River extended nearly to where Tenth Avenue is now. The Clarke homestead, though it was only about 200 feet west of Ninth Avenue on Twenty-third Street, was, therefore, only about 100 yards away from the river. With its magnificent view shaded by century old trees, there is no wonder why Mistress Mollie Clarke was so proud of the house she had built.

Mistress Mollie was a well known Loyalist of her day. During the Revolutionary War, much to her displeasure, she had to have some of General Washington's soldiers billeted in her home. She protested so violently against what she believed to be an outrageous violation of her personal liberty that General Washington finally removed the soldiers. It was about this time that an English frigate anchored in the Hudson accidentally shot a broadside into the big white house.[1] The scar could be seen many years later. Thus, the Clarke homestead suffered indignities from both belligerents during the Revolutionary War.

This house and the property extending from Eighth Avenue to the Hudson, from Nineteenth to Twenty-fourth Streets passed on to Mistress Mollie's daughter, Charity, who had married Bishop Benjamin Moore. The Bishop later became Episcopal Bishop of New York, and he was connected with Trinity for thirty-seven years. Bishop Moore was beloved and esteemed by all who knew him. He was President of Columbia College from 1801 to 1811, and when the Historical Society was founded in 1805, he became its first Vice-President. When Alexander Hamilton fell mortally wounded in his duel with Aaron Burr, it was Bishop Moore, his friend, who administered the last sacrament to the dying statesman.

Good Bishop Moore was violently opposed to the prevailing practice of settling differences of opinion with the sword. The day following Hamilton's death he wrote a bitter letter to "The Evening Post" which says in part, "Let those who are disposed to justify the practice of duelling, be induced, by this simple narrative, to view with abhorrence that custom which has occasioned an irreparable loss to a worthy and most afflicted family; which has deprived his friends of a beloved companion, his profession of one of its brightest ornaments, and his country of a great statesman and real patriot."

In 1813 the Bishop's son, Clement Clarke Moore came into possession of the house and grounds. With the advent of Clement Moore as squire, Chelsea began to acquire some of the character which made the place a favorite residential section of old Manhattan. It was conveniently located near the main thoroughfare of the day. There was the Fitzroy Road which ran about parallel to the present Eighth Avenue from Fifteenth to Forty-second Streets, and then continued as the Bloomingdale Road. Starting where the Great Kill (or Kiln) Road terminated and running uptown was the much frequented Southampton Road. This ran through a district known as Paisley Place or Weavers'

101

Row because it was settled by Scotch weavers. Also nearby was Love Lane or Abingdon Road. This originally followed the line of West Twenty-first Street from Bloomingdale Road to a point east of Eighth Avenue, where it turned slightly northwest to Chelsea. As late as 1894 traces of this road were to be found at Three Eighteen, Three Forty-two and Three Forty-six West Twenty-first Street, and at the southwest corner of Eighth Avenue and Twenty-first Street. It was met east of Sixth Avenue by Southampton Road, east of Seventh Avenue by Warren Road, east of Eighth Avenue it crossed Fitzroy Road, and east of Ninth Avenue by a Fourth Road.

The yellow fever epidemics of 1798 and 1822 had sent people scurrying away from downtown districts. In the latter year there were 1236 deaths from yellow fever. The fire of 1835 which wrought such havoc in lower Manhattan also encouraged people to rebuild in the lesser populated districts further uptown. In 1832, Don Alonzo Cushman built his home where One Seventy Ninth Avenue is. Many settled in Chelsea or Chelsea Village as it had come to be called. In 1831, Clement Moore opened streets and avenues through his property to conform with those laid down in the City Plan of 1811. The little community grew and prospered. Many factories sprung up. Ichabod T. Williams and Sons, cabinet makers, moved to Twenty-fifth Street in 1859. They are still there. The first real estate office opened at One Ninety-one Ninth Avenue in 1835 under the name James N. Wells. This establishment still operates from Chelsea, as a few years ago it moved to Three Forty West Twenty-third Street.

Population increased accordingly, so that it was not long until Chelsea Village was almost absorbed by the city. Janvier and Hemstreet found traces of the original village lanes passing through Chelsea as late as 1894, but today little or no traces remain of the roads described by these two historians.

On a July day in 1871 Chelsea was the scene of a terrible riot. The Orangemen had their headquarters at Twenty-ninth Street and Eighth Avenue, and when it became known that Governor Hoffman would permit them to parade large mobs of oppositionists gathered in front of this meeting place. There was bound to be trouble, and there was! Chelsea saw its share of bloodshed, violence, and such scenes as have never been witnessed there since. Riots broke out simultaneously all over the city, but the little community of Chelsea remembered for long afterward its part in the riot.

I often think of Chelsea as I knew it when the century was young. My family lived in Twenty-eighth Street. Later we moved to one of those fine old homes in front of the Rural New Yorker, on West Thirtieth Street. There were about sixteen rooms in the house and what a wonderful place it was to play in! There we would play "hide and seek" climbing up one flight of the mahogany staircase after another in our search for a good "bunk." At the head of each staircase, like in most of the houses of that day, there was a niche cut into the wall where a statue or stuffed bird could be placed. Those were the days when a green plush piano scarf with tassels of the same color decorated the top of every piano. Framed tintypes of members of the family grew up from the mossy scarf, while the family album, also covered in plush, stood on the square table in the center of the room. The "Front Parlor" to be complete had to have a sampler in which lovingly placed stitches spelled "Home, Sweet Home!"

Large bouquets of the most unnatural looking flowers I have ever seen sprung out of vases conspicuously placed all around the room. They popped up in profusion from the most unusual places! Some even seemed to be growing from the floor, but on closer observation one could see that they sprouted out of vases resting, of all places, on the floor. Such was our "Front Parlor" in our Chelsea home.

I remember wonderful mantel-pieces made of the whitest of marble, such as one seldom sees now-a-days. If I remember correctly, there was almost one in every room. The one in our "Front Parlor" was graced by two black and white China dogs that my mother had brought from Wales. We called one "Tom" and the other "Jerry." Sometime, throughout the years "Tom" has gone to the "happy hunting ground" of China-dog Land but "Jerry" is still with us. I wonder what he thinks sitting complacently on the top of a book-case; how he compares his present home with the old house on West Thirtieth Street.

Once a week we would go the the Grand Opera House on Twenty-third Street. The Opera House was old, even then, as it had been built in 1868, but we saw fine vaudeville shows there. In the Seventies Lilly Langtry played there, making her home in the same street just east of Ninth Avenue. Edwin Booth also appeared there, while his predecessor, Edwin Forrest, America's first great actor, lived at Four Thirty-six West Twenty-second Street. His house was a museum for a while. These players were all of an earlier day as we saw Weber and Fields, Pat Rooney, Eddie Foy and Eva Tanguay.

It may seem strange to present day New Yorkers, but Chelsea was then the center of the motion picture industry. Mary Pickford made some of her earlier pictures in an old building at Two Twenty-one West Twenty-sixth Street. There was the Kalem Company at Two Thirty-five West Twenty-third Street while at Five Twenty West Twenty-first Street there was another studio where such oldtime favorites as Wally Reid and Henry B. Walthall used to play.[8]

The motion pictures were still in their infancy and though a few years had elapsed since they were first introduced, people were still given to expressions of disapproval, and the forty foot kiss exchanged between May Irwin and John C. Rice in the racy comedy "The Widow Jones" did not help the situation any. But progress was made and the infant industry started in Chelsea on a shoe-string, grew to the robust proportions as we know the picture industry today.[4]

Though it was years later, people still talked about "Jubilee Jim" Fisk, famous in the "Black Friday" gold combine of 1869. He once owned the Grand Opera House in partnership with Jay Gould. At one time Fisk had the offices of the Erie Railroad located in the building. His life, culminated when he was shot by Stokes on the stairs of the old Grand Central (latterly the Broadway Central) Hotel, was familiar to everyone. We often heard older residents tell how Josie Mansfield, over whom the shooting was said to have occured, lived up from the Opera, at Three Fifty-nine West Twenty-third Street. Fisk's own house was at Three Thirteen West Twenty-third Street but he seems to have received most of the Tammany-Erie coterie at the home of The Mansfield. To this house, furnished to a queen's taste, came Jay Gould, Fisk's partner in the Erie enterprise; Tweed, who through his dishonest control of the city's politics, shielded and protected Fisk in many of his unscrupulous dealings; and Stokes, by whose hand the life of Fisk was terminated. Perhaps of these three men the character of Edward Stokes was the least obnoxious.

Across lavishly set dinner tables and between sips of expensive wines, these men plotted and planned with a single purpose—to get as much money as possible. Josie Mansfield had known privation and hardship in earlier days. It was not necessary for opportunity to knock twice on her door. In fact, the merest tap would have sufficed to open the door on West Twenty-third Street. The men manipulated with the stock market, more than once causing havoc and near panic. When it was profitable to sell, Josie sold; when more money could be had by holding, she waited for a more opportune time to sell.

When Josie Mansfield cast her lot with James Fisk, Jr. it is more than likely that love was not part of the bargain on either side. Fisk liked to exhibit Josie, for she was beautiful, intelligent and witty. Fisk was egotistical and sensuous enough to enjoy parading what was his. But it is safe to assume that he never loved Josie, and she, on her part, never loved the man who had precipitated the "Black Friday" of 1869. Nevertheless, they were well matched, these two, Fisk with his ruthlessness taking what he wanted and letting disaster fall wherever it might, and Josie, cool, beautiful, calculating enough to reap the spoils with the others. Yes, they were well matched.

To this menage Fisk brought Strokes with whom he had become associated in business. Stokes, though, according to the statement he made at Sing Sing, met The Mansfield as early as 1869 in Philadelphia. Fisk did not introduce the two as was popularly supposed. Both of these tycoons had one thing in common—they had both made and lost fortunes early in life. Aside from this they were completely different. Stokes came of a good family, was dignified and refined and had the best education money could buy. He was also somewhat of an athlete. Fisk was the very antithesis of Stokes. He lacked the culture of the man who was later to kill him, and no amount of coaching would improve his insatiable thirst for power and money.

How these two men could become friends is one of the enigmas of human nature. But they did become very friendly and on one or two occasions Fisk presumed upon this friendship by asking Stokes to intercede with Josie in straightening out some differences he had had with her. Again, this is from Stokes' statement made at Sing Sing: "At the time of the arrival of Mad. Monteland, Fisk gave her a banquet at the Erie Office. Miss Mansfield and several others of Fisk's friends were present. Fisk, elated with the brilliant surroundings, through an interpreter, a well known operatic leader, informed Mad. Monteland that 'if she had previously enjoyed the friendship of foreign nobility, she had now struck a prince indeed: that he owned everything, and that if he so desired, the name of New York City should be changed to Fiskville.' The interpreter was astonished. Miss Mansfield was offended, and left the supper-table and refused to be reconciled to Fisk. This was the real cause of their first estrangement."

Stokes goes on to relate how Fisk confided these troubles to him, begging his intercession with Josie.[5]

Such amicable relations, in which one friend could call upon another to act as his peacemaker, were not to continue. Soon disagreements between the two men cropped up; disagreements so bitter and acrid that Fisk and Stokes became deadly enemies.

On the day that Fisk was shot (January 6, 1872), Stokes had spent the morning in court pressing charges against Fisk for criminal libel. That afternoon Stokes was coming down the main staircase of the Grand Central Hotel when he chanced to meet Fisk ascending. Their eyes met in recognition and quick as lightening Stokes had fired two shots into Fisk, the first shot piercing his abdomen while the second entered his left arm. Fisk was mortally wounded and Stokes surrendered himself to the police.

Stokes was tried for the murder and was sentenced to serve four years in Sing Sing—the prison which, by a curious coincidence, is located on the ground once making up part of his grandfather's estate.

Fisk was buried in the Vermont hills which spawned him, while the beautiful Josie sailed off to Gay Paree, there to capture other hearts and other fancies.

In 1931, I remember reading in the newspapers how this same glamorous belle of bygone days died alone in Paris. Of all her prominent admirers in her younger days, there were none to follow her coffin to its final resting place. The only mourners of this former toast of Chelsea were her two servants. Thus was marked "finis" to the famous Chelsea triangle.

On the way to the Opera House we used to pass Miners' Eighth Avenue, but we were never allowed to go there. We heard Miners' originated "the hook" a device well known to would-be Hamlets of that day. It was not uncommon, either, for the audience to be armed with such choice bits of disapproval as tomatoes and eggs which had seen better days. These they had few qualms in introducing face to face with the aspiring Thespians who were intrepid enough to trod the boards before a Miners' audience.

Down towards Tenth Avenue on Twenty-third Street there was a row of dignified dwellings of three and four stories. In front there was a line of sturdy trees. This was known as "London Terrace" and today this site is occupied by one of the largest apartment houses in the world. It is still called "London Terrace." The apartment house includes the entire block from Ninth to Tenth Avenues, between Twenty-third and Twenty-fourth Streets. It houses a population between four and five thousand. It is a real village in itself, for it provides every conceivable necessity and almost every luxury the modern Chelseaite could require. It is constructed in small units around a lovely garden which has been landscaped English style. In this garden the Clement C. Moore memorial is erected. There is a roof deck, swimming pool, club and school located right in the building, but a most practical idea of London Terrace is its Main Street. This is really a hallway in the building, into which entrances lead to all the shops on Twenty-third Street and Ninth Avenue. Thus, one may do all one's marketing without going into the street. In keeping with its traditional name, London Terrace maintains a large squad of London "bobbies." These men patrol the grounds, also lending, at the same time, the English atmosphere for which Chelsea has always been noted.

However, aside from this agreeable modern invasion of Chelsea, and the Seminary, there are very few landmarks left. The two old houses, number Four Hundred and Three and Four Hundred and Five West Twenty-eighth Street appear to be throw backs to a former era. They are typical red brick three storied houses with the iron latticed front porches. A flight of stone steps leads down from each porch and is flanked on both sides by cast iron balustrades. On the west side of Ninth Avenue between Twenty-first and Twenty-second Streets there are two more old houses. These are one storied wooden dwellings consisting of a store on the ground floor and one apartment upstairs.

The neighborhood, even though it does contain London Terrace, is gradually passing from a residential district. The grand old houses in the side streets, now converted into furnished rooms, will gradually give way to office buildings and freight depots. Over on Seventh and Eighth Avenues is the center of an ever increasing clothing industry. New York City makes seventy-five per cent of ready made coats and dresses and eighty per cent of fur garments.[6] Most of this merchandise is manufactured in this neighborhood from which it is distributed all over the United States.

On the extreme west side is the railroad terminal where day after day hundreds of pieces of freight are unloaded from trains all over the country. On the river front are many piers. Warehouses are required to store this material for re-shipping, and Chelsea, located between these terminals, will eventually be swallowed up by them. Then, too, because of the nearness to transportation many factories are situated in the vicinity. In Thirtieth Street the pungent aroma of chocolate pervades the air; further downtown a very well known cracker factory is busy all day baking various cookies which are then shipped all over the country and exported, as well. There are piano factories, rag shops and paper cord lofts, some of them located in the old stoop houses, now abandoned and useful only as lofts. Truly, it is a sad district, not even permitted to rest upon its laurels.

However, older Manhattanites may still reminisce and modern New Yorkers may imagine the Chelsea that was. The Chelsea Hotel with its balconied front windows still lends quaintness and charm to a street that would otherwise be ordinary. When it was first erected over fifty years ago, it was one of the first fire-proof buildings in the city. Fire-proofing was so new in those days that in order to accomplish this feat the insulation between ceiling of one storey and floor of the next was two feet thick. The rooms are large and high ceilinged. The Chelsea also innovated another idea, that of cooperative housing. They granted fifty year leases to some tenants, and up to a few years ago two of these leasees were still residing at the Hotel.

The Chelsea has always been the home of distinguished writers and artists. O. Henry, that popular chronicler of life in the big city, was one of the hostelry's early patrons. Joseph Cummings Chase, the painter, and the well known editor of "Spoon River Anthology," Edgar Lee Masters, resided there. Until his death recently, the noted painter, Charles Melville Dewey made his home there, too. Hotel employees will relate with pride how the Chelsea was the only hotel in New York visited by Edward, Duke of Windsor, when he came here as Prince of Wales. The British Apprentice Club is located in the Hotel.

Cavanaugh's restaurant remains, too. Here, one may eat oysters and chops prepared exactly as they were seventy-seven years ago, for when John J. Cavanaugh bought the place in 1895 he kept the oyster bar as a very definite part of the establishment. Many a famous personage has been served in this restaurant, and many people have been regular patrons for years. It is said that one of the executives of the American Jersey Cattle Club lunched at the same front table for thirty-two years.

After dining, still in a reminiscing mood, one may walk over to the Seminary. Not much change here. The west building dates from 1835, but the rest of the Seminary was constructed in 1884. The houses facing Chelsea Square on Twentieth Street will carry you back some years. They form a neat little row of brick residences, set off by window boxes from which trailing ivy blows when there is a breeze from the Hudson. Shining doorbells and the trim appearance of these houses point out that their occupants are as proud of them as when they were first constructed years ago.

But walking around the block to Ninteenth Street one sees a different scene, sad, dilapidated houses which will soon have to perish. There is one all boarded up from which some one has torn away the boards covering the space where the front door should be. A door which once opened cautiously to the stranger upon a happy family gathered 'round the hearth, now opens into emptiness. It is only a wraith, a ghost of a house. Anyone may enter this dwelling which may have sheltered one of the "first families" of Chelsea. It is a tragedy of this generation that so many of these once proud homes are neglected and uncared for until they finally become eyesores and have to be demolished. But New York is a strange city, always progressing, building skyscraper apartments and offices to accommodate the increasing business and population. And Chelsea, as an integral part of the great metropolis, must suffer these changes to be wrought upon its face, too. However, just as its past has been a glorious epoch of staid conservatism and private residences, just as its present is a conglomeration of hotels and offices set off with tenements and furnished rooms, just so will Chelsea's future be a monument to commercial and industrial enterprise.

It is passing from a residential neighborhood into a commercial center of Manhattan. In the present transitory stage in which it finds itself, it appears to be like a boy entering the adolescent period—there are black vacant spaces where teeth should be, his skin is poor and blemished and his voice betrays signs of cracking at most inopportune times. But the boy outgrows all these symptoms which accompany his development from boyhood into manhood. Just so will Chelsea, by the mysterious process which certain regions undergo transformation, metamorphose from the present dismal reminder of the Chelsea Village that used to be into the future locality epitomizing the commercial and industrial strength of the city.

Already it shows signs of this future role which it is scheduled to play. Its proximity to the Hudson River on the one hand and the Pennsylvania Terminal on the other affords excellent transportation facilities. Raw material may be received, the articles manufactured, and the finished product shipped . . . all with the utmost speed and conveniences. By the same token, the large department stores and thousands of small retail shops are assured quick deliveries which they, in turn, are at liberty to pass on to prospective customers.

Chelsea is more or less of a retail trade center of Manhattan. It boasts of most of Manhattan's large department stores—Macy's, Gimbels and Saks, which are surrounded by thousands of smaller specialty shops. The aggregate yearly sales made in these stores runs into an enormous figure.

In addition, seventy-five percent of Mrs. America's dresses and coats are manufactured in the little village of Chelsea which houses the garment center of United States. The garments are designed and manufactured here, then shipped all over the United States to be sold. Needless to say, some of the dresses and coats are sold at retail in the small stores of Chelsea.

One of the richest industries of Chelsea is fur processing and manufacturing, as the seat of the fur center is within walking distance of what used to be Mistress Mollie's home. There are approximately 2,000 shops employing 15,000 people in them.[7]

From the village once considered beyond the city limits, Chelsea has now grown into a district right in the heart of Manhattan. Progressiveness, decadence, poverty and wealth walk side by side in Chelsea; the old making way for the new. It has always been so in all communities and Chelsea is no exception to the rule. Somehow, however, one laments the passing of this old Village. One feels a nostalgic longing for the Chelsea that used to be—not the dismal, left-over Victorian dwellings of my own youth, but the spacious homes of Clement Moore's time; the abundance of leafy trees in summer; a glimpse of the Hudson, frozen solid in winter. And in winter, too, the resonant jingle of sleigh bells and gleeful laughter coming from the direction of Abingdon Road. Looking at Chelsea today, it all seems so long, long ago!

CHAPTER NOTES

1. Janvier, Thomas A., "In Old New York," p. 170.
2. "The New York Evening Post" for July 13, 1804, p. 2, c. 3 & 4.
3. Federal Writers' Project, "New York City Guide," p. 154.
4. Hays, Will H., "See and Hear," p. 13.
5. Sutton, Charles, "The New York Tombs; Its Secrets and Its Mysteries," p. 649, 650.
6. Federal Writers' Project, "New York City Guide," p. 160.
7. Ibid., p. 163.

Eighth Ave. and 23rd Street. Grand Opera House, Gift of the Essex Institute

CHAPTER ELEVEN

The Naughty Tenderloin

"Who profits by a crime commits the crime."
Seneca, Medea, 1.500

MANHATTAN has played host to many disreputable neighborhoods some of which have lived on in poetry and song and others which have been allowed to lose their personality in the mist produced with the accumulation of years. The Bowery will always bring to mind thoughts of questionable gaiety because of the many ballads and poems written about it. No one wrote a "tear-jerker" about the Tenderloin and so this part of Manhattan—which was just as scandalous as the Bowery—is permitted to disappear in the enveloping haze of past decades. It was every bit as bad as the Bowery, yet, select anyone from any-part of the United States, and the chances are that he will know all about the Bowery while the Tenderloin remains as mysterious and unknown to him as the Ming Dynasty.

This naughty part of Manhattan—for other than this it cannot be called—reached the zenith of its notoriety in the early Eighties. The Tenderloin came of its name by a member of "New York's finest." "I've had nothing but chuck steak for a long time and now I'm going to get a little of the tenderloin." Thus spoke Captain Alexander S. Williams and though he did not know it at the time, Williams had given the district a name by which it became notoriously famous. To look at the erstwhile Tenderloin today, with its great department stores jutting out all along the Avenue of the Americas, the casual observer would find it hard to believe that in the last century it thrived as the wickedest part of "the modern Gomorrah." The latter was one of the favorite epithets which the Rev. T. De Witt Talmage applied to New York City

111

of that time—a name which he claimed singularly appropriate and applicable to any city which would tolerate a "Tenderloin" within its midst.

The boundaries of the Tenderloin really should be considered as arbitrary inasmuch as some people held the opinion that this region of gaiety, vice and graft extended from Fourteenth to Forty-second Streets. However, most of those who knew the old Tenderloin agree that it actually began at Twenty-fourth Street and extended north as far as Forty-second Street, occupying the region between Fifth and Seventh Avenues. At least, it was within these confines that the places which gave rise to its nickname were located. The Captain, later Inspector, was clairvoyant when he coined the name "Tenderloin" for he waxed wealthy on the revenue received for protecting the organized vice which grew up within his patrol. At one time the artful Inspector boasted a diamond shield which he is said to have received from some of the Tenderloin business men. During the Lexow Committee's investigation it was brought out that Williams was not averse to accepting donations and that he exercised little or no discrimination as to the donors. Thus we find that he "accepted from Louise Smith, a keeper of a house of ill-fame, various valuable presents,"[1] The testimony goes on to recite the items which Williams was accused of receiving. He had a yacht, a seventeen room summer home at Cos Cob, horses, coaches plus the retinue required to service such luxuries. No, there was nothing backward about the Inspector. Williams, it appears, made hay while the sun was shining and nowhere on Manhattan Isle was the sun shining as brightly for those who would make money quickly and easily.

The Tenderloin reigned as one of the most vicious parts of the city for a period of around twenty-five years during which time it was entirely given over to vice and to those who would prey upon the proceeds gained from vice in all its ramifications. Williams was not to blame for the growth of the Tenderloin, as such, but he was largely responsible for its continuation. New York had weathered the corruptive wave of bribery and graft set loose by the Tweed Ring but after a brief period of honest politics, the city government suffered a relapse whence it came to be dominated by the corpulent "Boss of New York," Richard Croker. Williams, therefore, in closing his eyes to conditions existing in his precinct was only imitating on a small scale what his superiors were doing on a larger scale.

New York's politics were in such a state of corruption that the leading journals of the day called for an investigation which was not long in forthcoming, and which, when it had been concluded, brought to light a very sad state of affairs. The crux of the situation was that rodents were gnawing at the municipal cheese and the largest and

112

fattest of them was Croker—in comparison with whom Williams was a neophyte. And so while Croker and his cohorts were robbing the entire city in diverse manners, Williams restricted his graft to the "Tenderloin" which was content to pay tribute to him as long as he permitted them to run their businesses in accordance with their own standards.

These "standard"—using the term in a most elastic sense—were far from commendable. True, the naughty Tenderloin did attract some of Manhattan's elite who, upon tiring of their daily round of pleasure descended upon the district in search of a change. On the whole, though the majority of habitues were culled from the lower strata of Manhattan's citizenry—people of questionable repute. In this respect, the proprietors rated no better than their customers. Owners of Tenderloin establishments maintained no qualms as regards the process of "rolling" a customer. Knock-out drops and the subsequent robbing of patrons were frequently employed. Hence, it can readily be seen that though on the surface the Tenderloin may have presented another aspect, in a final analysis, it was no different from the Bowery when that locale was the purveyor of unrestricted gaiety.

The scandalous conditions prevalent in the Tenderloin soon made the place the habitat of fallen women as well as a rendevouz for criminals, blackmailers and gangsters—all of whom were given full sway to operate unmolested—as long as they paid their protection money. Once in a while the police tried to control some of the lawlessness and with great enthusiasm they would swoop down upon the district. But their raids were only half-hearted and instead of accomplishing the desired end, which was to quiet public opinion periodically aroused by leading journals and ministers of the day, these sporadic farces only served to throw the spotlight upon conditions as they then existed. As early as 1878 the entire area was given over to some form of wickedness soon earning for itself the opprobious title of "Satan's Circus."

Women habitues shocked the city with their brazen exhibitions of the Cancan which had just been imported from the French capital and which was considered risque according to Victorian standards of our grandmother's day. In all justice it must be pointed out that in the evolution of muscle dancing—an evolution which produced such dances as the hoochy-coochy, hula and shimmy—the cancan certainly was no more suggestive than its later day counter-parts.

If Sixth Avenue had any inkling then that it was destined to be the present Avenue of the Americas, it gave no sign. It was gay and merry with its many amusement houses where wine, women and song were the order of the day. Slumming parties often frequented the Tenderloin.

They would go there expecting to be shocked, and they usually were. It harbored several establishments catering to the "pursuit of happiness" among which was the French Madame's over on Sixth Avenue and Twenty-first Street. Though the name which Madame bestowed upon her establishment is suggestive of delicacy, the proprietress was diametrically opposite to what one anticipated. She is described as a bewhiskered shrew excellently ripe for the modern beautician's "spot reducing" treatments. Madame served no food but large quantities of black coffee were always available in addition to the abundant supply of liquor.

One of the most abandoned "dives" of the period was the Cremorne on Thirty-second Street west of Sixth Avenue. It was the usual type of the time and place and its greatest attraction was the bar along which men would stand five and six deep drinking and telling ribald stories to the accompaniment of loud guffaws. The Cremorne was exceedingly popular for drinkers soon gaining the reputation of receiving perpendicular patrons only to turn them out horizontal. At the same time as the Cremorne was doing a flourishing business a reformed drunkard who also had an eye for his particular business (keeping people perpendicular) hit upon a scheme whereby he could capitalize upon the Cremorne's popularity and at the same time achieve his own purpose. Jerry McAuley, the name of this altruistic gentleman, rented a large room on the same side of the street as the Cremorne. Above the entrance to this room he had a large sign erected bearing the name "Cremorne" in huge letters. Confused drunks bent upon getting themselves more confused would wander into Jerry's place in search of a drink. One night Jerry locked them all in, mounted a chair, and tried to preach to the befuddled crowd. His attempt was very unsuccessful, the drunks forcing him to unlock the door, whereupon they all poured into the street in quest of the genuine "Cremorne." McAuley later opened another mission, but he did not interfere with the Cremorne's customers again after this experience.

Buckingham Palace, Sailor's Hall and Tom Gould's were other places well known as Tenderloin "joints" but the most notorious was the Haymarket.

Here was an establishment which would bring exclamations from the quietest of mortals! It plied its trade at the southeast corner of Sixth Avenue and Thirtieth Street, operating as a combination dance hall and cafe. Originally, the Haymarket opened as a variety theatre similar to those in vogue in London of that time. Soon, however, it found itself unable to compete with the Tivoli and Tony Pastor's both of which were very popular with theatre crowds of the time. So the Haymarket closed its doors reopening soon afterward as the dispenser of a different kind of entertainment. In remodeling, the tier of private boxes which ran around the upper walls was allowed to remain. Sixth Avenue woke up one morning to find a new sign gracing it. "Haymarket—Grand Soiree Dansant" fluttered in the breeze and after sundown the rollicking rhythm of the cancan sent its gleeful strains into Sixth Avenue. There were times when these gay notes would fall upon the ears of some passing bumpkin ready to be plucked. And if he looked ripe for this process, the twenty-five women entertainers employed by the Haymarket saw to it that he was. While they did not employ such violent methods as prevailed in the Bowery, the result was the same and the yokel would leave the Tenderloin a poorer, but wiser man. The Haymarket was closed several times and often the horse drawn patrol wagon would pull up under the "Grand Soiree Dansant" sign and to the clang of the old bell carry away customers and entertainers alike. But the Haymarket always managed to reopen. Some pressure would be exerted over at West Thirtieth Street Police Station or somebody's palm would be greased and the next day the catchy strains of the cancan would again be released upon an all too willing Sixth Avenue.

With the appearance of the new Century, the notorious character of the Tenderloin underwent one of those metamorphosis so common to districts of Manhattan. This change was brought about by many factors, but perhaps one of the precipitating causes was the gory Craft murder. At the time of the murder the Tenderloin was wide open. Gambling, prostitution and other vices had found fertile teritory in which to grow and the police tolerated the outrageous situation with an attitude almost akin to indifference. Captain Michael Sheehan was in charge of the district the night of September 27, 1902 and it was during that night that the cellar of one of the Tenderloin's "dives" yielded the decapitated torso of a respectable Glen Cove resident. The head had been hacked from the body and thrown into the furnace to burn in the roaring fire which the murderer had prepared.

Newspapers for the next day decried the "laissez faire" attitude of the police, creating such a scandal that an investigation was in order and there was an inquiry into the activities of the New York Police, especially in connection with patrol of the Tenderloin region.

The locale of the crime was a typical Tenderloin saloon operating at Thirty-eight West Twenty-ninth Street. It had the high-sounding name of Empire Garden Cafe. The Empire Garden was owned by Eddie McCann who came from the Eighteenth Assembly District of which Charles F. Murphy was leader. From this it can readily be concluded that McCann was naturally prominent in Tammany Hall circles and like most politicians of that day his scruples were not lily-white. It was shown that in addition to harboring a clientele more or less shady, his employees were likewise of questionable character. It was certainly not the best place for a man like James B. Craft to spend his leisure, but the evidence showed that he was a frequent patron at the Empire Garden where he was known as "Captain Jim."

On the night of the crime, Captain Jim ordered drinks for himself and a Tenderloin woman companion whom he had met at the Empire. Thomas Tobin was the waiter. The woman left the room and at the same time the bartender went downstairs to tend the furnace. When he returned Tobin was standing over the unconscious form of Craft. Tobin then carried the victim downstairs and before the horror striken eyes of the bartender began to decapitate Craft, using a meat cleaver borrowed for the purpose from a neighboring Chinese restaurant. The bartender called the police but when they arrived Tobin had tossed the head into the furnace.[2] Tobin was convicted and paid the death penalty but many believed that he was hopelessly insane both at the time of the murder and when he was executed.

When these gory details became public Captain Sheehan was transferred from the Tenderloin and a drive initiated to clean up the district. Retail merchants who were finding the downtown area inconvenient, began to look to the Tenderloin with a view to establishing there. Some had already moved into the area before the murder but with the assurance that the neighborhood would be open to respectable business enterprises other merchants followed and by the early Nineteen Hundreds the Tenderloin fringes had several retail stores.

Thirty-five or forty years ago the southern outskirts of the Tenderloin proper—depending upon what boundary one imposes—was quite a shopping center. In fact, most of New York's large department stores of that day could be found on Sixth Avenue between Fourteenth and Twenty-third Streets. Macy's was divided, having two stores, one on each side of Fourteenth Street and their "ads" read "from 13th to 15th Streets on Sixth Avenue." Adams Dry Goods Co. were on Sixth Avenue from Twenty-first to Twenty-second Streets. O'Neill's was on Sixth Avenue between Twentieth and Twenty-first Streets. Siegel Cooper Company, of "meet me at the fountain" fame was on Sixth Avenue between Eighteenth and Ninteenth Streets. Some of these establishments have perished during succeeding years but others have prospered and their names are by-words in merchandising fields in this country. Macy's, since moved up to Herald Square, is known throughout the world. This Department store carries nearly every conceivable article and no one was astonished when a few years back, Macy's announced that live stock and prefabricated houses were available. The latest thing they are selling is perhaps the airplane which I recently saw on display there.

Siegel Cooper's have been out of business for many years. The old store on Sixth Avenue is dearly associated with pleasant childhood memories for it was here that I used to visit Santa Claus. Jovial, robust old Santa from whom a pat on the head and a few trite phrases were much-to-be desired bounties. As soon as the month of December approached, butter would melt in my mouth for that was the month when my father would take me to the city to see Santa. The old gent was no different in those days than he is now and his interview was the same. Santa Claus is one tradition remaining unchanged in a changing world. I would sit upon his knee and after asking my name he would look down upon me and altruistically inquire what I wanted him to bring me. This was my cue to commence naming all the objects of my affection. The list was long and well rehearsed, I assure you. For days before the prospective visit I thought of nothing else except new toys to add to my growing list. We were living in New Jersey and as the ferry plied its way across the Hudson's icy waters, I would be memorizing my list so that when it came time for Santa to reach the point in his interview, "And what do you want me to bring you, little girl?" I knew exactly what to reply. Santa always terminated the visit with admonishments to "be a good little girl" and I would return to Jersey with a feeling of such exalted happiness as only a child can experience. My photograph album still boasts a fond memento of one of these cherished visits. It shows a four year old girl mounted on a pony as dear old Santa looks on approvingly.

O happy days of childhood!—gladdened and brightened by the legend of Santa Claus! And when I hear modern child psychologists blithely advocating abolishment of this legend, I am inclined to wonder whether they ever examined their own childhood and whether they, as children, didn't derive many happy moments in joyful acceptance of the jovial old man with the reindeers. He contributed a great deal to my own childhood, I know, and was as much a part of my life in those early formative years as the reading of fairy tales was later. I hope he will always remain to gladden the heart of childhood.

Once, however, my meeting with Santa Claus did not terminate as successfully as it should. This was no fault of the genial old man, but was due, rather, to my unbounded curiosity. At the time of the visits, Siegel Cooper's had installed escalators. They fascinated me, carrying people, as they did, into new worlds of foodstuffs, furniture, linens, etc. Mysterious realms where large stocks of beautiful things were available for all to see. All, that is, who were brave enough to allow the escalator to lead one into this kingdom of mystery and plenty. Curiosity, which I had often been told "got the cat" got me, too. I was overpowered. I stepped on one of the escalators and disappeared. But the worlds which

117

I had expected to see frightened me, for I was alone. Tremendous waves of fear engulfed me. Resorting to childhood's formidable defense, I began to cry. Finally, I turned up at the "lost and found" department where I was claimed by a worried father who came upon me in a vale of tears. For a long time thereafter, escalators held a dreadful feeling of calamity for me.

Things have changed since the days of Inspector Williams when every street offered its variety of amusements for now nearly the entire vicinity is devoted to merchandising and the purveying of entertainment has been left to the Times Square sector adjoining the Tenderloin on the north. The section is far too busy to admit of ghosts of the past. In fact, should a former habitue of Satan's Circus return to his old haunts, he is almost sure to be struck by one of the many vehicles with which the Avenue of the Americas, formerly Sixth Avenue, pulsates. And if echoes of the old police siren are heard around the site of the old Haymarket, one may be certain that the echoing clang will soon be drowned and obliterated by the modern sounds of Manhattan.

CHAPTER NOTES

1. Lexow, Clarence, "Investigation of the New York City Police Department, 1894," (5 vols.) p. 5459.
2. "The World," for September 28, 1902, p. 1 c. 8.

SIXTH AVE. and 30th Street, Haymarket Bar

CHAPTER TWELVE

Gramercy Park

"Old thanks, old thoughts, old aspirations,
Outlive men's lives and lives of nations."

A. C. Swinburne, "Age and Song"

G RAMERCY Park with its aristocratic mien of the mauve decade
seems to sleep in the heart of Manhattan, almost oblivious to the
passing of time. There it lies, serene and elegant, a throw-back to a fine
period when houses were built to be lived in and family life, even in the
city, centered more around the hearthstone. Even today, as time is
gently passing its irrevocable hand over Gramercy's countenance, the
few remaining homes have lost none of their original charm. On the
contrary, their beauty has become enhanced because in comparison
with the taller buildings silhouetted against the sky, they carry us back
to a period when life in Manhattan was much simpler. Throughout the
years the Park as well as part of this neighborhood has maintained a
simple conservative aspect where residents may live in comparative
privacy. There have been several threats to the Park's existence but the
merest hint of cutting through it has always been fought and rejected by
the residents. And one cannot but agree with the prevision of such an
attitude.

Gramercy is a quaint little nook of Manhattan. One expects to see
coaches driving around the Park or lovely belles in crinoline, instead of
buses and automobiles and glamor girls. It is as though one were atten-
ding a nineteenth century play where the stage manager had mistakenly
supplied twentieth century "props." This is the main reason why
Gramercy has always exerted an intriguing influence over so many,
your faithful chronicler not excepted. Yet, be that as it may, we have
never really paused long enough to "discover" Gramercy.

So, on a bright January day when the air is briskly invigorating, and the last pleasant odor of burning Christmas trees pervades the air, we decide to "set forth upon our journey" as though we were a Twentieth Century Marco Polo aventure in Manhattan. This neighborhood, which extends from Third and Fourth Avenues between Twentieth and Twenty-first Streets, has long held a peculiar interest for us. Thus it is with an expectant air of discovery that we descend from the Fifth Avenue bus and wend our way eastward through Twentieth Street. Maybe we shall find the spell which Gramercy has cast over four generations of New Yorkers. Perhaps we shall find the charm which attracted O. Henry, Washington Irving, Edwin Booth, Robert Ingersoll, Samuel Tilden, James Harper, Peter Cooper, and the Hewitt family, Cyrus Field and the many other Knickerbockers who knew Gramercy when it was young.

Of course, the Park is more lovely in early spring or late autumn, when nature has wielded her inimitable brush over the folliage, painting the exquisite colors which no artist has ever been able to duplicate. Yet, even on a cold winter's day we are told by those who know that Gramercy still retains its charms. Especially, they will tell you, is the Park alluring when it dons its white coat for winter, when in all sense of the expression, it becomes a white Fairyland as its glistening trees sparkle in the sunlight.

The district which we pass through is a wholesale merchandise center. Offices and showrooms of rug manufacturers occupy much of the floor space in the cloud capped buildings which soar up all around us. Here are also located the fabric industries and many companies dealing in undergarments. A great many leading American publishers have their New York offices on Fourth Avenue, so that we can truly call this neighborhood the "cradle of Booklandia." Many a new manuscript has grown into a robust "best seller" because it was successfully nursed in a Fourth Avenue publisher's office. Scattered about are a few office supply houses and the inevitable tea rooms and restaurants which spring up wherever there are numbers of workers.

This is also the center of social and welfare work, as well as the central location for much of the missionary work carried on throughout the world. The Russell Sage Foundation and the Welfare Council of New York City are situated here; the latter being the coordinating force of some 600 health and welfare agencies. The New York School of Social Work, Commission on Social Service, Society for Improving the Condition of the Poor, Childrens' Aid Society and the State Charities Aid Association all distribute their good work from this center.

Crossing Fourth Avenue the west wind strikes our back firmly. What was it that the Latin book used to use for an example? Oh, yes! "It is folly to complain of the fickleness of the wind."[1] And so it is! But as soon as we reach the open Park some of its strength is diverted and we are able to walk about undisturbed. We meander about peeking through the iron palings to obtain a better view of the Park and try to settle in our mind the derivation of its name. As is the case with many street designations in New York—names so familiar and "every dayish" as to be commonplace—the name "Gramercy" seems to be a corruption of a very indefinite origin. According to some the farm which included Gramercy was shaped like a "crooked little knife" so that the Dutch called the locale "Krommessie" taken from the two words, "Krom" meaning crooked or bent, and "Mesje" meaning little knife. A booklet issued by The National Arts Club in 1906 has the following to say about the name: "Gramercy is Anglicized from 'Crummashie' the name given by the Dutch settlers to a hill which stood where the Park now lies and also to a rivulet 'Crummashie Vly' which rose west of Madison Square and after forming a pond, crossed the present Fourth Avenue, skirted Crummashie Kop and fell at Kip's Bay into the East River." The name has been explained from a word meaning crooked knife, but a more probable derivation is Cramoisy, a word common to French, Dutch and English, signifying red. Red Hill and Red Brook may have been the original meaning owing to the red clay of the hill and the brilliant autumn folliage along the stream. Shackleton goes on to suggest that the name may have come from the olden time English expression, "Gramercy" meaning many and unusual thanks.[2] Certain it is that this last derivation of its name could apply to Gramercy today, for the residents who use the Park are more than thankful for the privilege. In the summer it is pleasant to while away an hour or so in the Park, provided, of course, that one is fortunate enough to possess a key. Watching evening descend over Manhattan is another way of taking full advantage of the Park's possibilities. As the city grows darker, lights go on in nearby office buildings, timidly at first, but gradually increasing in bravado until entire floors are illuminated. The great battalion of office cleaners and charwomen are swinging into action. Armed with dusters, mops, brooms and such miscellaneous articles as are required to obliterate the ravages left by the thousands of day workers, this little known regiment falls upon the city's offices. An entire realm of activity must be put into condition before the next business day arrives. The army descends and begins its job, each worker preoccupied with his own problem. And all the while the chimes from the Metropolitan Tower gentle but irrevocably toll away the quarter hours. One may sit in the Park and thus muse to oneself while enjoying the little plot of grass and trees. It is like a lone green spot in this desert of Manhattan skyscrapers. It is no wonder that people should be willing to present many and unusual thanks for this retreat!

The hill has long ago been graded out to conform to the level of surrounding ground, but the rivulet or "crocked little knife" as the Dutch called it, still flows far beneath the surface. It is said that when old Peter Cooper built his house over on Lexington Avenue, he had to erect the building on stilts because the land was so marshy.

But there is no appearance of marshiness about the Park as on this winter day we make our way hither. One would never suspect that a little more than a hundred years ago the entire tract was uninhabitable and that it was necessary for Samuel B. Ruggles to have the land drained before he could put up his lots for sale. In the center a winter sun casts oblique shadows of light across faded patches of grass as it strikes the Quinn statue of Edwin Booth. The statue faces Irving Place and the Players' Club which the generosity of the great actor made possible. It depicts Booth in his well known role of Hamlet, a tribute to one of Gramercy's best beloved residents and a reminder of all that is artistic and noble in the theatre.

Surrounding the statue are some trees, now barren and withered trunks of wood, but in the summer they enliven the picture with their lovely green leaves and branches which seem to beckon one to come and enjoy their shade. However, now they are very bare and lonely looking, gracefully waving their nude branches in the penetrating January wind. Maybe they recall the days when Gramercy was part of an extensive farm, when there were hundreds of trees to keep them company. Now, they shrivel in shame at the comparison, these few trees, very few indeed, solitary sentinels of the Park. But we learn later that these trees are not old and that we have been off on a reverie again. The oldest are a "fine old elm and a willow tree" which were planted when the Park was landscaped in 1844.

Leading away from the Booth statue in crisscross directions are trim gravelled footpaths with hedges and shrubbery planted on both sides. Nestling among the easterly shrubs there is a delightful statue of a nymph, moved to this part to make room for Booth's statue. Formerly, it occupied a place on top of the old fountain, but now it graces a newer fountain and is more in harmony with its present setting. The westerly end also has a fountain, the base of which contains a marble shaft embellished with a bronze medallion portrait of Samuel B. Ruggles, The inscription, "Samuel B. Ruggles,—Founder of Gramercy Park—1831" is written beneath the portrait. The memorial was placed there by Mr. John R. Strong, a grandson of the founder.

122

The caretaker of the Park, Mr. James A. (Tech) Hannan has been tending the little oasis in Manhattan since 1902. He knows most of the key holders by name, and as he himself will tell you, three generations of residents have watched the tulips bloom and fade under his careful guidance. When "Tech" Hannan completed thirty-five years as the Park's superintendent, the people of the neighborhood tendered him a party. It was a gala affair in which most of the children of the vicinity took part. Mr. Hannon received a presentation of a $1,000 purse which had been subscribed by neighbors. The presentation was made by Dr. John M. Finley, Editor-in-Chief of "The New York Times" who delivered the address which he concluded by reciting the following poem which he had written for the occasion:

"Of the Green Hills of Shannon an Irish bard sang
'Til the hills and the vales and the forests all rang.
Of the Green Park of Shannon the rather would I
Sing a Gramercy song, were my Lucy but neigh.
On my harp I would play all the fair afternoon
And the "Green Banks of Shannon" would be my one tune.
But the words would all be of our loved Gramercy,
And Hannan, St. Peter's Assistant would be."

The silence which sometimes characterizes places that are conservative and aristocratic is broken for presently our attention is drawn to the gleeful shrill voice of a little girl gayly rolling her hoop, black curls blowing rebelliously in the wind as her nimble feet carry her up the gravelled path towards the statue. Not very far off an English nurse follows sedately pushing a carriage with an infant. Aside from the nurse and her charges, the Park is empty of people. The nurse soon reaches the little girl and after a few words of caution she seats herself on a bench fronting the statue and prepares to knit.

This scene looks so peaceful here in the heart of New York's turmoil. There is something staidly orderly about the Park reminding one of some of the private squares of London. This is the only private park in the city, each resident contributing a yearly sum to its upkeep. Gramercy Park has steadfastly refused to allow business to enter its bounds, yet one can see that protest as they will, the long tentacles of Manhattan's skyscrapers are gradually replacing the Nineteenth Century dwellings which used to face all around the Park. Only the south and west sides contain these residences now; the north and east sides having been built upon by apartment hotels.

The Park is not open to the public. Those who are residents of the houses surrounding the Park have keys to the huge gates which are located in the center of each side. They are kept locked. When it was deeded by Mr. Ruggles in 1831 for the "use, benefit and enjoyment of the owners and occupants of sixty-six surrounding lots of land belonging to the said Samuel B. Ruggler and with a view to enhance the value thereof," special keys were given to each family privileged to enter the Park. Today, there are over two hundred keys issued for the Park, twelve of which are in possession of the Gramercy Park Hotel. It is interesting to note that the first time since Civil War days that Gramercy Park was opened to the public occured in 1931 during an unemployment rally.

The land once belonged to James Duane, first Mayor of New York, in 1784. He called it Gramercy Seat. A portrait of this James Duane painted by the reknown Trumbull may be seen hanging in the Governor's Room in the City Hall. James Duane bought Gramercy Seat in various parcels which he acquired over the period from 1761 to 1786. The land where the Park is belonged to the Watts family. Another deed to land in the vicinity came from Gerardus Stuyvesant. This covered approximately four acres lying on the present Broadway between Nineteenth and Twenty-first Streets.[3] In 1674 the widow of Peter Stuyvesant referred to this latter parcel as "Crommessie." Her grandson was the Gerardus Stuyvesant who sold the land to Duane in 1761. In an earlier transaction (1746) Stuyvesant's sister, Mrs. Anna Pritchard conveyed a large parcel of Gramercy Farm to a James Delancey, who, in turn conveyed it to John Watts in 1747.

The records show that change of title in connection with land in Gramercy Park were as follows:

1. June 23, and 24, 1746: Anna Pritchard conveyed to James Delancy over 131 acres;
2. November 12, and 13, 1747: James Delancy transferred his title to the above to John Watts;
3. July 21, and 22: Gerardus Stuyvesant conveyed over 4 acres to James Duane;
4. December 28, and 29, 1763: John and Ann Watts conveyed over 10 acres to James Duane;
5. In 1786, by forfeiture of John Watts' estate and a transfer by John Watts Jr., James Duane acquired "all that part of the Gramercy Farm lying east, and a part (north of Twenty-first Street) lying west of the Third Avenue."[4]

Ruggles acquired the entire tract consisting of parcels obtained by Duane from the Watts and Stuyvesant families, through conveyance by the heirs of Duane. It was Mr. Ruggles' foresight and liberality which preserved the Park as a heavenly breathing spot for the harassed city dwellers of today who are fortunate enough to be able to use the grounds.

He deeded over forty-two lots to be used as a private park by the owners of the sixty-six adjacent lots.[5] It was this early city planner's belief that the city was bound to grow, but by allotting this land as a park, there would always be preserved a plot of ground where one could look up into the sky. Twenty years after Gramercy had thus been deeded, President King in addressing the Mechanics' Institute recalled how, while walking around the Park with a well known minister of the day, Mr. Ruggles said, "Come what will, our open squares will remain forever imperishable. Buildings, towers, palaces may molder and crumble beneath the touch of time, but space—free, glorious open space—will remain to bless the city forever."[6]

At the time of its establishment Gramercy was considered as being on the outskirts of the city. The fact is that like Greenwhich and Chelsea, it did not become popular as a residential neighborhood until after yellow fever epidemics and the great fires had exacted their toll. Previous to these events it had been used as farmlands but when fever and fire wreaked their vengeance upon the inhabitants of New York, most of whom resided in the lower portion of the Island, it was decided to rebuild further north. This decision had been reached by Clement Clark Moore in 1823 who planned and cut streets through Chelsea and organized Chelsea Village. In 1831 Samuel B. Ruggles divided Gramercy Seat into city squares, preserving Gramercy Park for the use of the sixty-six adjacent lot owners.

The Ruggles family stables were over on East Fifteenth Street; number One Hundred and Three it is today. Here the Ruggles and the Griswalds and Costers who lived on Union Square used to store their horses and carriages. Later, Richard Watson Gilder, who was editor of Scribners, had the stable altered and with his well known wife made his home there. Mrs. Gilder had studied art and naturally numbered among her friends many well known artists, while her husband's interests inclined toward the written word. Together, they entertained Stanford White, La Farge, Joseph Jefferson, Saint-Gaudens and Mme. Modjeska. President and Mrs. Grover Cleveland were frequent visitors to the little house on Fifteenth Street, as was the poet, Walt Whitman. One may still see this modest little house nestling between a bank and an apartment building. It is picturesque and has a romantic and interesting history.

Theodore Roosevelt probably used to frequent the Park, as a boy, for he was born at Twenty-eight East Twentieth Street. Peter Cooper lived at Nine Lexington Avenue with his daughter, Amelia, who had married Abram S. Hewitt. Hewitt was elected Mayor of New York in 1889 and the two lamps which distinguish the Mayor's residence were placed in front of Number Nine. Three former Mayors and one Governor have lived in Gramercy, one of the Mayors being Edward Cooper, brother-in-law of Hewitt and son of old Peter Cooper. Edward at one time occupied the house which stood at Number One Lexington Avenue. His father, Peter Cooper, once ran for President on the Greenback ticket in 1876, securing 81,737 votes. He was eighty-five years old at the time. James Harper of the publishing firm, another Mayor, lived at Number Four and the two lamps which distinguish the Mayor's residence have never been removed until today.

Some historians claim that when Washington Irving forsook his Battery haunts, he lived for a while at the corner of Seventeenth Street and Irving Place. The three story brick building has been preserved and it stands there marked by a tablet to commemorate that a beloved Knickerbocker once choose this as his home. At Number Fifty-five lived our favorite chronicler of Manhattan, O. Henry. He caught something of the pulse of Manhattan and transcribed it into those human stories which find their appeal to all classes. We can picture him walking down Irving Place to Luchows over on Fourteenth Street, there to discuss "The Four Million" over a stein of beer. The surrounding territory was well known to O. Henry's characters. Some had special benches they preferred in neaby Union and Madison Squares, and when his character was a conservative New Yorker, he sometimes had his home in Gramercy.

However, we should return again to the Park. There are still those few aristocratic brown stone mansions which we should see. Let us leave the "Old Petes" and other typical New York characters who lived so vibrantly between the covers of O. Henry's books, and return to our starting point. This used to be known as "Club Row" because so many clubs were located in the houses facing the Park. Today, however, Gramercy shelters only three clubs, The Players', The National Arts, and The Netherlands Clubs.

Samuel J. Tilden's home, numbers Fourteen and Fifteen, today houses The National Arts Club. Mr. Tilden, a former Governor of New York and well known lawyer, has long been remembered for his fine appreciation of books. His bequest of 20,000 volumes and $2,000,000 led to the formation of New York's wonderful Public Library. Mr. Tilden was also instrumental in bringing about the final dissolution of the Tweed Ring. It was Tilden's able handling of the prosecutor's case against Tweed which led the Tammany leader to jail and the prosecutor to the Governor's mansion. Great lover of books that he was, he had his residence designed with a view to be the home of the Tilden Library.

126

However, Mr. Tilden's will was broken by collateral heirs, and the home which he had lovingly created to be the great Tilden City Library eventually became a boarding house. Then The Players' Club opened next door. That changed the picture, for it was then that a group of spirited men seeking a location for the newly organized National Arts Club, selected the Tilden mansion. They remodeled it, saw the possibilities of building studio residences on the Nineteenth Street side, and made it the headquarters of a very noted group of people.

Now in the home which was once the pride of Samuel J. Tilden, and which later passed through so many vicissitudes, eventually bearing a "Boarders" sign in front is a very distinguished group of people congregate. Some reside in the newly built studio apartments in Nineteenth Street which is connected to the main building by a private garden running through from Twentieth to Nineteenth Street.

When Gramercy Park celebrated its Hundredth Anniversary in 1931, the Club helped to organize a very interesting exhibit of portraits, scenes and articles contemporary to the period and district. Hamlin Garland read a poem written for the occasion.

Next door is The Players' Club. It was the home of Valentine C. Hall until Edwin Booth bought it and had it remodeled by Stanford White. Booth lived there until his death. In 1888 The Players' was founded and ever since it has been the meeting place of noted artists, writers, actors and musicians. The room where Edwin Booth spent his last years remains exactly as he left it; ashes lie untouched in the fireplace, even a book is opened at the page where Booth left off reading. Among other important members such as John Drew and Maurice Barrymore, The Players also boasted the membership of Samuel Clemens, better known as Mark Twain, and Richard Mansfield. The Players' Club possesses a very fine collection of paintings including masterpieces by Gainsborough, Sargent, Inman and some by Gilbert Stuart's daughter, J. E. Stuart. They also maintain collections of old theatre programs and photographs of great actors and actresses.

Number Twenty-one was owned by American Minister to France, John Bigelow. Mr. Bigelow was also the biographer and friend of his neighbor, Tilden, as well as joint editor of "The Evening Post" with William Cullen Bryant. Horace Greeley, a contemporary lived at Thirty-five East Nineteenth Street.

Passing over to Lexington Avenue, at Number One, there is a tablet on the corner of the large apartment house occupying the site which tells the passerby that this is where the Atlantic Cable project was conceived. After eight years of determined efforts and perseverance the story of the cable was written with a happy ending on this spot in the home of Cyrus W. Field. United with Field in this enterprise were Cooper, who lived at Number Nine, Moses Taylor, Marshal O. Roberts and Wilson G. Hunt. When the Atlantic Cable was completed there was a great celebration in aristocratic old Gramercy.

On the opposite corner, where the Gramercy Park Hotel is now located, there is another plaque which proclaims that "On the site was the home of Robert G. Ingersoll. He knew no fear except the fear of doing wrong." It is interesting to note that this famous agnostic and exponent of Freethinking, the son of a Congregational Minister, lived within walking distance of four churches, The Calvary Episcopal Church, The Church of the Epiphany, The Evangelican Lutheran Church and The Quaker Meeting House. Ingersoll's home adjoined that of Stanford White, and both houses stood where the Gramercy Park Hotel is now situated.

A particular significant fact about Gramercy is that it has housed more distinguished residents than any other section of a like area in Manhattan. This is an outstanding characteristic of the little region which Duane called "Gramercy Seat." It appears that since Ruggles divided Gramercy into lots, the sites have always been occupied by men of distinction, men who were to contribute greatly to the cultural, political and scientific annals of our nation. Working in their respective fields they achieved wide recognition which in turn brought distinction to Gramercy where they had established their homes.

Gramercy has given us four Mayors of New York, one Governor and two presidential candidates. It has given us Booth, the great tragedian whom Fate designated to play the role of America's foremost actor; Booth who was to attain a most elevated and noble place in the hearts of his countrymen while his brother descended to a most ignoble concept among Americans. It gave us Col. Robert G. Ingersoll of whom Walt Whitman said, "America don't know to-day how proud she ought to be of Ingersoll." It gave us orators, men of letters, scientists, diplomats, philanthropists, politicians—great men all—and men who are today held in affectionate regard by modern Gramercyites.

But reflections are very well when one is snuggled in a cozy chair before a crackling fire. The chill blasts of winter wind are becoming more frequent. The sun is casting its rays over the benign countenance of Booth as the children's nurse leads her charges through the west gate. Snow is in the air. The charming Park which has seen so many winters fade into summers is alone, entirely free for the spirits of yesteryear to romp and cavort as they used to in days of old. Adjusting our coat collar high around our throat, and with a final glance at old Gramercy and a thought of praise for the man whose foresight and generosity preserved this Park, we wend our way west on Twenty-first Street.

Truly, we feel like a Twentieth Century Marco Polo who has discovered a place reeking with tradition and aristocracy right in the heart of our beloved Manhattan.

CHAPTER NOTES

1. Ovid, Heroides, Epis. XXI, 1.76.
2. Shackleton, Robert, "The Book of New York," p. 162.
3. "American Scenic and Historic Preservation Society, Twenty-fourth Annual Report, 1919." p. 98.
4. "Outline of the title of Samuel B. Ruggles to his lands between Fifteenth Street on the south, Twenty-eighth Street on the north, the Bloomingdale Road and Old Post Road on the west, and the First Avenue on the east." c. 1832, pp. 24, with a 17 page appendix of documents.
5. Lamb, Martha, "History of The City of New York," Vol. II, p. 750.
6. "The New York Times," for May 16, 1931, p. 16, c. 3.

GRAMERCY PARK WEST, November 27, 1935

CHAPTER THIRTEEN

The Old Gas House District
Not So Good — Not So Bad

> *"Political democracy, as it exists and*
> *practically works in America, with*
> *all its threatening evils, supplies a*
> *training school for making first-class*
> *men. It is life's gymnasium, not of*
> *good only, but of all."*
>
> Walt Whitman

A city, like a person, is made up of good and bad elements, a composite of both extremes. No one person has ever been found to be perfect, so too, there has never been discovered what can be considered an Utopia of cities. No matter how beautiful a city, no matter how genial and hospitable its residents, no matter how efficient its municipal government, there always exists some underlying defect to mar its perfection.

New York, while it is progressive and as modern as tomorrow's newspaper, does not deviate from this general rule. It has its sections of grandeur and opulence, but it also contains localities where drabness and poverty hold sway. Such a place is what used to be called the "Gas House District," deriving its name from the gas houses located in the vicinity. Though the original Gas House District extended as far north as Thirty-fifth Street today its boundaries may be considered as from Fourteenth to Twenty-third Streets between Third Avenue and the East River.

Years ago the gang known as the "Gas House Gang" terrorized everyone for blocks around. Approximately two hundred strong, they roamed the district where they excelled in footpadding and other questionable practices which made them neighborhood pests. It is said that this gang averaged about thirty robberies nightly.[1] The gang disappeared during intervening years, but it left in its stead the slums for which it was partly responsible, though it was not only because of the gangs that the better classes shunned the district. The odor of leaking gas from the tanks was forever present in the vicinity, contaminating the air with its presence. Such a condition was not conducive to good health and so it was only to be expected that those who could afford to do so moved elsewhere leaving the Gas House District free for the poorer classes and the renegades who preyed upon them for many years.

The community was associated for many years with slums and all their accompanying evils, a condition which prevailed for a great number of years. Today, however, despite the fact that some tenements remain and one solitary gas tank, soon to be demolished, the old Gas House District has been completely changed from the pest-hole of former years. The region boasts a hospital, one of the foremost in the country, in addition to many large office buildings, the well known Tammany Hall together with a miscellaneous assortment of stores and tenements.

The hospital is Bellevue. Like all large institutions of its kind, it presents a pattern of life greatly accellerated—for here life appears and disappears—all in the space of seconds. A child is born at the moment its mother draws her last breath. Here, daily contact brings out the wonders of life, the mysteries of death, making both commonplace. Bellevue, where, in the words of William Ernest Henley . . . "——grey, quiet, old, When Life and Death like friendly chafferers meet."[2]

And life in its exhultant joy and death in its unfathomable finality fraternize.

The oldest general hospital in the Continent, Bellevue Hospital was moved in 1810 from the City Hall Park region. Harboring so much that is vital to us Knickerbockers, it has steadily grown throughout the years until today it covers twelve square city blocks fronting the East River upon which seventeen buildings loom forth in bewildering confusion.

All sorts of diseases eventually find their way to Bellevue including some of the strangest known to medical science. It seems to be a clearing house for many of the most unusual cases extant. For this reason it is an ideal place for the medical student to gain general experience. In addition to observing the progress of many uncommon diseases, the Bellevue interne also has the advantage of participating in a huge turnover of cases. When it is realized that in the year 1945 Bellevue treated a total of 62,766 patients of which 19,517 were psychiatric cases, one can calculate the value of a Bellevue internship.[2b]

This famous institution is credited with having inaugurated the first ambulance service in the world and its New York Training School for Nurses was also the first of its kind to be established in the United States. The date of this auspicious advancement in the nursing profession was 1873, just eight years after the Civil War and during the height of Clara Barton's activities.

Of interesting note is the fact that Bellevue was not discouraging in its attitude toward women in the medical profession. While many other hospitals were barring them as internes, Bellevue admitted women physicians in 1913. Today, of the 215 resident physicians and internes—25 or 30 are women which shows that Bellevue has been consistently helpful in fostering medical careers for the gentler sex. And since the old institution has been first to promote other projects, one naturally expects that it would be one of the first to admit women physicians to their staff.

I suppose I am partial to Bellevue. It recalls to mind many an interesting experience, for some years ago I had the good fortune to take my student dietetic training in the Bellevue kitchens. In those days we had a night chef who had decided to become a "landlubber" after twenty years as a cook on an oil tanker. The kitchen was never spoken of as such; it was a "galley." He never threw anything away; it went "over the side." And when he went off duty, he went "up on deck." In truth, many a time I had to cope with the impression that I was far out to sea, miles and miles away from East Twenty-sixth Street.

And during the long hours when I was on night duty he used to recount some of his experiences to me. His tales were interesting, even if greatly exaggerated, and they served to while away the lonesome night hours in the eerie quietude of our hospital kitchen. There were typhoons and semi-mutinous crews demanding all his ingenuity to weather; there was a shortage of items from which he could make his menus, and as many other difficulties to contend with as would try the patience of a Griselda. No, according to Mac, there wasn't a cook sailing the seven seas who had as much to put up with as he did. There was never smooth sailing for poor old Mac, like the time when the old tanker took such a buffeting in the English Channel that it was a miracle when they made port. He told fabulous stories, did old Mac—stories that could have been an adventurous liaison between those of a Conrad and the dashing tales of a Scott.

He proved to me, though, that just the right amount of nutmeg gave lamb gravy that intangible "all-to-be-desired" flavor and no one at

Bellevue made better mashed potatoes than he. Mac had very definite ideas and such a violent temper that few of the dieticians dared to cross him. He was the culinary embodiment of a high strung opera star. Mac consumed more gargles and cough medicine than an entire ward. Whether or not he ever cured his cough, or, in fact, whether he really had a cough, are matters the mystery of which I never have been able to pierce.

I recall that there were many passages through the basement of Bellevue, the one I avoided most being that leading to the Morgue. I would come on duty, happy, and imbued with the enthusiasm of youth, only to meet an attendant heading towards the Morgue with the basket and its lifeless contents. If there is one thing which forces the young to pause pensively in the thoughtful conjecture of the future, it is death with all its revocableness. It was as if the warm ardor of my enthusiasm was chilled by Artic blasts of reality. Such thoughts, happily, could not for long abide in a healthy individual. Yet, the depression caused by such encounters made itself felt.

It is estimated that there are 20,000 bodies delivered to the Morgue yearly of which 8,500 are never claimed.[3] The latter figure of unidentified dead seems appallingly high. Yet one must take into consideration the fact that it includes non-residents and transients who die either naturally or violently, leaving no means of identification.

These cadavers are kept for two weeks in refrigerated vaults. If, after that time they are not identified, their bodies are photographed and described and the records turned over to the Police Department Bureau of Missing Persons. Some bodies are given to medical schools for dissection while others are allotted to embalming schools. An average of 170 coffins a week are carried to Potter's Field.[4]

The Pathological Building or Morgue looks just as one would expect it to appear. Symbolizing the termination of man's mortality, oft by foul means, it stands on the corner of Twenty-ninth Street and York Avenue, a gloomy structure of red brick and stone.

But it must not be thought that the neighborhood surrounding Bellevue is all poverty, death and despair. It is not. And contrary to what one would expect, the residents of this section are not depressed and sad. The locale has its better aspects, foremost among these being the Davenport Theatre, which is the only free theatre in the world.

Manhattan has its free libraries, its free concerts, its free museums; in short, the city provides unlimited facilities for improving the cultural perceptions of its inhabitants. However, it remained for Mr. Butler Davenport to conceive the idea of a free theatre. The site selected for this achievement was One-Thirty-Eight East Twenty-seventh Street where, in 1915, this remarkable undertaking was inaugurated. Since

133

then the Davenport Theatre has been presenting plays of such well known playwrights as Shakespeare, Shaw, Ibsen, Victor Hugo, Galsworthy, Chekhov and a host of others.

There is no admission charged to attend these worthwhile performances. The Theatre is maintained by donations and supporting donations. During my student days at Bellevue, I spent many an enjoyable evening seeing Davenport presentations of the great dramatists. Best of all, and most appealing to a student, it was all as free as the air we breathe. I have thought since of this wonderful experiment of this far sighted man. Certainly our City Fathers should devise some means for continuing this meritorious initiative.

Like in many sections of Manhattan's other districts, the neighborhood around Bellevue is home to a large number of foreign born citizens. There are said to be around 10,000 Armenians in New York City, many of whom live in the side streets west of Bellevue. They have their own church at Two Twenty-one East Twenty-seventh Street. Other Armenian influences have crept into the neighborhood. There are restaurants and cafes where these people so far from their homeland may gather and speak their native tongue, enjoy their special dishes and nostalgically talk about places and things they have left behind. That is one of the good things about Manhattan. The foreigner need never feel alone for he is sure to meet a compatriot within the friendly confines of Manhattan.

Tammany Hall is located on the westerly fringes of the Gas House District, as it is situated on Seventeenth Street slightly east of Union Square. A meeting place for members of the Tammany Society or Columbian Order, Tammany Hall has been for long a part of the Gas House District and the Gas House District in its turn has supplied many leaders to the "Hall," thus the two have become allied in the thoughts of New Yorkers.

The first Tammany Hall was in "Brown" Martling's tavern (Abraham B. Martling), located at Nassau and Spruce Streets. The building was typical of those days, made to serve practical requirements rather than to enhance the city's esthetic appearance. It was constructed of rough wood, unpainted with its entrance on Nassau Street. The Tammanyites held their meetings in what was known as the Long Room which was situated in the rear. Due to the unusual disorderly state of the room, it was derisively dubbed "The Pig Pen" by the Federalists who were then the opposing party.[5] By 1802 the Society was outgrowing the room set aside for use in the tavern and it was decided to move to more commodious quarters. The sum of $28,000 was pledged for the erection of a more suitable "wigwam," but the move was not accomplished until

1811 when the Tammany Society took possession of its own building at Chatham and Frankfort Streets.[6]

There it remained through many a political uproar until after the Civil War. All Manhattan was expanding and the Society followed along with the crowd. In 1867 it moved to Fourteenth Street and Third Avenue next door to Tony Pastor's. The "Sachems" gathered in this edifice until 1929 when the "wigwam" began to hold its "pow-wows" in the building which it now occupies.

Though the building can be called famous without deviating from the thin line described by veracity, the Sons of St. Tammany were very oft infamous, as shown by their own deeds. Certainly, it cannot be claimed that the Gas House District was ever singularly distinguished by either the presence of the edifice or the groups of scheming men who met within it, there to mold the political thoughts of voters. We, who have often looked askance at the corrupted governments of some of the other nations, must preforce hang our heads in shame when we think of many of the nefarious schemes employed by Tammany in its insatiable greed to obtain money.

It started altruistically enough, and its inception (which took place three weeks after the Constitution was adopted), had the best conceivable motives. To understand the founding of the Tammany Society or Columbian Order one must picture the American political stage after the Revolution. There was a distinct class separation. The aristocrats were well represented by the Federalists who had Alexander Hamilton as one of their leaders. These were the people who owned property, who had family and background and who voted, for according to the New York State Constitution of 1777, the franchise was held only by those who owned property to the value of one hundred pounds free of debt. Hamilton was sympathetic to having the President and Senators of the United States hold office during their good behavior. He further felt that the President and the Senators should appoint Governors of States.[7] They also had their political tenets which naturally were partial to their own class.

But what about the great number of people who owned no property and to whom the rights of man were paramount? To them the Tammany Society represented a formulation of ideas resulting in political power. It meant the possibility of their taking part in the organization of the young Republic, a Republic which they had a part in proclaiming. To these people, who, in a last analysis, were the pioneers and the workers upon whose industry America grew and prospered, Tammany supplied a crying need. For this reason and for the honorable achievements rendered by the organization during those splendid begin-

135

nings, we must be prepared to forgive, or at least condone, some of the iniquities of Tammanyites who came later.

In his desire to name the organization with a real American name, William Mooney, the founder, delved back into Indian lore and fell upon the legend, if such it was, of the Indian Chief Tammany, or Tamanend. This Chief was so wise and ruled his tribe of Delaware Indians so sagaciously that his wisdom spread, increasing as the years went on until by the time of the American Revolution his exploits were legendary. Whether or not Chief Tammany existed we are not sure, though tradition has it that William Penn, in exchange for a few handfuls of tobacco, needles, knives, scissors, and miscellaneous articles, received in return 300 square miles of rich fertile land. It was, then, to the fame of this first American that William Mooney went for the name of the Society. And to commemorate the Indian origin of its name in the early days of the Society its members indulged in many Indian rituals and ceremonies. Even now the terms "wigwam" and "sachem" are employed in connection with this political organization.

In its early days Tammany devoted itself to the propagation of genuine Americanism. Its ideals were lofty, so lofty in fact, that the warriors once offered a unanimous nomination for Mayor to Washington Irving. The organization numbered amongst its friends such spirits of democratic thought as Jefferson, Madison and Jackson. However, the latter day history of Tammany has not been a happy one to contemplate. There have been scandals, graft and corruption bobbing up every once in a while to mar the altruistic purposes for which the organization was founded. There have been unprincipled rogues who appeared and attached themselves to the safe confines of Tammany, like barnacles clinging to the hull of a ship, there better to weather the storm of political strife.

William M. Tweed, boss of the notorious "Tweed Gang" was one of these men. He was also a member of the "Forty Thieves" by which name New York City's Board of Aldermen was popularly known. This body of men, together with other Tammany politicians controlled the city's politics. They dipped their greedy hands deep into the city's coffers, apparently withdrawing only when no more gold would cling to their palm. Seemingly dissatisfied with this source of revenue they proceeded to impose a percentage or "shake-down" on all the vices then rampant in the city of New York.

They sold naturalization papers; city officers and public jobs were auctioned to the highest bidder; they protected crime and prostitution from which they were not too fussy to extract their share of the profits. Lawlessness, vice and corruption flourished. Bribes and graft were accepted and often solicited—by the political "boss" clear on down to the patrolman on the beat.

Tweed, christened William Marcy, was born on Cherry Street in 1823, while twenty years later Richard Croker saw the light of day in County Cork, Ireland. Tweed, therefore, had twenty years head start on Croker in perfecting the fraudulent machinations for which both were noted. Between the two they succeeded in besmirching the name of the honorable Indian warrior after whom Tammany was so hopefully called. Which of them did more damage to this good name is hard to judge. Both did not hesitate to accept bribes and graft and close their eyes to the source of their ill-gotten revenue.

One of the greatest frauds perpetrated by the Tweed Ring was the naturalization of foreigners in order to control their votes. In House Report No. 31 on Election Frauds in New York City we find that Tammany Hall engaged the New York Printing Company, which Tweed owned, to print 105,000 blank applications and 69,000 certificates of naturalization.[8] Tammany Hall also paid the fees required by the clerk of the court for naturalization papers and gave foreigners red tickets which entitled them to their papers free; more than 40,000 such tickets were issued in 1868.

In a city where the majority of votes was foreign, it is not surprising that the Ring came to be the most powerful political organization of the city. Elections were a farce, repeating a common practice, and once the Ring's candidate was in office another greedy hand was extended to be "oiled." Tweed had his friends put on the city pay rolls. In some instances the names of dead people were allowed to remain, the money thus received going to the Ring. Sometimes, one individual held several sinecures, many times receiving thousands of dollars yearly for doing nothing. A notable example of such political chicanery was the case of Mr. George H. Lynch, father-in-law of Senator Genet. This gentleman held not one city job, but three.

On commenting upon the sad state of municipal politics then prevalent in New York City, the New York Times for October 3, 1871 published that "One of the members of the Citizens' Committee has stated that his examination of the Records of the Finance Department had convinced him that at least thirty-three and one-third percent of the money expended by the various Departments was stolen by the Ring."[9] There was plunder on a large scale.

By far and large the very worst practice of the Tweed Gang were the methods used to control an election. In a table prepared by John L. Davenport which shows the number of votes cast from various polling places in the city during that year, one address alone shows a record of seventy-four fraudulent votes. These votes were cast from Compton

House, owned by Scannel and Fagin. This Scannel was a brother of Florence Scannel of whom we shall hear more later.[10]

Yet, bartering of votes was mild to other devices by which the Tweed Ring sought to carry an election. The nefarious practice of repeating was extensively employed during the Tweed regime. The fact is that the presidential election of 1868 brought about its use to an extent undreamed of in the previous history of elections held in New York. That year the evidences of repeating were so flagrant as to be undeniable.

To a good citizen his vote represents the results of hundreds of years of strife. There was a time in our history when Jews were disfranchised, when Catholics could not hold office and when one had to be a property owner to vote.[11] It is as much a part of the citizen as his liberty. To deprive him of suffrage is to take away part of the freedom which he has fought so hard to attain. He should no more think of selling his enfranchisement than he should his liberty. Yet, conclusive evidence showed that sometimes a repeater would vote as many as thirty times during an election. Ballot box stuffing and illegal canvassing were also prevalent during those times.

As is to be expected, such a state of political corruption could not continue indefinitely. The major responsibility having been fixed on Tweed, at long length his corrupted practices caught up with him, and in December 1872, he was indited by the Grand Jury on the overwhelming charge of one hundred and twenty counts.[12] From that time until his death in Ludlow Street jail (April 12, 1878) Tweed was beset by the many troubles accruing from his own wrong deeds.

Meanwhile, the neighborhood of the Gas House District was undergoing some changes. As the city spread uptown, more and more people moved within the confines of the District. Tammany, which had fallen into ill repute following the revelations connected with Tweed's exposure and conviction, was now located on Fourteenth Street. Tony Pastor's was next door to the smoke filled rooms where the "sachems" of old were wont to gather. Over on the north side of Fourteenth Street near Irving Place, the Academy of Music resounded with operatic arias, until the Metropolitan opened and attracted the elite clientele of the Academy. The Academy of Music was opened in 1855, burned May 21, 1866 and rebuilt and reopened in March, 1867. The Metropolitan's opening brought people further uptown, and society, which had followed the amusement center up from the Bowery, again betook itself, with its jewels, furs and high hats, up to the Metropolitan, then, as now, the city's foremost music center.

Irving Hall which is now the Irving Place Theatre was built in 1859 on Fifteenth Street and Irving Place. Fine hotels and restaurants began

138

to appear in the neighborhood bringing with them their aristocratic clientele. Though in the intervening years many of these famous places have deserted the district, Luchow's still maintains its well known restaurant on Fourteenth Street, little changed from the days when O. Henry would sit at his special table and dream of his characters in the "Four Million."

Well known families appeared in the vicinity and fine residences were established. Residential neighborhoods were shifting just as the population was increasing with a result that quite a few of New York's first families were moving into the district from the neighborhoods of lower New York. The city was progressing at a rapid rate, like a youngster who shoots up all at once and apparently becomes a man overnight. But just as a boy cannot be a boy one day and a man the next, so a young city cannot be a town one day and a metropolis the next. Both must pass through intermediate stages of learning, of adjusting themselves to new conditions, to new environment. In the last twenty-five years of the Nineteenth Century New York was like the twelve year old boy who sneaks behind the barn to smoke his father's cigar. It is not a feat of the imagination to know the unhappy results occasioned by the boy's intrepid action. He became deathly sick. So did New York.

One thought, and with sufficient reason, that the conviction of Tweed would put an end to corrupt city politics. But meting out punishment to Tweed did not achieve the desired results for during ensuing years the honest hard working man fared little better than he did when the Tweed Ring milked his pockets dry. Commercialized vice was on the increase, organized crime flourished, and outsiders were beginning to comment, with due cause, that the citizens of New York were incapable of self government.

The fleecing which the lambs underwent at the hands of the Tweed Ring had not been forgotten, least of all by the lambs themselves—the lambs being, in a last analysis, none other than Mr. and Mrs. John Q. Public. They were slightly wary and distrustful of Tammany. It was a time of political reconstruction and whoever assumed the leadership of the "Wigwam" had to manouver the bark of politics through some very muddy waters. But it was accomplished, the braves of Tammany quieting down to a more or less quiescent state for the next few years—or until Richard Croker, by brain and brawn, had fought his way up to be master of the Tammany Tiger.

When Croker assumed leadership of Tammany, Tweed's way of operating was restored, with, of course, modifications adopted to meet the changing times. Once again the Gas House District, always a Tammany stronghold, and all New York for that matter, reverberated with

139

hints of corrupted politics emanating from the "Wigwam." Graft was the order of the day. Politicians received their cut by allocating city contracts to their friends, who would "kick back" making up the difference by supplying inferior materials or cutting down on specifications. Illicit trades were permitted to continue provided some public official received his share of the profits. In many instances vice and debauchery were even encouraged so long as some public servant was paid to close his eyes.

The Lexow and Mazet Committees brought to light many of the evils existing in New York during 1894-1899. Certainly, these conditions had existed previously, but even allowing for the rapid growth of the city, had the municipality's paid officers dispensed with their duties efficiently and conscientiously, there would have been no need for such investigations. As it was, however, the debauched state into which the city had fallen grew yearly in proportion to the city department's susceptibility to graft. But under the "Spoils System" of Croker, graft as practiced by the city employees of the day hit a new high. In Crocker's own words "To the Party belong the Spoils." And the Party went after the spoils in a manner befitting the grandiose Croker, then boss and ruler of Manhattan.

During this period there was published a brochure called "Dr. Parkhurst's Crusade or New York after Dark." The book states, "In nineteen years there were in New York 881 recorded homicides, of which 679 were committed by persons known, but not in every instance punished, and 202 were committed by persons unknown, and never arrested. There are in New York about 3000 professional thieves, including bank robbers, burglars, dwelling-house and chance sneaks, panel thieves, forgers, shop-lifters, pickpockets, confidence men and receivers of stolen goods. The casual thieves are more numerous but less daring, rapacious and successful. All the thieves are estimated, from sources more trustworthy than the records kept in Mulberry Street, to steal $6,500,000 yearly. The police claim to restore to the owners about $2,560,000 worth of property a year; though much of the property thus reported has been lost instead of stolen. Crediting the whole of it as recovered from thieves, there is still left to the latter and their fences a revenue of $3,940,000 directly extracted from the wealth of private citizens. But this is not all the thieves cost to the city. The police and criminal judicial establishments, which they render necessary, are supported at an expense of $3,212,000 more. This runs up the cost of the criminal and disorderly classes to $7,000,000 a year."[13]

Now, at the time this was written, New York's population was a little over 2,507,414. It can readily be seen that based upon the population the cost of caring for the criminal element in New York was a relatively high expense for the city to sustain.

The power so vilely weilded by Tweed and Croker had provoked public antipathy toward New York City's municipal government. Coupled with this there grew up a strong reform movement and the focal point of the reformer's wrath centered upon New York City and specifically upon the Gas House District, from whence emanated all the evils of Tammany.

It was an era and a set of conditions which perforce had to produce a Dr. Parkhurst. Here was a fighter and a crusader whose weapon consisted neither of armor nor sword. But woe betide the wrongdoer who was the target of his vituperative accusations! Words were his weapons—words based upon facts which were later proven beyond the shadow of a doubt. Dr. Parkhurst's scathing denunciations of the Police Department and other city officials rocked Tammany to its very foundations, and even the excess weight of Croker failed to balance the throne upon which he sat and to save him from toppling in the face of the impending disaster.

In the Nineties bribery among the police officers was so open that vaudeville skits of the day made frequent use of the fact. Dr. Parkhurst did not spare his words in accusing the New York City Police of fostering crime and immorality. He asserted: "that social vice has been so protected and encouraged by the filthy officials who control the department, that the number of abandoned women and disorderly houses now existing in the city is no measure of what it would be if we had a police force from top down, who conceived of sexual crime as an evil to be suppressed, not as capital to draw dividends from. I have had women of this class tell me in my own house that they did not belong here, but that they came here from outside because they knew that in New York the police would protect them."[14]

Dr. Parkhurst would visit the saloons and dives of the city hiding his identity so as to get the unbiased facts of the situation. Many times his visits to places of questionable reputation were criticized by the press, but the determined clergyman went on with his crusade. He hired a detective, Charles W. Gardner who promised to guide him into the city's vice dens. Once he visited a place called "The Golden Rule Pleasure Club" over on West Third Street. It must have been a place like "Parisis Hall" where both men and women of homosexual tendencies cavorted and performed for the amusement of patrons. It was the only scene from which Dr. Parkhurst fled, exclaiming, "Why, I wouldn't stay in that house for all the money in the world."[15] Gardner later wrote about the venture of Dr. Parkhurst and himself into the

141

city's vice dens in a book called "The Doctor and the Devil, or Midnight Adventures of Dr. Parkhurst."

The eminent clergyman's vitriolic denunciations were made from the pulpit. He made startling accusations; he fomented public wrath against the political machine until finally his untiring efforts aroused public indignation. In January, 1894, a resolution was introduced into the State Senate authorizing an investigation of the Police Department of New York. This was approved, a committee was formed and Clarence Lexow appointed Chairman.

The Committee carried on its investigations for a year after which the testimony was published in five volumes. It seems incredible that such a state of affairs could exist as to have provoked five volumes of accusatory testimony. Startling conditions were revealed; the cancerous growth of corruption and vice was bared to a shocked city, its malodorous stench offensive even to the strongest olfactory organs. The lid was finally blown off the top of New York's vice situation. Testimony produced substantiation of many of Dr. Parkhurst's accusations. It was conclusively shown that police officers accepted bribes—witness the testimony of Captain Schmittberger who swore that while he was Captain of a number of precincts there was a well organized system for collecting from disorderly houses of the city.[16] At one time the Board of Education asked for a list of these houses in order to have them suppressed. They complained that they were so numerous in the vicinity of Wooster Street School that the children could not attend school in safety. Captain Williams testified that there were eighty-three such houses of ill-fame in the Eighth Ward at the time his testimony was given.[17]

Women of abandoned character paid patrolmen on the beat to walk the street.[18] The alternative of refusing to pay this bribe for protection meant arrest.

But if the Lexow' Committee's Investigation uncovered the deplorable state into which Tammany had plunged the city, the Mazet Committee brought the situation home like a "blow to the jaw." As in Tweed's time, prostitution, vice, gambling and crime afforded a very good source of revenue, but Tammany, under Croker, extended its rotten tentacles to "big business." Its manipulation of the Ice Trust was one of the most flagrant violations of public confidence.[19] In this it took issue with the Great Ramapo water deal, another scheme evolved for making money. The hearings before the Mazet Committee brought out the fact that although the Ramapo Water Company involved a $200,000,000 city contract to supply water to the "City of New York" the company possessed neither pipes nor right of way to conduct water into New York City.[20] Yet, they issued stocks even going so far as to offer Hon. William J. Gaynor who was then Judge of the Supreme Court in Second Department, a block of shares worth $50,000 to accept the Presidency of the company.[21]

The Ice Trust was little better than the Ramapo deal. As pointed out by the New York World of October 17, 1901, Robert A. Van Wyck, who was the Mayor at the time, his brother Augustus and the confidential clerk of a third Dock Commissioner were in possession of a combined number of 9,425 shares preferred and 9,550 shares common of American Ice Company stock. The total par value of this stock was $1,957,500.[22] These figures were taken from the stock books of the American Ice Company.

And what was Croker doing while public opinion mounted steadily against the infamies committed by the Irish born lad and his cohorts of the Wigwam?—Croker, who was raised on the fringes of the Gas House District and who had irrevocably bound himself to the destinies of Tammany Hall, thus doubly linking himself to the district. The rotund, grizzled squire whose caricature was familiar to all and sundry, was devoting himself to racing in which he was very interested and in raising English bull dogs, another hobby to which he gave much attention. At one time Croker wanted to have a race course laid out in Central Park, but the plan met with opposition and was never realized. He made repeated trips to Europe, where he cavorted with royalty, giving subject to many cartoons of the time. One cartoon shows the King of England bidding farewell to the corpulent Croker. The King's crown is padlocked, and so is his purse.[23]

At the turn of the Century, Croker began to take less interest in politics. Slowly he was casting aside Tammany and the Gas House District with which he was so closely associated. He spent more and more time abroad living like a country squire, racing his horses and breeding his dogs. The Gas House District and Tammany were left to their own devices.

Crocker outlived his supreme political triumphs by about fifteen years. Though the grizzled former boss of Manhattan returned annually to the scenes of his triumphs, he took no active part in politics nor in the destinies of Tammany. He lived to be eighty years old and though the winter of his life was peaceful and uneventful, he could look back upon hectic and turbulent days spent in the summer and autum of his manhood.

In 1929 Tammany moved over to the building which it now occupies. The Hall still plays an important part in American politics. That is undisputed. Today if you walk along Seventeenth Street east from Union Square you will see the "Wigwam" of these erstwhile Sachems of Tammany. A three storied building with a neighboring bank to lend

143

respectability, it has the innocent appearance of a school. Looking down on the passerby from an honored niche above the center of the third floor stands the wise and mighty Indian Chief, Tammany. Could he but talk, what we could learn from him! Placidly watching Seventeenth Street's traffic, he was the inspiration for Gus Edwards and Vincent Bryan's "Tammany." This song, coming out in 1905, perhaps best exemplifies the attitude of that year towards Tammany. Though the authors gallantly dedicated their work to Hon. Timothy D. Sullivan, one of Tammany's foremost leaders, the lyrics cannot be considered as of an entirely complimentary nature. A few verses follow:

TAMMANY

Hiawatha was an Indian, so was Navajo,
Pale-face organ grinders killed them many moons ago.
But there is a band of Indians, that will never die,
When they're at the Indian club, this is their battle cry:

Tammany, Tammany, Big Chief sits in his tepee,
cheering braves to victory. Tammany, Tammany,
Swamp 'em, Swamp 'em, get the "wam-pum" Tammany.

Chris Colombo sailed from Spain, across the deep blue sea,
Brought along the Dago vote to beat out Tammany.
Tammany found Colombo's crew were living on a boat,
Big Chief said: "They're floaters," and he would not
let them vote,
Then to the tribe he wrote:

Chorus: Tammany, Tammany,
Get those Dagos jobs at once, they can vote in twelve
more months.
Tammany, Tammany,
Make those floaters Tammany voters, Tammany.

Fifteen thousand Irishmen from Erin came across,
Tammany put these Irish Indians on the Police force.
I asked one cop, if he wanted three platoons or four,
He said: "Keep your old platoons, I've got a cuspidor,
What would I want with more?"

Chorus: Tammany, Tammany,
Your policemen can't be beat, they can sleep on any street.
Tammany, Tammany,
Dusk is creeping, they're all sleeping, Tammany.[24]

In latter years the gas tanks with their ugly bulks silhouetted against the East River have gradually undergone demolishment. Today only one remains and its future is as doomed as the horse car and bustles.[4] Civic improvements are always underway in the "Gas House District" and though Father Knickerbocker has already done much, there still remains much more to do. It would appear that razing the tenements would be a step in the right direction and something is being done along those lines. In fact, a project has already been initiated which will mean the rehabilitation of the Gas House District. The Metropolitan Life Insurance Company have undertaken the task of constructing two massive low cost housing units which will be known as Stuyvesant Town and Peter Cooper Village. Stuyvesant Town will provide housing facilities for 8,761 families while Peter Cooper Village will accommodate 2,000 families. It will be a wonderful face lifting operation on the old District when these two projects are completed. But there will still remain block after block of old tenements, their fronts disfigured with the familiar iron balconies and ladders which the fire law makes mandatory.

These fire-escapes are a typical New York sight and in few other cities do they mean as much to the inhabitants. This is very true in the Gas House District. Besides serving as a means of escape in the event of fire, as well as the divers other purposes to which ingenious Manhattanites put them, fire-escapes also reveal a great deal about the lives of those who dwell behind them. If you pass on a Monday, the "Great American Washday" you will get an idea of the size of the family and the ages of its members. If you pass towards the end of the week (in late Fall or early Spring) you may spy what the family are going to have for Sunday dinner. A few days before Christmas the Christmas tree appears. Potted plants and flowers come in the "good old summer time." In between seasons the friendly fire-escape lends itself as a quick expedient from which Mrs. Murphy can exchange a choice morsel of gossip with Mrs. Goldberg. Fire-escapes are a New York institution and though fire ordnances state that they be kept free from obstructions, in these congested areas of New York City one notices that such restrictions are not strictly observed.

Thus the Gas House District goes along in its way, with Tammany Hall lending a colorful and exciting past and constant improvements to ensure an interesting future. The Gas House Gang is gone, having received its death blow in 1914 when its last chief, Tommy Lynch met his end during a violent battle with the Jimmy Curley Gang.[25] Tony Pastor's is gone; the gas tanks are gone except one and that is doomed; Bellevue Hospital progresses with the times, modernizing, improving its equipment and treatment to meet the exigencies of a changing world.

What was once a fashionable neighborhood of refined entertainment and elegant shops has disintegrated into a cheap shopping center and a place of tawdry amusements. Shooting galleries and burlesque theatres, hawkers and peddlers line Fourteenth Street. Perhaps the erection of Stuyvesant Town and Peter Cooper Village will change all that and rejuvenate the area, but that remains to be seen. The Gas House District has been in such a rut for so long that it will take such drastic measures to jog it out. But if ever things do change, I hope Luchows will remain. I always feel when I am there that if I am quiet enough I may almost hear O. Henry breathing in the very essence of his "Bagdad on the Subway."

CHAPTER NOTES

1. Asbury, Herbert, "The Gangs of New York," p. 253.
2. Henly, Ernest, "In Hospital."
2b. Statistics taken from a letter from the Dept. of Hospitals to the author, dated January 20, 1947.
3. Federal Writers' Project, "New York City Guide," p. 316.
4. Ibid., p. 317.
5. Bayles, W. Harrison, "Old Taverns of New York," p. 376.
6. Harlow, Alvin F., "Old Bowery Days," p. 284.
7. Smith, Nelson, "Tammany Hall; A Sketch of its History," p. 32.
8. "House Report No. 31, submitted by Hon. William Lawrence of Ohio, from the Select Committee on New York Election Frauds," p. 12, 13.
9. "The New York Times," for October 3, 1871, p. 4 c. 4.
10. Davenport, John I., "New York Election Frauds and Their Prevention," p. 169.
11. Payne, George Henry, "History of Journalism in the United States," p. 218.
12. Werner, Morris Robert, "Tammany Hall," p. 233.
13. Walsh, Robert F., "Dr. Parkhurst's Crusade; or New York after Dark," p. 104.
14. Parkhurst, Rev. Charles H., "Our Fight with Tammany," p. 155.
15. Gardner, Charles W., "The Doctor and the Devil or Midnight Adventures of Dr. Parkhurst," p. 58.
16. Lexow, Clarence, "Investigation of New York City Police Department, 1894," p. 5575.
17. Ibid., p. 5470.
18. Ibid., p. 4875.

19. "The World" for October 15, 1901, p. 6 c. 2.
    "The World" for October 16, 1901, p. 4 c. 1 & 2.
20. "Investigation of the Public Offices and Departments of the City of New York" (1899) p. 3411.
21. Ibid., p. 3624.
22. "The World" for October 17, 1901 p. 3 c. 1 & 2.
23. "New York Evening World" for August 31, 1901 p. 8.
24.
25. Asbury, Herbert, "The Gangs of New York," p. 358.

"GAS HOUSE," New York City WPA Art Project

CHAPTER FOURTEEN

Murray Hill

When greater perils men inviron,
Then women show a front of iron;
And, gentle in their manner, they
Do bold things in a quiet way.

Thomas Dunn English "Betty Zane"

WHEN the actions of a man serve to alter the destiny of a nation, little wonder is evinced at this feat. The world is quite accustomed to having its concepts and fate molded and changed by members of the masculine sex. Should, however, the course of natural events be transformed through some manipulation performed by the gentler sex, then there is cause for universal awe, the obvious reason being that the world is more used to having its destiny shaped by men.

Nevertheless, there are some stories in history which are extraordinary accounts of how a woman has changed the course of events. There was the face that launched a thousand ships and which caused the Trojan War. Had Helen of Troy not preferred Paris to her husband, it would not have been necessary for countless generations of students to study causes and effects of the Trojan War. History tells us that it was largely through the aid of Queen Isabella of Spain that Christopher Columbus was able to equip his three vessels and set forth upon his journey. Would subsequent historical events been different had another monarch financed this venture? Assuredly they would, though one can only theorize upon the probable outcome.

But this subtle influence which women sometimes exert may be employed both ways. There have been many instances when, after man's strategy has failed—after man has employed all available arguments at his disposal—a frail woman has appeared upon the scene

148

and deftly turned the tide of events. Put this down to what influence you will—sweet persuasion or shrewish nagging or any other methods women are prone to employ to have their own way. The fact remains that it happened and right here in our own Murray Hill.

The heroine of our story is Mrs. Murray whose husband Robert, had a country house probably situated about where Thirty-seventh Street and Park Avenue is. There is a copper plaque on this site marking the location of the Murray home. Though the Murray's son, Lindlay was a very prominent grammatician, considered an authority by both English and American men of letters, the family name has won considerable fame in New York in connection with Lindlay's mother who saved the day for Washington's Army.

The Murray farm house was called "Inclenberg." Relatively isolated, it was surrounded by farm lands and spacious lawns extending from Thirty-third to Thirty-seventh Street between the present Broadway and Third Avenue.

At a time when Washington's Army was beset by hardship and impending defeat, the mistress of this domain sympathized with the American cause. It so happened that by the time September rolled around—in the year 1776—the Continental Army found itself in a very precarious position. General Israel Putnam and four thousand of his men were in imminent danger of being captured. The British, under General Howe, had taken Staten Island in July, but no attempt was made to cross the bay until that historical September 15, 1776. Aaron Burr and Alexander Hamilton both saw action in this battle. Burr, who was familiar with the terrain, was appointed Aide de camp to General Putnam, and he was supposed to guide the General and the army up to Harlem Heights. Hamilton was heading his company of New York Artillerymen.

On September 15 five British men-of-war anchored in Kip's Bay announcing their presence with accurately directed cannon shots which fell into a part of a regiment of Continentals. General Washington tried to rally his fleeing soldiers in the open field which we know today as Bryant Park, but it was to no avail and the regiment became completely disorganized. The terrified soldiers fled in retreat and try as he would the great general could do nothing to prevent the rout. According to his own account, ". . . and on the appearance of a small party of the enemy, not more than sixty or seventy in number their disorder increased, and they ran away without firing a shot."[1] This cowardice so infuriated the great General that he is said to have drawn his sword beating the soldiers and some of the officers, as well.

It was then that the charming hostess of "Inclenberg" entered upon the scene and turned the tide of events for the discouraged Continentals.

149

This gracious lady, famous for her hospitality in England as well as with the Colonials, gave a dinner party in honor of the British officers, whose soldiers surrounded the territory through which Putnam had to pass to reach Harlem Heights. Washington had been a guest at "Inclenberg" but two days previous, but if the British were aware of this fact, they did not consider it was relevant to their own safety for they accepted. Mary Murray's invitation to rest awhile and partake of the refreshments which the noted hostess herself assisted in preparing, was cordially received, inasmuch as the officers and men had had a difficult time and the prospects of a brief rest mingled with pleasant company and surroundings looked very promising. Mrs. Murray wined and dined the officers in true colonial fashion, taking care that the Murray hospitality endured long enough to enable the General to remove his soldiers and rejoin the main army at Harlem Heights. General Putnam marched his soldiers past the British to whom the Murrays were playing hosts and thus evaded capture which would have been inevitable had he remained separated from the main division.

Mrs. Murray's dauntless courage in delaying the British had succeeded in saving the day for the Continentals who, while the British were regaling themselves with good food and good cheer, marched past them to Harlem Heights rejoining the main army. Whether the region took the name of Murray Hill because of Mrs. Murray's brave deed or because all the property belonged to the Murrays, is open to discussion. Most historians, however, devote more attention to Mrs. Murray in connection with this incident than they do to other members of her family. At any rate, long after the Murrays disappeared, the name remained and the hill, too. The hill is still evident, streets and carlines having conformed to the general contour of the land. The Murray Hill section today is considered as the land lying between Fifth and Third Avenues from Thirty-fourth to Forty-second Streets. This includes Grand Central Terminal, which occupies one of Murray's cornfields, Tudor City, the New York Public Library as well as the Empire State Building and many fine stores.

This is the terrain which saw many important happenings in our early national life. Though desperate battles of the Revolution occurred here, generally the Murray Hill was calm and peaceful—a quietude disturbed only by the song of the thrush or the cry of some domestic animal. Ah! Days of yore and yesteryear, when life was so simple, uninhibited by modern devices which serve only to complicate; when New Yorkers could leisurely stroll around Murray Hill without having to contend with determined crowds eager to reach their destination. Life was assuredly simpler, and there were fewer problems to confront my progenital Manhattanites. Hawthorne wrote, "Time flies over us, but leaves its shadow behind."[2] In the case of Murray Hill the only shadow left is the hill itself, for all else has gone into the limbo of the past.

That includes Jacobus Kip who also owned property in the vicinity. The house he built for himself in 1655 predated the construction of "Inclenberg" by a number of years, and it remained standing for well neigh onto two hundred years.[3] Kip's farm was located near Second Avenue around Thirty-fourth or Thirty-fifth Streets while the house was at Thirty-fourth Street and the East River. The bay took the name of Kip's Bay. There is no bay today as it was filled in, but older Manhattanites still refer to the section as Kip's Bay. There are several industrial enterprises operating in the neighborhood, now, among them, the New York Steam Corporation. This Corporation, a subsidiary of the Consolidated Edison Company, pumps steam into down town buildings forcing it through underground pipes at a speed equivalent to two hundred miles an hour.

At the time the Murrays lived in "Inclenberg" and old Jacobus Kip had long been forgotten by the Colonials, the site now housing the New York Public Library was only an open field. The only historical association with it was that it had been the scene of the shameful rout of Washington's soldiers. Later, in 1822, the city acquired the land now known as Bryant Park for the use of a Potter's Field. It is a curious coincidence that many of New York's principal squares were once used as burial grounds for the city's destitute. In 1823 the Potter's Field of Washington Square moved uptown to Bryant Park and it was used as such for three years.

Twenty years later the reservoir was completed at a cost of $500,-000. The opening was a great day for New Yorkers who deigned to commemorate the event with a procession seven miles in length. Many commercial houses closed for the day and evening editions of the press were suspended in order that their employees could witness the celebration. The reservoir gave its name to the land known as Reservoir Square. Later, the name was changed to Bryant Square in honor of the great editor and poet who had contributed so much to Manhattan's cultural and political life. I can recall my grandfather often speaking about the resevoir which, when it was built in 1842 was on the outskirts of Manhattan. It was surrounded by a huge blue granite stone wall about seven feet in height. The water was not visible from the side walk adjoining the wall, but if one crossed Fifth Avenue, ripples of water could be seen gently tossed to and fro according to the passing breeze.

The reservoir was razed in 1897 to make way for the Public Library. This action caused deep concern among the older generation, grandfather not excepted. I am sure to him the reservoir represented an integral part of Manhattan. And when it passed he must have felt that as

151

the stones making up the bulwark were razed, an epoch in Manhattan's life went with them. But the old makes way for the new, and who among us can deny that the magnificent New York Public Library lent more charm and beauty to Fifth Avenue than the old reservoir? With its majestic lions looking down on Fifth Avenue and its hundreds of pigeons hovering around or fluttering from cornice to cornice, it completely harmonizes with the fabulous Fifth Avenue.

The Public Library which now occupies the Fifth Avenue end of the park where the old reservoir used to be, was completed in 1911. In it repose the combined treasures of the Tilden, Astor and Lenox collections. The rare book room contains, among 50,000 other treasures, the Lenox copy of the Guttenberg Bible. While all is serene and tranquil inside, one has but to walk down the stone steps to Fifth Avenue to be caught in the maelstrom of human activity distinguishing the spot. People walk to and fro as the ever moving traffic of Fifth Avenue scurries by, flowing like two rivers in opposite directions.

Uptown or downtown, starting from this point, the fashionable shopper will find the world's smartest stores displaying luxurious furs, costly perfumes, elegant clothes and expensive jewelry. There are also to be found Five and Ten Cent stores which in their design, appointments and fixtures, are the height of luxury.

The Kress Five and Ten Cent Store on Thirty-ninth Street and Fifth Avenue is one of these stores. There is a plaque on the corner of the building reminding the reader that on this ground stood the home of the Wendel family, one of the last midtown mansions to be demolished. This house, built in 1856 by John D. Wendel remained in the family until the death of the last surviving member, whence it was willed to the Drew Theological Seminary of Madison, N.J.

The Wendel family had many eccentric ideas. Their motto was never to sell property. They had extensive realty holdings in Manhattan but would never sell and were independent and wealthy enough not to care whether or not they rented. Another quaint notion they had was that a building any higher than three stories was dangerous for their employees to clean the windows. Ah! Could they but see the Empire State with its one hundred and two stories and sixty-five hundred windows, what would they say? Upon the death of the last member of the Wendels there grew up a great deal of court litigation for the distribution of the estate, claimants appearing sporadically up to the present time.

The Murray Hill Hotel is an old landmark in this district. Sixty years ago when it was built it was one of the most lavishly appointed hotels in the city. The rooms are spacious and they are furnished in Victorian style. When Cleveland had his inaugural dinner in Washington, the entire meal was planned and prepared in the Murray Hill and then shipped by special train to Washington.

The New York Daily Tribune for March 5, 1885, in describing the Inaugural Ball at the Pension Building states, "The supper was furnished by Messrs. Hunting and Hammond of the Murray Hill Hotel, Park Avenue, New York City." It goes on further, "Every feature of the supper, except the tea and coffee and colored waiters, was brought on from the Murray Hill Hotel in New York. A wooden kitchen was erected alongside of the building and communicated with the supper rooms through the window."[4]

Another account for the same day appearing in the New York Herald reports, "The Murray Hill Hotel chef, Mr. J. P. Campazzi, has had an army of white capped assistants busy for a fortnight in fashioning the ornaments for the more elaborate dishes. A small menagerie of stearine animals and bevies of tallow angels and babies await further manipulation after reaching here, these delecate structures being hardly able to stand the rough usage of travel."[5]

It must have been a grand and proud day for Murray Hill on this day when it was selected to play one of the steller roles in the functions centering around the Inauguration. The Murray Hill Hotel will soon be demolished and when it goes so, too, will disappear much of the "atmosphere" of Murray Hill.

My father, whose remarkable memory for facts and faces has always seemed extraordinary to me, and who has often made appear to my mind's eye the Manhattan of a bygone era, tells of another hotel which used to be located in the Murray Hill district. It was called the Park Avenue Hotel and its location was Thirty-third Street and Park Avenue. My father tells me that the Park was old in his time and that it was frequented by many famous people. When the Seventy-first Armory burned as the result of an explosion in the powder stores, the conflagration spread to the Park Avenue Hotel trapping many of the guests.

Mrs. John Foster, known to New Yorkers as the "Angel of the Tombs" was one of those who perished in the disaster. The Angel of the Tombs was a familar figure in the Criminal Courts Building and in the Tombs where she used to go to comfort prisoners. At the time of her death, February 22, 1902, Mrs. Foster was one of the best known social workers in the city. There was not a court room in New York into which this gentle lady could not enter. She was a friend and a confidant of criminals as well as judges, lawyers and court reporters, and the tragedy surrounding her passing was mourned equally by these different classes of New Yorkers.

Murray Hill was for many years strictly a residential section where the affluent residents dedicated themselves to good living confined within the limits of good taste. In past years both sides of the streets boasted those familiar residences of the Victorian era—three or four stories of brown stone with a flight of stone steps leading up to the vestibule. The avenues were distinguished by wealthy homes; the neighborhood was quiet and peaceful and had all the attributes which one desired in which to establish a refined home.

Many of New York's first families resided on the "Hill." Wendels, Robinsons, Rhinelanders, Tiffanys, Gerards, Pells, Kips, Belmonts, Morgans—all lived there at one time or another. Though these families have all contributed much to community life of Murray Hill, perhaps the most prominent benefactors of the locale were the Morgans, father and son.

J. P. Morgan Sr., the great financier, owned all the property on the east side of Madison Avenue between Thirty-sixty and Thirty-seventh Streets. He occupied a brown stone house on the northeast corner of Madison Avenue and Thirty-sixth Street. His son lived in the same style house on the southeast corner of Madison Avenue at Thirty-seventh Street. The Morgan property ran east almost to Park Avenue. At Thirty-nine East Thirty-sixth Street another Morgan residence was located. This belonged to Ann Morgan, sister of J. P. Morgan Jr. A great deal of the Morgan property was covered with spacious green lawns tended by the well known Morgan gardner, Jock. Jock, as can be deduced from his name, came from Scotland. There were those who still remember the figure of the Scotchman, pipe dangling from one corner of his mouth, as he cut the beautiful lawns surrounding the Morgan homes.

The elder Morgan attended the Church of the Incarnation which stands on his property at Thrity-fifth Street and Madison Avenue. He used to pass the collection plate there every Sunday morning when he was in town. J. P. Morgan, Sr. was a stocky man, a powerful figure in international finance and at one time director in many corporations. He lived in an era when great single fortunes were being amassed and the times were really gay. It is said that Morgan used to smoke cigars which cost into two or three figures for each cigar. This, it must be remembered was nearly fifty years ago and sufficient time has elapsed since to color even the simplest tale.

The Morgan Library enhances the Murray Hill of today. Located at Thirty-three East Thirty-sixth Street, it was erected in 1924 by the elder J. P., while the Annex was completed in 1929 by the son. The collection housed in these two buildings is a notable one. There are included Michelangelo's "Infant Hercules" and the Morgan ruby. Among the manuscripts there are the very rare Mainz Psalter of 1465 and the Ashburnham Gospels of the Ninth Century, together with several other volumes of great value.

Most of the families owning land or houses in Murray Hill are gradually releasing their holdings in favor of commercial advances, as the neighborhood is gradually going commercial. The section still boasts a few Victorian dwellings, reminiscent of the era of tasselled portierres and plush covered family albums. For the most part, though, Murray Hill has been turned over to large hotels and stores, many-storied office buildings, an air terminal and Grand Central Station. The domains of "Inclenberg" remain only in memory.

Manhattanites are more or less conditioned to the constant modifying of this Twenty-four Dollar Isle of ours. They are attuned to the fact that there must always be a certain percentage of the island under construction and the constant excavations which the buildings of a new subway entails. They take all this for granted and are not surprised to find that something which was here one day, had disappeared the next. Nothing surprises the blasé New Yorker. O. Henry's "Bagdad on the Subway" changes from day to day and New Yorkers are too busy to worry about it or to focus the lens of retrospection upon various spots within the city. They live only in the future.

This leads one to wonder whether it is not wrong to live too much in the future, just as it is wrong to live too much in the past. A happy medium is desireable and ideal. However, as the tendency of the New Yorker is to anticipate rather than to recollect, one may safely inquire whether as an antidote for the speed and high pressure of this modern age in this modern city, it is not a wise and healthy idea to refresh oneself with the glow emitting from events and places in our island's past.

Surely, by so doing one cannot be accused of wool gathering or aimless day dreaming! The study of history has always been an asset to mankind. Yet, when it comes down to actualities, Manhattan's past is a very little known entity in this vast realm.

Murray Hill is a good place to start. Not so rich in historical associations as lower Manhattan—nor quite so new as some of the uptown sections—it supplies an in-between subject into which the Manhattan historian may delve and find sufficient information to wet his appetite. He may start his investigation with Mrs. Murray and the story of how she saved the Continental Army and find himself peering into the intricacies of New York's transit system. That is the way historical research works; one event leads up to another and the relationship may be connected by a series of analogous happenings.

Yes, begin with Murray Hill. Here, you will find the key which will open new doors to romance—to adventure and to the glorious past of this fabulous island.

CHAPTER NOTES

1. Wilson, James Grant, "Memorial History of New York," Vol. II, p. 517.
2. Hawthorne, Nathaniel, "The Marble Faun."
3. Federal Writers' Project, "New York City Guide," p. 208.
4. "New York Tribune," for March 5, 1885, p. 5, c. 3.
5. "New York Herald," for March 5, 1885, p. 4, c. 5.

"THE OLDEST HOUSE, FOOT OF MURRAY HILL, Cor. 3rd Av. & 34th St."

CHAPTER FIFTEEN

Grand Central Terminal
A City in Motion

*"The progress of invention is really
a threat. Whenever I see a railroad
I look for a republic."*
Emerson, "Journals" 1866

MANHATTAN without its labyrinth of track, both on the surface and below the surface, would be like a person without arteries or veins. The transportation systems—of which it can boast many—carry the life blood of the Island from one end to the other, and far beyond to neighboring states. They are the commercial arteries which make it possible for the farmers of the middle west to exchange their produce for manufactured goods of the east. They are the link between a carload of iron ore from Pennsylvania and a shipment of automobiles from Detroit. If the history of the United States could be written in terms of its railroads, we should have a comprehensive record of the country from Andrew Jackson's time up to the present. We should cover the opening of the west, the Industrial Revolution, the Reconstruction Period as well as the rise and growth of political and economic thought—a truly wonderful phase in American history and one which runs parallel to the extension of rail facilities throughout the country. Development and control of strikes as well as the formation of large single sources of wealth appear to have some direct bearing upon the expansion of railroads. Legislation to restrain stock market manipulations is also directly attributable to growth of railroads in this country.

Railroads are the means which equilibrate labor and industry, supply and demand. They have replaced the covered wagon of yore in transporting new settlers to where they are needed, thence carrying the results of these peoples' labors to marketable regions. They play a stellar role in the evolution of the locale through which they pass, thus their importance cannot be overestimated.

But if the railroads are of such importance to a country, think what they do for a city! Think of the influence upon a city like New York! Think of the tremendous effect rail facilities exert upon the average New Yorker, even though he himself, in blissful content as is his wont, appears not to notice the boon rendered by the "iron horse!" Just as the railroad made its effect all over the Continent, so was its presence felt in New York City.

On land, in the air or on the sea, many routes lead in and out of Manhattan. Should any interruption occur in any one of these transportation systems, dire results would be felt throughout the city. Undoubtedly, the railways play a major part in keeping the Island open to communication and to them belong the responsibility of transporting not only the larger part of the millions who yearly pour into New York, but also the materials necessary to support the ten million or so people who live in the Greater New York area and to carry the results of their labors to other parts. Yes, railroads bear a heavy responsibility for upon them depend the progress and life of the city.

New York—ever mindful of its debt to these rolling wagons of steel—has not been amiss in furnishing its railroads with two terminals—Pennsylvania and Grand Central—both of which are worthy examples of railroad terminal construction and design and both of which exemplify the importance New York attaches to its railway systems. Into these Terminals hundreds of trains enter and leave each day. In and out they wend their way, this circulatory system carrying life with each revolution of the engine's wheels. They come from the sunny South, from the West, the land of opportunity. They come from Northern timberlands, from the great Atlantic Seaboard States, from Seattle and Miami, Boston and San Francisco—tired dust covered trains—chugging their way into home stations. Trains carrying passengers, food, livestock, manufactured goods—trains carrying mail—all huffing and puffing their way into Pennsylvania or Grand Central Terminals.

The former Murray cornfield has provided the site for one of these terminals, Grand Central, where the New York, New Haven and Hartford and the New York Central systems converge upon New York City disgorging their long-distance passengers and commuters. This is the nucleous of such activity as is seldom seen. Everything resolves itself

158

into motion, incessant motion; motion that is quiet and suggestive, like the swish of a piece of taffeta or the flapping of a bird's wings. Then there is the motion the result of which manifests itself by screeching and ringing in one's ears as terrific claps of thunder bursting upon the stillness of the night. Grand Central epitomizes motion in all its degrees for at no matter what hour one enters the station something is always in progress.

The present location of Grand Central is due to Commodore Cornelius Vanderbilt and his son under whose guidance the original Grand Central Depot was constructed in 1871. No discussion of Grand Central can be complete without bringing in salient points in the careers of the Commodore and his son, William, for the lives of these two men, especially that of the Commodore, are closely linked with the establishment of the New York Central Railroad and its Manhattan terminal, Grand Central Depot.

Enterprising and equipped with unusual foresight, the shrewd Commodore felt that Forty-second Street would someday be the hub of the city. United States was then in the throes of great industrial development. The terrible panic and the demonitization of silver, occuring in 1873, had not had an opportunity to curtail industrial enterprise nor to effect the financial activity which made rapid progress and in the year 1871 was surging to very high index figures. The Reconstruction Period had had ample start in repairing the chaos and utter destruction wrought by a nation divided against itself. Great strides had been made in agricultural as well as industrial pursuits and the South, whose resources and agricultural assets had been badly depleted by ravages of war, began to recover its former position in the agrarian and economic structure of the country.

It appears that the development of railroads in United States, that is, the addition of thousands of miles of track, advanced at a rapid pace during this year. 1869 saw the opening of rail transportation between the Atlantic and Pacific Oceans and from that time on rail facilities were extended throughout the United States. In 1860 the railway mileage was 30,000 and by 1890 it had reached 166,000.[1] By the turn of the Century the railway mileage had jumped an additional 74,000 miles.

It was little wonder, then, that Vanderbilt saw a means of huge profits in this expansion of the new mode of transportation. The astute Commodore had made his fortune through the operation of a fleet of steam boats, though as early as 1840 he had dabbled in railroad stock, maintaining at that time the position of stockholder and director in the Long Island, the New Jersey Central and the Stonington Railroads.[2] Though in later years Vanderbilt was to become one of America's greatest railroad magnates, in the earlier part of his life his real interest manifested itself in steamboating wherein he is said to have amassed the sum of twenty millions of dollars at the onset of the Civil War.[3] As soon as he had made up his mind to go into railroading Vanderbilt devoted all his energy and resources to his objective. He bought up small lines here and there until he had made himself a power to be reckoned with in that field. The Commodore, though, did not fare so well when he attempted to get control of Erie, then in the hands of Daniel Drew, Jay Gould and Jim Fiske, Jr. The Vanderbilts, father and son, ordered their brokers to buy up large blocks of Erie stock. The latter railroad kept issuing additional stock so that after buying up to an amount reputed to be $16,000,000 the Vanderbilts were no nearer controlling the rival company than they were at first.[4]

Erie stock was undoubtedly "watered," the manner in which this was accomplished later being revealed in the series of court actions accruing from the Commodore's attempt to corner the road. As a matter of fact, it was in connection with the psalm singing Drew's early business ventures that the term "watered" came into significance. In his youth, Drew had been a cattle-drover, buying and selling cattle in New York State. To him is credited the practice of depriving the cattle of water until just before they were to be weighed by prospective purchasers when the crafty Drew would allow the thirsty animals to satiate themselves with water. Thus Drew is responsible for the term "watered stock" and for inventing the process. It was an easy task for him to apply his youthful habits to his more mature enterprises. Uncle Daniel brought to Erie all his peculiar practices for making money.

According to a statute of New York then in force a railroad could issue stock in exchange for the stock of any other railroad which was under lease to it. Thus, in order to create large blocks of new stock, Erie had only to lease another road and issue stock in exchange for that of the newly acquired road. And as Drew, Gould and Fiske rolled off new stock from the printing press they had installed in the Erie offices, Vanderbilt issued orders to buy up all the gilt edged certificates upon which the printer's ink was still wet. The Commodore, who had been accustomed to coming out the victor in his business deals, was infuriated at the turn of events ensuing from his abortive attempt to gain control of Erie. The matter was taken to court and a series of court battles took place the outcome of which was the recommendation that a bill be enacted to prevent further manipulations of a similar nature.

The fight for Erie is regarded as one of the most notorious examples of attempting to make a "corner." Large interests were at stake, to be sure, for whoever plucked the Erie plum would be assured of one of the most lucrative enterprises in America. The battle waged continuously for a period of five years and at one time it was necessary for the Erie coterie, consisting of Daniel Drew, Jim Fisk and Jay Gould and even some lesser luminaries involved, to flee to Jersey City as the New York courts had issued warrants for their arrests on charges of contempt of court. Then there began a series of episodes in this strange affair which were so ludicrous as to nearly border the burlesque. Once arrived in Jersey City the pious Drew accompanied by the boisterous Fisk, with his diamonds glistening in the Jersey sunshine, and Jay Gould, who later earned the sobriquet "Mephistopheles of Wall Street," barricaded themselves in Taylor's Castle which later became known as "Fort Taylor." These men—the three controllers of Erie—were as different in character as they were in appearance. Before embarking on their spectacular dash across the river—in which they only managed to be a couple of steps ahead of the process servers—they had first looted the Erie offices on West Street of every tangible asset they could carry. The Erie group are said to have taken with them six million dollars in greenbacks and their pockets were stuffed with Erie stock and other securities as they made their wild dash across the Hudson and out of the jurisdiction of the New York courts. They settled themselves sumptiously in Fort Taylor which was guarded by a formidable array of bodyguards, detectives and Erie employees. There the three men set up court and to the amusement of the public established themselves in luxury and splendor while the outwitted old Commodore fumed and ranted on the other side of the Hudson. Though at least seven million dollars were involved, it was as melodramatic a situation as could only provoke smiles from disinterested outsiders who had nothing to lose through the large scale shannanigans indulged in by the empire builders of that day.

When the smoke of battle had cleared, Vanderbilt had lost a million and a half dollars,[5] the dissimilar Erie partners were still the lords and masters of that line and Mr. and Mrs. John Q. Public had had unique entertainment at the cost of the capitalistic interests then looming to the fore on the American horizon.

It must be remembered that at the time of the Erie incident great financiers of the day were not averse to resorting to sharp practices, following procedures which at times were flagrant violations of common decency, and such legislative measures as could have prevented the refined privateering engaged in at this period had not been taken. Therefore, it is not surprising that many of the men whom we credit as possessing unusual financial ability at some stages of their careers indulged in deals so shady as to be almost obscure. The so-called "empire builders" who launched upon their careers in the hectic ante bellum days very often were unscrupulous in their insatiable thirst for wealth and power. Some of their actions would have put to shame the reckless deeds of the privateers of yore, because while the bucaneers of yore plied their trade openly, a great many of the financial wizards did their plundering insidiously and the fact that they were dishonest very often was not even perceptible. They stole and plundered from each other and from outsiders and withal exhibited such magnificent aplomb and finesse as is seldom seen outside of the gaming room. Yet, oft times, like in the case of Drew, when the Sabbath rolled around there they were in their pews, praying and singing hymns in loud fearless voices. A curious paradox, to be sure. But cheating and plundering appears to have paid heavy dividends and formed many of the large fortunes founded in this ephoch when scruples were elastic enough as to permit off color deals.

In this connection, one of the most amusing examples of how one of these wizards of Wall Street was bested, is the story Edward R. Hewitt tells about his father's deal with Jay Gould. It seems that the firm of Cooper and Hewitt were under contract with Erie to re-roll their iron rails at a price of twenty-four dollars a ton but when Jay Gould became associated with Erie he proposed that Hewitt raise the price to thirty-five dollars and divide the difference between them. When Hewitt refused, Gould found some legal pretext to break the contract though it had five more years to run. Hewitt did not forget the incident, so some years later when he heard the Goulds wished to purchase a box at the Opera, Hewitt offered his box for $14,000. The opera at that time was given at the famous Academy of Music on Fourteenth Street and Irving Place. Gould, who was anxious to enjoy the prestige which a box at the opera would entail, completed that transaction and paid the sale price of $14,000. Three days later the papers heralded the fact that New York's opera would be given at the Metropolitan. Mr. Edward R. Hewitt, who tells the story, goes on to say that Gould never once sat in his $14,000 box at the Academy.[6]

At the time Vanderbilt decided on the erection of the Grand Central Depot, he had become President of the New York and Harlem Railroad as well as President of the New York Central which was combined with the Hudson River Railroad in 1873. Station facilities for these lines were very poor and the idea of a new depot met with immediate favorable reaction. There were two terminals into which these lines discharged their passengers. Both of these depots were small, inconvenient and incapable of adequately handling the increasing numbers of passengers which were carried by the various rail lines running into the city. One of these terminals was located at Madison Avenue and Twenty-sixth Street on the site which later became the old Madison Square Garden and today houses the Metropolitan Life Insurance Company. The Harlem and New Haven Railroads carried their passengers into this depot, which had its entrance on Madison Avenue.

An arrangement existed whereby the cars were pulled out of the station in Twenty-sixth Street by horse through Fourth Avenue where the locomotive was attached. A similar arrangement existed in connection with operation of the Hudson River Railroad. The passenger coaches were horse drawn through Hudson Street and Tenth Avenue to Thirty-second Street. Here, the locomotive was attached and the train proceeded on its way.

The new terminal, called Grand Central Depot, was to be a consolidation of both these stations. Grand Central Depot was opened in 1871 when the city was experiencing a wonderful period of growth. Telegraphic communication had made great strides while the use of steam as a source of energy had become widespread. Gas companies in Manhattan were supplying this fuel to thousands of homes and railroads kept pace with this rapid industrial expansion. The new Depot was designed by Isaac C. Buckout, superintendent and chief engineer of the New York and Harlem. The trainshed was six hundred feet long and two hundred feet wide while the building, a typical affair of the period, consisting of red brick and simulated marble, met with national acclaim. Many said it was second in architectural beauty only to the national capitol at Washington. The Vanderbilts under Buckout had achieved their purpose. They had succeeded in erecting a railroad terminal second to none in the United States and this opinion was shared by all who beheld New York's newest edifice. It appeared that nothing wasleft out of consideration in its construction. Fifty pounds per square foot allowance was calculated for expansion or contraction caused by natural elements. All possibilities were considered by the engineers who designed the Depot. It was no wonder that the building which some claimed was very like the Tuilleries, evoked national comment.

In 1898 three stories were added to the Depot and the red bricks were substituted by a stucco finish. These improvements, though, were insufficient to serve the augmented demands which the ever growing city was imposing upon the Depot and Terminal. By the turn of the Century the Depot which the discerning Commodore and his son had caused to be erected, was hopelessly outmoded and entirely unequal to the task of meeting the exigencies which a city no longer in knee breeches exacted. The consensus of opinion was that the red brick depot was fast becoming as obsolete as the Pony Express. The need for a more modern terminal was apparent.

Thus the "gingerbready" Grand Central Depot which in its earlier days was the pride and joy of Manhattan, was razed and in 1903 construction initiated on the present Grand Central Terminal. And for the second time the Murray cornfield became the site of a railroad station. Grand Central Terminal was not completed until 1913. Representing an engineering marvel largely due to Mr. William J. Wilgus, the innovation of building the trainshed on two levels was instituted. The Terminal is a city within itself. Underneath its surface, extending in all directions like the tentacles of an octopus, are thirty-four miles of yard track while within the Terminal itself are fifty-four stores, a hospital, a police force, a motion picture theatre and an art gallery. As a matter of fact, it is quite possible for a person to enter the Terminal and find all the necessities required for a normal life without ever having to ascend to the street. There are entrances to some of the large office buildings, a hotel, barber and beauty shops, restaurants, wearing apparel stores, drugstores, in truth, the Terminal is actually a miniature city.

The plans for the Concourse were drawn by Warren and Wetmore, Reed and Stem whose combined ideas have resulted in one of the most beautiful stations in the world. This is true both of the exterior as well as the interior. The Concourse is one of the most striking rooms in all New York. It is dignified and austere, yet there is a certain warmth to it. It is the locale of excitement, pathos and happiness—running through all the gamut of human emotions. One may glimpse a tear lined face, a farewell full of the uncertainty of parting or an expectant look, then a fond embrace to culminate a joyous reunion. In the Concourse we find both extremes together with all the intermediate stages of greetings and farewells. Varied emotions register upon the countenances of the crowds who shuffle about the Terminal, hither and yon. Fond hopes of great success as well as unmistakable signs of dimmed aspirations find their way to the faces one sees. Life with all its joys and follies, heartaches and sadness looks out upon you. The Terminal is romantic, stimulating, animated by the thousands of people who pass through it. It is colorful with its famous personages one encounters daily boarding or alighting from any one of the five hundred trains which enter and leave the yards each day. Yes, it is exciting, and strange to relate, one is always conscious of this quality. The excitement and motion may diminish, but not disappear, because these active qualities are produced by people. And when have you seen a railroad station—least of all Grand Central—entirely free of travellers? One might add, if these prospective travellers are New Yorkers, what more natural than to expect them to be in a mad rush, even if the reason for such speed may only be their desire to buy a newspaper from one of the twenty-two stands in Grand Central? Can you conceive of a New Yorker who is not in a hurry? It is a natural attribute of the average Knickerbocker. People expect it from him and what better place to run than Grand Central with its long ramps? Yes, here at Grand Central Terminal Mr. and Mrs. New Yorker can give full play to their running prowess and amid such attractive surroundings as few other railroad stations may boast.

Yet, through all the commotion, one is always conscious of the presence of the great Commodore whose foresight saw Grand Central years before the ordinary citizen was aware of its possibilities. The history of Grand Central may almost be said to represent the history of railroads in America—a saga of the men whose manipulations brought railroading into one of the foremost enterprises in this country.

CHAPTER NOTES

1. Beard, Charles A. and Mary B., "Basic History of the United States," p. 293.
2. Lane, Wheaton J., "Commodore Vanderbilt," p. 185.
3. Ibid., p. 84.
4. Knickerbocker, Jacob, "Then and Now," p. 184, 185.
5. Josephson, Matthew, "The Robber Barons," p. 134.
6. Hewitt, Edward R., "Those Were the Days," p. 83, 84.

GRAND CENTRAL DEPOT, ca. 1870

CHAPTER SIXTEEN

"The Great White Way"

"The signs in the streets and the signs in the skies
Shall make a new Zodiac, guiding the wise,
And Broadway make one with that marvelous stair
That is climbed by the rainbow-clad spirits of prayer."

Vachel Lindsay "A Rhyme about an Electric
Advertising Sign."

NEW York is an industrious city, a city where life is difficult and tense, a city which admits of no drones. When the Manhattanite works, he works. It is not unusual, then, that he who does everything to the extreme, also takes his recreation to the hilt of his endurance. And when he feels like "tripping the light fantastic," or to use a typical expression "having a good time," there is no other place in all Manhattan like "The Great White Way." Even in times of tribulation and concern, the troubled Manhattanite may betake himself to Times Square and there find in the divers amusements which the area affords, a temporary surcease from the worries of this tired old world.

Here is the panacea for all the ills of the bored Manhattanite. When he is tired of the daily grind, when he feels that a change from the usual routine is necessary, then he seeks out "The Great White Way" area. This, with its diversity of amusements, welcomes him: it permits him to escape for a few hours from the ticker tape of Wall Street, the schoolroom, the factory or the office. It drones out the sound of his daily occupation, it relaxes him so that on the morrow he is more altruistically equipped to confront his worries and problems. The bright and glaring lights, the pushing, milling crowds, in many instances sooth and cheer him, rather than irritate him as one might expect. The average person is not the only one who finds a gratifying relief from his usual routine in the tinsel and glitter of Broadway. Here come, too, the abnormals—masochists, hypochondriacs, neuresthenics, seeking temporary alleviation from their troubles.

It is difficult to conceive of this section of Manhattan as differing much from its present appearance. "The Great White Way" is such an integral part of the city, and has been taken so much for granted, that the idea of it as not existing seems fantastic. One would as lief have New York City without Manhattan, as Manhattan without "The Great White Way." Yet, there are people still living, and they are not very old either, who recall a very different Times Square than the one we know today. It was not always theatres, huge electric signs, snarling traffic and crowds. Many present day New Yorkers who would wince were they to be referred to as "old" can recollect when horse drawn cars ran along Broadway from Bowling Green to Fifty-seventh Street. The horse drawn street car ran on tracks which were set along the same route previously serviced by stages, and old Dobbin remained to supply the power. Electric traction was not introduced until the spring of 1901.[1]

The Times Building made its appearance around the same time and was the highest structure in the city. Photographs taken shortly after it had been erected show it towering high above all the other buildings in the vicinity, like a giant oak in a field of grass. This was the second building known by that name, as the original Times Building was down in "Newspaper Row." Work on the underground was commenced around the same time, its construction necessitating the tearing up of surrounding streets, a condition from which the city has been spared only at intervals ever since. The I.R.T. line to One Hundred and Forty-fifth Street was opened in 1904 which date marks the time when the Times Square area was serviced by rapid transit facilities. Yes, in those days "The Great White Way" was different. It was a youngster with big ideas—gay, youthful, vivacious, as it enticed the "Rialto" from the Union Square area which it used to occupy.

In passing through this stage it was inclined to be boisterous, not perhaps to such an extent as The Bowery—where things were said and done in a bombastic manner, too, but it leaned more to the showy, spectacular side. Reformers, though they still found a fertile field in The Bowery, fell upon the section like thunder out of a hot summer's sky. They came with epithets, with psalms, with dire warning of a calamitous end. Most turgent of them all was Carry Nation who not only denounced the powers of evil but many times resorted to the use of her hatchet which was usually accessible and which she let fall upon many a saloon of her day. The time she visited John L. Sullivan's saloon at One Hundred Seven West Forty-second Street was typical of the way Carry swung into action. Carry was infuriated when told that

John L. Sullivan had flamboyantly boasted to reporters, ". . . if that old woman ever comes to New York and tries to poke her nose into my business, I'll push her down the sewer."[2] It so happened that on August 28, 1901, which was a week or so after the big John L. had thus boasted, Carry did come to New York. As was to be expected, she headed for Sullivan's saloon, brandished her hatchet and pursued the saloon's owner to the cellar where he had barricaded himself. There was no damage done, except to subject the mighty John L. to public ridicule. The city never did recover from his encounter with the buxom Carry.

It appears that the politicians of the time fared little better with the hatchet wielder. When Carry called upon Police Commissioner Murphy to inquire if he didn't think "a little agitation or hatchetation would do any harm" Col. Murphy had a police officer show her out, emphasizing his unwelcome gesture with "Don't come back again." Carry Nation was not easily discouraged for she continued to defy the public officials in her quest to have the "hell holes"—the name by which this spectacular personality from the Kansas plains described saloons—close their doors. Though saloons of the time jocularly exhibited signs over their bars "All Nations Welcome Except Carry," the lady of the hatchet liked to quote the following doggerel about herself:

"Sing a song of six joints,
With bottles full of rye.
Four-and-twenty beer kegs
Stacked up on the sly.
When the kegs were opened
The beer began to sing:
'Hurrah for Carry Nation.
Her work beats anything.' "[3]

Carry's concern in connection with the quantity of "hell brew" and tobacco consumed by sinful New Yorkers did not receive the approbation she would have desired and after many vain attempts to show them the error of their ways, she gave up her mission as far as New Yorkers were concerned, a resolution which evoked no regrets on the part of Manhattanites, and concentrated her efforts and talents on other parts.

After Carry there were others for as the Broadway sector attracts those who would abandon themselves to the wreckless gaiety the area affords, it likewise follows that reformers would find a prolific field in which to practice their calling. Yet, the "Great White Way" manages to go on a glittering and a twinkling as its millions of Mazdas outline merry dancing figures and colorful advertisements.

168

One of the most interesting sights in Times Square is its celebration of New Year's Eve. Reservations in clubs and hotels are usually made well in advance. When the old year's last day is at hand store owners in the vicinity construct wooden reinforcements as a protection for their plate glass windows. The day wanes and as night approaches the gay crowds walk back and forth along Broadway. They are prepared to welcome the birth of the New Year with assorted noise makers, confetti and horns, in addition to boisterous spirits which even the dreary weather of many a December 31st fails to dampen. As midnight approaches, there is a general tendency on the part of the celebrants to congregate in Times Square. It seems as if all Manhattan is grouped in this area. The police are everywhere. Crowds start to gather as early as three hours before midnight and their number is swelled around eleven o'clock when audiences come pouring out of the theatres. An extra large police detail is required to preserve any semblance of order and to keep traffic moving. This last New Year's Eve more than 1,600 policemen were deployed in the sector and out of this number 320 were traffic men while 100 mounted men rode back and forth amidst the exhuberant spirits which gravitated as though drawn by some magnetic power to the "Great White Way."[4]

Thousands of revelers crowd themselves around the Times Building, in front of the Hotel Astor, and in the side streets, optimistically attempting to move simultaneously in various directions. Of course, it cannot be done. Fortunately, no one cares whether his ultimate destination is reached or not. One may try to cross Forty-second Street at Broadway only to desist and eventually find that he is carried along by the surging crowds and deposited blocks away from his goal. This is one time when independence of motion is impossible.

It makes no difference to the pedestrian as eagerly he awaits the whistles and honking of klaxons which herald the arrival of midnight. He is gay, he is eager and good-natured. Tonight you may push him and he will return to wish you a "Happy New Year." No scowls, no hurrying, no visible sadness. Just an atmosphere of "Hail-fellow-well-met" which later in the evening may reach the proportions of boisterousness. Thousands of people jam "The Great White Way" until at last the moment arrives: the climax is here: the moment which brought them all to "The Great White Way" as though this were one time which called for the presence of an immense crowd. It is here! The old year dies with its disappointments and heartaches while the youngster is hopefully welcomed to bring what it may. Bells ring, radio loud speakers resound with the tune of "Auld Lang Syne"—greetings for a "Happy New Year" are exchanged—it is all over. The crowds disperse, some going to their homes, other to finish the night in one of the clubs or restaurants along the way. New Year's Eve is over for the merrymaker. The next day Broadway is its old self again. On January 2nd the barricades around the shops are removed, the city's "white wings" go into action. Confetti, serpentine, noise makers, paper hats, horns that have been flattened by the thousands of feet which pass over them—all find their way into the Department of Sanitation trucks waiting to dispose of the rubbish thus accumulated. Broadway resumes its old character once more. The exhilaration of New Year's Eve is gone but there is still much animation. "The Great White Way" is ready to get back into its old routine and take up its normal life again.

And of what does its normal life consist? Many novelists and writers whose interests have been aroused by the locale have attempted to picture Broadway, to depict its people; its habits. Most of them can readily succeed for Broadway is composed of all the human factors and attributes encountered in large communities. Any description may be adapted to fit Broadway. It consists of good and bad people, gladness and sadness, poverty and wealth and all the other elements and human idiosyncrasies which go into the composition of large cities. The writer may take his choice.

The chief interest of the amusement center lies in the different types of people one encounters there. In contrast to other parts of Manhattan where the onlooker may be awed by great canyons of man-made skyscrapers, the dazzling beauty of a sunset on the Hudson, or Central Park in all its winter splendor, here one is struck by the diverse kinds of people the thoroughfare presents. If there is one place on Manhattan Island where the playwright and novelist may find a rich field of material for character depiction, he need search no further. This is it! All sorts of personalities may be recognized in the passing crowds. Look closely and you will see the famous film star rubbing elbows with the shop girl whose idol she is, or the broken-down vaudeville performer whose main ambition is to achieve a come-back. If you are adept and up on your social register you will also recognize the scion of one of New York's First Families whose arm is graced by his latest fancy, a hostess in a nearby taxi dance hall. Literary lights are wont to frequent the streets, as well as politicians and diplomats who seek out this region for a brief respite from the pressing affairs provoked by current events. Mingling throughout the passing crowds are the big and small time racketeers. Broadway is their favorite haunt. Here they come to trim the sucker and sometimes each other, and to spend some of their easy earned money. Last but not least, in this passing parade of Broadwayites come the thousands of plain John and Jane Does, who also make up an important part of this heterogeneous group which one encounters in the old Longacre Square vicinity.

Watch the facial expressions on the people you meet. Look at that lonely soldier. Perhaps he is in town on a week-end pass, a stranger in New York. But he will not be lonesome very long. Just let him get his bearings. There is a well known playboy. His every move is copy for the columnists. Who is the lady with him? There is another story about that, a long story, but let us designate its telling to the hands of more able chroniclers of "The Big Stem."

With such a conglomeration of rich literary material from which to choose, it is no wonder that Broadway appears in the title and subject matter of numerous plays, stories and songs. The late George M. Cohan found Broadway a fertile source of material for his songs and plays. O. Henry also used the locale for settings in many of his stories. The neighborhood abounds with interesting situations and characters awaiting only the delicate brush of the word artist.

It goes further, it provides these characters with a variety of backdrops and locale. Crammed into an approximate area one mile in length and about a half-mile in breadth, this section, as "The Broadway Association" defines the theatrical district, "is that rectangular portion of Manhattan extending from 38th Street along Broadway North to 59th Street and from Sixth Avenue West to Eighth Avenue." The assortment and number of recreational facilities offered within its confines are worthy of note. There are eighty night clubs and two hundred restaurants located in the Broadway area. It also houses a total of ninety-three theatres, fifty of which are classified as legitimate theatres while the other forty-three are cinema houses and six radio broadcasting studios with two radio theatres within this district.[5] This centralization of amusements has made "The Great White Way" one of the best known entertainment focal points in the world.

Every visitor to America wants to see Broadway just as every performer wants to be seen playing before a Broadway audience. Millions of people from all over the world have cherished the ambition to visit Broadway, to see Radio City and Rockefeller Center, the venerable Metropolitan Opera House and all the other places associated with the bright light district. Millions have achieved their desire, returning to their homelands carrying with them memories of happy days, for Broadway does not disappoint.

It has been called a bad influence—its bright lights drawing strong people to it like a flame attracts the helpless moth; then when it has sapped its life, tossing away what remains as it seeks a fresh victim. But I do not think that is true. There is as much kindness, as much good-heartedness and sympathy here as there is in any other part of New York. And for all its air of hardness and sophistication, I will warrant that there exists more sentimentality along "The Main Stem" than in many a country village. Broadwayites are not as blasé and unsympathetic as some would have us believe. They may look hard, but once one pierces the outer shell in which Broadway habitués enshroud themselves, one finds that they are not as hard as they are reputed to be. Fundamentally, they are softies and if the denizens of the Bowery only knew this fact they would walk a little further uptown to do their panhandling.

I guess I am partial to this part of New York town for this is where I was born. As a wanderer always reserves a niche in his heart for the place of his birth, so I have for New York City and particularly for Times Square. And so if it appears that I condone its faults and emphasize its virtues my partiality should be pardoned. I grew up with Times Square, entering the scene just as the star was launching out upon the role which was to be cast as "The Great White Way." (Because of its many twinkling lights, this name had been coined by O. J. Gude, the advertising man.) Shortly before I was born the Café de l'Opera opened. It is said to have cost over a million dollars. It lasted four months.* Thus was exhibited at an early date the fickleness of New Yorkers. They build one day only to demolish the next. They are forever on the move, the epitome of all that is progressive and modern, though there are times when such movement is detrimental.

The Metropolitan Opera House and the Empire Theatre had already established the enviable reputation which they enjoy today. The Metropolitan, from whose stage have resounded the voices of Caruso, Calvé, Tetrazzini, Sembrich, Melba, Chaliapin, etc. had its premier in 1883 when "Faust" was presented to a discriminating audience composed of the cream of New York's society. A decade later the Metropolitan was swept by flames necessitating its rebuilding. At the opening, due to the jewelled display of the parterre boxes, the tier was called "Diamond Horseshoe," a name which has been associated with it the past fifty years.

The Metropolitan is not a beautiful structure. On the contrary, in a city as modern as New York, it presents a very drab appearance, not at all as one would expect the opera of New York to be. It is ante-dated, ugly and its interior so poorly designed that only half the stage is visible from certain parts of the house. Nevertheless, one can hardly conceive of Manhattan without the tradition of the old Metropolitan. Year after year, music lovers from all over the world have assembled at the Metropolitan to listen rapturously to the glorious voices with which the old walls resound. The Metropolitan is one of New York's traditions. One wishes, though one is quite certain that it cannot be, that the old Met might be spared a few more years. No matter what New York builds—and the time is drawing closer each year when a new opera must be constructed—it will be many years before another building can be mellowed with the tradition hovering around the Met.

Ten years after the Opera opened, the Empire Theatre began its successful reign with the play "The Girl I Left Behind Me," produced by David Belasco. To name the famous stars who have graced the stage of the Empire would be to call out a roster of well known personalities of stage and screen. Maude Adams played there, as did Mrs. Fiske, Margaret Anglin, John Drew, William Faversham and many others. Among present day stars who have played at the Empire during their careers are Katherine Cornell, Billie Burke, the late Jeanne Eagles, Mary Boland, Helen Hayes and others. Recently, the Empire Theatre celebrated its Fiftieth Anniversary. The festive occasion was enhanced by the presence of several luminaries of stage and screen who came to do honor to the home of their former triumphs. Telegrams were read, speeches delivered and the good old Empire found itself cast in the limelight for that one brief evening. Through it all, however, I wonder what Mr. Frohman or John Ryland, two figures very closely associated with the Empire, would have said about the celebration. Certainly, their spirits must have been somewhere off in the wings proudly observing the proceedings.

Charles Frohman was the producer who guided the Empire through the first twenty-seven years of its career. John Ryland started as a bootblack in a barber shop located in the Empire Theatre Building. Later, he became personal valet to Frohman who lived in the building. In his spare time John acted as a handy man in the theatre. Soon Ryland became a permanent fixture in Frohman's household and his sincerity earned for him the friendly regard of many influential and prominent white people.

When Frohman died his will recommended that John be taken care of and so John Ryland became superintendent of the Empire. I can see him still, a husky man, standing in front of the Empire talking to celebrities, his lighted cigar posed between his fingers and the diamond horseshoe pin Frohman bequeathed him sparkling in the Broadway sunshine. He would stop me everytime I passed the theatre and inquire as to the health of the family. Sometimes he gave me passes to see the show. Once, when he saw my brother walking along Broadway, hatless, like most boys do, John rebuked him with "Don't you know, boy, that no gentleman ever goes without a hat!" Before I was born he would stop my father and have a chat with him. In fact, it seems as if John and the Empire belonged together for he was as much a fixture of the Empire as the marquee displaying the current attraction. One expected to see him there and if he were not around one had the feeling that something was missing. On opening nights John could be found at the entrance of the

173

theatre, a picture of sartorial elegance as he welcomed noted personalities.

To many people, the names "Great White Way" and "Broadway" are synonomous and are used interchangeably. Broadway in itself, is one of the longest streets in the world, "being surpassed in length by two of ancient Roman construction: the Appian Way from Rome to Brundusium, 350 miles, and Watling Street in England, from Dover via London to Chester and York, thence in two branches to Carlisle and the Wall near Newcastle.[7]

It started out as a cow-path, gradually grew wider and longer until it traversed the whole of Manhattan Island. Then it grew bolder and gathered confidence with its own progress increasing its momentum until it had nearly reached Albany. Though we have always known it as Broadway, this venerable thoroughfare has been called by anyone of fourteen different names. They are: Heere Waage, Wagh Briedweg, Great Public Road, Public Highway, Great Highway, Common Highway, Broad Wagon Way. After it crossed the Common it was known as Great George Street, Middle Road, Boston Road, Bloomingdale Road, Manhattanville Road and Kingsbridge Road.[8]

"The Great White Way" actually consists of only a small part of Broadway—a mile or so—yet, it is inconceivable for anyone to visit New York and fail to traverse this small distance. All steps gravitate towards this incandescent highway with its myriads of twinkling lights constantly splashing the Broadway night with great daubs of color. Everyone gazes upon these wonderful signs carries away the gay impression they create. And when war time exigencies imposed that they be dimmed out, no other section of New York was so altered in mien as Times Square in its dim-out attire. It was a sad spectable.

Now all that is over and "The Great White Way" rejoices in its restoration. It goes on as before, singing and dancing, telling its "corny" jokes, popularizing its flashy clothes, feuding, cheating, and loving; beckoning all to come and see its lavish displays of lights advertising everything from "soup to nuts." It tries painfully hard to capture and hold one's interest. Every day some new type of amusement appears upon the scene; something novel is devised to entertain.

A few years back a flea circus was located some doors away from the taxi dance hall on West Forty-second Street. And, curious as it may seem, there were many who paid admission to see these fleas. These supposedly erudite insects drew their audiences from the Broadway crowd, people reputed to be sophisticated and too smart to be fooled, yet actually as gullible as poor Mortimer Snerd. Many such places spring up in this locality. Sometimes, it is an Ajax, leopard skin thrown across his torso, bally-hooing the elixir which will produce an

174

equivalent specimen of physical culture. Once, an outfit engaged in selling a patented hair grower engaged many hundreds of square feet of Broadway store space. There are shooting galleries, amusement centers, nickleodeons and other novelties which impart a circus atmosphere to a locality which was always associated with all that is fine in the theatre.

One of the most curious things "The Great White Way" offers are its taxi dance halls. To one who has never seen how they operate, the notion of buying a ticket to dance with a paid hostess is unusual, but on Broadway this is the source of considerable revenue. There are at least four taxi dance in this sector and they have been operating in the same respective locations for a long time. They have an ambulent clientele culled from all strata of society. One of these dance emporiums has a sign above its door reading "Through these doors pass the most beautiful girls in the world"—a very far fetched statement, if not actually misleading. Impressed by this assertion the potential customer may look at the photographs flanking both sides of the entrance unaware that most of the beauties pictured therein are no longer employed there. Hopefully, he may even enter in a vain attempt to spend a moderately priced evening.

If he enjoys dancing and has plenty of money, or if he enjoys talking to the girls and has plenty of money, he will have a good time. But if he thinks that the entrance fee entitles him to an evening's entertainment, nothing could be further from reality. Once upstairs, he is sold some tickets for which he pays ten cents apiece. Perhaps the customer, in a typical "out-for-a-good-time" mood still thinks that a dollar's worth of dance tickets will last all evening. Still, nothing could be further from the truth. Each dance is scheduled to last approximately one or two minutes, thus a dollar will only provide ten minutes of actual dancing, or twenty minutes at the most. Quite an expensive form of recreation!

The dance hostesses usually work on a percentage basis, that is, they receive perhaps fifty percent of the total value of the tickets they collect. Their average salaries run from fifteen dollars a week to as high as fifty dollars. When a prospect enters, they stand in line all eager to "trip the light fantastic" with whatever Fate sends them. Although there is a law preventing girls from approaching men, there is no restriction against their attracting attention by the various means peculiar to them, and which they have had to cultivate because of keen competition amongst themselves. Expressions such as "Hi, Toots, wanta dance?" or "Hello, Mister" serve their own purpose. The timid male who is not accustomed to such familiar salutations oftentimes is embarrassed clear off the premises. For the most part, however, the men are mildly amused and remain to dance.

Here, one sees not only a cross section of Broadway, but also the several types of men one finds in a cosmopolitan city. One would suspect that a taxi dance hall would be the refuge of the lower classes of men; mentally and morally. A visit to any typical place would soon dispel that false conception. Among the dancers any unskilled observer may easily detect brokers, professional men, merchants or even a henpecked husband out on a rampage, as well as the adventurers, racketeers and a harmless specie known in the vernacular as a "Broadway hangeron." All are drawn here by an urge as old as civilization itself.

To the man of average intellect, this environment affords a continuous source of interesting material. To a person interested in people, here is a veritable encyclopaedia of knowledge. More than in any other station in life, more than in any other situation in life, here each person really has a story behind her or him; a story in many instances which is worth hearing and often times worth recording. They are not people whose lives move by in slow, drifting currents: they live in continuous maelstorms of uncertainty, very often crowding years into a few brief days or hours and the quickness of the pace is easily discernible in the taughtness of their facial muscles, now and again relaxed into a forced smile or a half-hearted laugh, for after all this is the place where one is supposed to be gay and enjoy the passing moments.

"The Great White Way" of the past few years has taken on a tinsled "honky-tonk" appearance. The glamor and certain degree of refinement of twenty-five years ago are lacking. Although sporadic attempts to deviate from Broadway's main attraction, the theatre, have usually met with eventual failure, they succeed for a time. Then one day they disappear, like the flea circus, the leopard-clad Ajax and all the others. These nomadic forms of entertainment never linger long on "The Great White Way," but the theatres and supper clubs remain, as of old, the staple types of amusement. True, the old time ten acts of vaudeville is a thing of the past, talking movies having sounded vaudeville's death knell. Lavish dinners of champagne and lobster at Rectors and Delmonicos have no substitute. Rectors Café Metropole, hour-glass figures, the Floradora Sextette, have all lapsed into a memorable past, an era which means nothing to some, but to others awakens a host of nostalgic memories.

There was Mae Murray dancing her famous "Merry Widow Waltz" in Reisenweber's, the era of the Ziegfield Girl and the Stage Door Johnnie, Marie Dresser singing "My Gal Sal" in George Considine's Café, the coming of the motion picture, which, in the opinion of those who first saw them, my father included, "were doomed to failure because they flickered so," Bert Williams' plaintive rendition of an early blues

song, "I Ain't Got Noboby" and the Wintergarden extravaganzas. . . .
All water under the bridge!

Today the younger generation is busy culling what will be their future recollections. They have had the opportunity to witness one of the greatest achievements ever undertaken on this island, the erection of Rockefeller Center, an enterprise which was severely criticized when the project was first undertaken. It was called "wasteful and useless" and "inartistic." Yet, it rose to house twelve acres of skyscraper offices, the world's largest indoor theatre and underground concourses which connect the buildings rising thus with a sudden brutality from all the land of the Center. The twelve buildings comprising Rockfeller Center are gigantic in stature, yet lean in width; it almost seems like the earth buckled and thrust these towering hulks into the sky. The younger generation witnessed this miniature city go up before their very eyes, an undertaking of such magnitude that it would have been undreamed of as little as forty years ago. Even in 1929 the venture was considered as foolhardy.

It is useless to try to inhibit the hands of time. Just so is it of no avail to expect growth without progress or change. This is the situation confronting "The Great White Way." If it is to progress and go along with the time, certain concessions or departures from customary habits are called for. New theatres are erected, new restaurants make their debut while others give up the struggle and close their doors. New faces appear, regular habitués disappear, new versions of old jokes make the rounds, rackets become streamlined to adapt themselves to modern conditions. There is a continuous process of evolution taking place which may be imperceptible to the Manhattanite, but which is decidedly apparent to the infrequent visitor.

Irregardless of the style of amusement offered, the underlying factor which brings everyone to "dear old Broadway" remains the same. They all come to be amused. Broadway supplies this important need of a hard working people, for a people, at all times require relaxation and amusement. During the war, the War Department in its recognition of this fact recruited Broadway stars, and arranged tours for them to appear before large audiences of men and women of the armed forces. The idea was to raise the morale of those in the services. Whether at war or at peace, that is "The Great White Way's" function, to elevate the spirits. It is as much a necessity to the city as the sunlight which replaces the millions of Mazdas when night is done. A toast to "The Great White Way!"

CHAPTER NOTES

1. Jenkins, Samuel, "The Greatest Street in the World," p. 234.
2. Asbury, Herbert, "All Around the Town," p. 124.
3. "The New York Sun" for August 29, 1901, p. 3 c. 4 & 5.
4. "The New York Times" for January 1, 1947, p. 1 c. 2.
5. Letter from "The Broadway Association" to the author, dated July 17, 1942.
6. Jenkins, Samuel, "The Greatest Street in the World" p. 258.
7. Ibid., Introduction.
8. Callender, James H., "Yesterdays in Little Old New York" p. 166, 167.

Times Square

CHAPTER SEVENTEEN

Hell's Kitchen

Hell's Kitchen is no longer hot
Since we've electric stoves;
And you will not in that fair spot
Find racketeers who hatch a plot,
Or gunmen out in droves.

"Hell's Kitchen" from "Nursery Rhymes of
New York City" by Louis How.

WHEN one dissects Manhattan, viewing its component parts so
that each may be analyzed separately, one finds in some instances that there is a marked semblance between different sections.
Chelsea and Gramercy show a distinct similarity as to their origin and
composition. The same is true of the Gas House District and Hell's
Kitchen. Whereas, in their heyday Chelsea and Gramercy were the
epitome of respectable gentility, the same cannot be claimed for Hell's
Kitchen and the Gas House District. These two places were as lurid and
obnoxious as their names imply. Yet, were one asked to decide which
was the most notorious, it would be difficult to decide between them.
Both were the haunts of hoodlums, thieves and murderers. They were
generally acknowledged as places of ill repute, yet, withal, they differed
from other neighborhoods enjoying a similar reputation in that they
lacked both the merry abandon of an early Bowery as well as the crude
gaiety of a Tenderloin of the vintage 1870 or 1880.

It is a curious fact that a place can be catalogued into various classes
of infamy, that is, it can be disreputable and still present a cheerful attractive appearance. The same idea is true of people, for very often one
meets somebody whose very manner is so charming that one is instantly
captivated, yet closer inspection reveals him to be a scoundrel. The

179

Bowery and Tenderloin were like that, but not the Gas House District and Hell's Kitchen. These two did not misrepresent. One saw, one became aware and one knew them for what they were—the refuge of undesirables and the abode of crime and criminals. Happy to relate, both regions have been merged into Manhattan's mad history, for today slight vestiges remain of their inglorious past.

Hell's Kitchen came of its unsavory reputation in the turbulent days culminating in and following the Civil War. In those days the area from Ninth to Twelfth Avenues was beset by organized gangs of hoodlums. The Hell's Kitchen gang came into existence around 1868 with Dutch Heinrichs as its leader and their domain covered from Thirtieth to Fifty-ninth Streets between Ninth and Twelfth Avenues. As in the case of the Gas House District, Hell's Kitchen also derived its name from the gang which ruled it. The neighborhood included yards of the Hudson River Railroad which later merged with the New York Central under the direction of Commodore Cornelius Vanderbilt. The Hell's Kitchen gang drew its spoils from systematic raids on the Thirtieth Street yard of the railroad and even after it had merged with the Tenth Avenue gang, the railroad continued to be a lucrative source of revenue for the gangs preying in the vicinity.

They were a bad lot—these early counterparts of later day gangsters—committing every crime on the books. Though they were well organized, many times they fought among themselves and the neighborhood was often the scene of violence and bloodshed. And when they were not fighting each other, they fought other gangs and the winner would automatically take over the hegemony of its vanquished rival. It was thus that the Gophers came into control of Hell's Kitchen and continued terrorizing the neighborhood until 1910 when the New York Central Railroad organized its own police force.

The Kitchen was then composed of streets upon both sides of which were the red brick and brown stone tenements—an ever familiar sight in poorer districts of Manhattan and one which, thanks to unremitting efforts of social workers and public spirited citizens, is gradually disappearing from Manhattan's horizon. Looking back at the tenement, one wonders, indeed, how they were permitted to exist so long and why they continue to do so in certain sections of Manhattan. At any rate in 1910 Hell's Kitchen consisted of block after block of these tenements, three to five stories in height, called "cold water flats." Unheated in winter, dark and dreary in summer, lacking very often even basic plumbing facilities, usually these barrows were filled to capacity with the poorer classes of the city. Bred in such places, one is led to speculate as to why there were not more gangsters than there actually were. Certain it is that there was much sickness as an outgrowth of the prevailing poor living conditions—an expected state since unsanitary living, going as it does hand in hand with poverty, can only breed illness and crime.

January 1, 1862 the city opened the Eighteenth Precinct which controlled such disorders as should arise in this unwholesome neighborhood. As the years went on, this building was located at 345 West 47 Street, became one of the most noted of the Kitchen. Its rosters were not confined to those feuding denizens of the underworld whose methods of eliminating their rivals consisted in packing their bullet-riddled bodies in wet cement then tossing the incriminating "corpus delecti" into the Hudson. Very often the portals of the Eighteenth were graced by famous personalities of the stage and sometimes a leading member of society would be hailed into the station house. Due to its proximity to Broadway, most of the cases originating on "The Great White Way" were brought to West Forty-seventh Street where the offenders were arraigned. No matter whether it was day or night, the station house was a lively place. Newspaper reporters used to consider an assignment to West Forty-seventh Street as rather important for they never knew what spicy items of news would turn up, and in order that they should be on hand for all eventualities, they rented a basement across the street where they kept their typewriters uncovered and a weather eye on the entrance at 345. It is said that the famous Richard Harding Davis was one of these "fly-beaters" which was the term applied to those reporters assigned to cover the station house.

The Eighteenth Precinct served its purpose until a few years ago when it was replaced by a newer edifice. Statistics state that 500 men worked out of the old Eighteenth and they made as many as 15,000 arrests a years.[1] The law enforcement accomplished by this one situation was more than that done by many good sized American towns.

During the long reign of the Eighteenth, perhaps the most exciting time experienced by it was in July 1863 when all Manhattan had turned into one made riotous mob. The dreadful draft riots had enveloped the entire city. In view of the fact that resultant casualties were as high as some of the key battles of the Civil War, it is not surprising that the stone building on West Forty-seventh Street had more than its share in quelling the riots. The estimated damage for that week was between $1,200,000 and $5,000,000, Hell's Kitchen contributing its part to the general disorder.[2]

The predominant nationality of Hell's Kitchen was the Irish who had fled from famine and oppression only a few years before. They settled in Hell's Kitchen and when the conscription laws were passed they were the ones most vitally affected. The precipitating causes of the Draft Riots were not only that there existed certain lawless elements who objected to prosecuting the war on any terms, but in addition, the

181

fact that soldiers were conscripted by lottery vision was greatly protested inasmuch as anyone with $300 could evade induction. Thus the army was entirely recruited from the laboring classes of Irish which made up most part of the Kitchen, it being a fairly reasonable assumption that any man who could afford the $300 was not going to risk his life in combat.

Rioting broke out simultaneously in all parts of the city. People congregated in angry mobs, stormed public buildings and smashed the lotteries which had been set up to induct them. They assaulted policemen and burned and plundered the buildings which happened to be in their mad path of destruction. Their anger was directed mainly against the civil authorities and the negro population of the city, though the latter were innocent of any of the events which led up to the riots. The people reasoned, however, that the negro was the cause of the Civil War and if there had been no Civil War, there would have been no draft—ergo—the negro was the cause of the draft. Any negroes who happened to be so unfortunate as to be at large during that dreadful week met with a sad fate. Brutality, plunder and death stalked the streets of New York. The populace assembled into riotous masses determined to make all negroes bear the brunt of their grievances. Reason had been replaced by a violent rage and madness gripped the island from end to end. In one instance the mob set upon and brutally attacked a Mohawk Indian, whom, because of his dark complexion, they mistook for a negro. The unfortunate victim subsequently died from injuries received resulting from the terrible beating he sustained at the hands of the frenzied mob.

Another victim of that week was a seven year old lad who fell prey to the fury of the rioters. After they had seized him, his fiendish captors beat the frightened child with sticks and cobblestones, completing the atrocity by felling him with a blow from a pistol barrel from which the child died. But summary inflictions of their revenge upon negroes in general did not satisfy the mobs. They hit upon a plan to destroy large numbers of blacks through the firing of the colored orphans asylum. Bereft of all reason the angry crowd thereupon marched to Fifth Avenue until they arrived at the asylum which was located between Forty-third and Forty-fourth Streets. The building contained upwards of two hundred children ranging in age from infants up to twelve years. A tragedy was averted by the quick action of the Superintendent for while the rioters were gaining entrance at the front door, he was hastily evacuating his charges by way of a rear door. The ruffians smashed their way in after which they proceeded to do as much damage as possible. They destroyed the furniture by chopping it up and then set fire to the entire building. Once or twice the gallant firemen nearly had the

182

blaze under control but the rioters soon rallied and completed the job they had undertaken. There was nothing for the firemen to do but retreat into the streets and watch the massive four story structure go up in flames.

At the end of a week the city quieted down and the Draft Riots went into history. Hell's Kitchen, which had not been so affected by the passionate outbursts as some other parts of Manhattan, resumed its normal mode of living, erecting factories and warehouses amongst the tenements and freight yards still prominent in the vicinity. The only damage suffered by Hell's Kitchen during the affray was when the rioters marched down Eleventh Avenue where they wreaked their vengeance upon the yards of the Hudson River Railroad. During this melee they made it a point to destroy as much of the railroad's property as possible.

The blocks of railroad track on Eleventh and Twelfth Avenues upon which the trains of the Hudson River Railroad used to run were one of the most outstanding features of the Kitchen of those days. I can remember as a child watching the freight trains go by and sometimes counted the cars which often were so numerous that my attention would be distracted and I would lose count. This was a very dangerous place for a child and there would always be trouble when my mother found out where I had been, for while I was judged competent to roam in other parts of Manhattan, Eleventh and Twelfth Avenues were taboo. Besides, as Mother would point out, what was there to see aside from the factories, their chimneys belching whiffs of black soot into the air and the warehouses from which a steady stream of merchandise passed in and out. It was the "other side of the tracks" as far as she was concerned and Central Park or the Botanical Gardens were far more to be desired for her daughter's visitations.

But the waterfront seemed so much more romantic! Although one could not see much of the Hudson adjacent to the New York side, for it was hidden from view by the dock buildings along the shore, one could see clear across to Jersey. One could see the ferry boats carrying commuters back and forth, the garbage scows on their journies out to sea, a regular turmoil of activity. There were the boats plowing their way up and down the Hudson and on the Avenues the trains chugged along. Until a few years ago the New York Central used to have a "cow-boy" who would trot his horse in front of the freight trains and lead them into the terminal. Many times I have witnessed this sight, for it was strange indeed to see a locomotive chugging its way along Eleventh Avenue preceded by the cow-boy. This ritual was followed in accordance with a city ordinance ninety years old.

In addition to the danger to which one was exposed as a result of the heavy traffic pouring along the Avenues of Hell's Kitchen in a steady current, as constant and inevitable as the continuous onward movement of the Hudson, there was always the possibility of harm from other sources for the Kitchen was the known habitat of many gangsters. The gangsters used to roam the region subsisting on the raids which they occasionally staged against the Thirtieth Street yards of the Hudson River Railroad. When this activity did not yield enough loot the outlaws would break into houses or beat and rob those who came across their path. They managed in this way to create and maintain a continuous state of terror in the district which clung to it for many years and still enveloped the neighborhood at the time of my childhood.

After the railroad installed its own police force, in 1910, some of the heat went out of Hell's Kitchen and although it continued to be a source of trouble for those who would enforce law and order, gradually the Kitchen cooled off. Due to its proximity to river traffic as well as to the freight yards, the neighborhood assumed the role of freight depot for Manhattan. The Kitchen now contains many warehouses into which merchandise is stored before it is loaded into boats or freight trains or distributed by the trucks which monopolize the streets. The tracks have been removed from Eleventh and Twelfth Avenues and entire blocks of old tenements were demolished to make room for the West Side Improvement project launched by the New York Central. Whole city blocks of old tenements were torn down to make way for the Lincoln Tunnel approach and the West Side Improvement project. There are still some blocks lined with tenements but these two improvements eliminated hundreds of rat infested dilapidated houses.

Hell's Kitchen was more or less prominent as the site of Paddy's Market which used to convene on its easterly fringe. It was as much of a conglomeration of nationalities and commodities as I ever expected to see; an actual Bedlam let loose in Manhattan. But if you were to look for Paddy's today, you would not find it.It has passed from reality to the stage where it only exists in our memories. Some few years back the City Fathers decided to prohibit the gathering of pushcarts in the area of the Kitchen. With the passing of the market, there went, too, an interesting custom, for other than a custom it cannot be called. It was more consistent with Old World habits than what we like to think of as modern American. Yet, when one considers what a huge melting pot this city of ours is, the tenacity with which we cling to many customs of the Old World is readily understandable. This tendency is apparent in some neighborhoods more than it is in others, obviously appearing in direct proportion to the amount of foreign born in a given section. As an example, one has only to travese districts which are predominantly

Irish or Italian, German or Jewish, noting different racial customs observed in each. New generations, as they come upon the scene, are prone to accept what they find, soon adopting the imported customs and habits of their progenitors as native. This predisposition on the part of native born New Yorkers is very evident for if one delves into the origin of many of our customs, he will find that oft times they have been transported from other countries and bequeathed to us. New generations accept what they find and adopt the existing state. That is how most Manhattanites felt about Paddy's. It was completely foreign in origin and concept yet it was as much a part of Manhattan as the Metropolitan Opera or Central Park.

The many pushcarts aligning themselves under the elevated on Ninth Avenue from Thirty-ninth to Forty-second Streets made up Paddy's Market. The Market only existed on Saturdays and on that day the distance on Ninth Avenue from Thirty-ninth to Forty-second Streets would be covered by pushcarts selling every conceivable commodity—from the ingredients of a rabbit pie to the makings of a house dress. Glorious Day! Saturday! To be allowed to do the family shopping for the coming week; to go out with the fabulous sum of six or seven dollars and to return laden with supplies for the next four or five days. What an independent and "adultish" feeling it gives to a little girl of nine and what progressive educational ideas were displayed by a mother unafraid to foster such a responsibility! It was always a sensation of tremendous pride when she showed the lean meat or the trim grapefruit that she had selected. The pride in the child's judgement would be shared by her mother who was always highly appreciative of the purchases for it was a known fact that one had to be rather clever to shop at Paddy's. One had to keep a sharp eye on the shrewd pushcart vender and to be on the alert. In fact, it was a game of matching wits. One had to be sure the vender's hand was not deftly weighed in with the peaches. One had to be sure the butcher ground the meat fresh and did not take it from the tray marked "chopped meat." One had to watch that the tomatoes were firm and not over-ripe ones taken from under those on display. Yet, it was a game—and if one were to play it wisely, one had to know the rules.

Every Saturday was an adventure. It is hard to say why that was so for seldom did anything change at Paddy's. Take the horse radish man. Week after week and year after year, the old man ground his horse radish. He was a stocky man with a moustache that, were it a half inch longer, could be designated as the "handle-bar" type. In winter time he never wore a coat. He used a long dark red skating sweater which was never doffed until mid-summer. Week after week and year after year the old man could be found grinding his horse radish. He had a cellar on

185

the west side of Ninth Avenue near Forty-second Street. One was always sure to find him at the top of the stairs which led to the cellar. His grinder was there and the pungent odor of freshly ground horse radish pervaded all the surrounding air. It was a good smell and sometimes it carried clear across Ninth Avenue and the children would cross the Avenue just to watch him.

A few doors away there was a man who had a parrot which would pick out your fortune. It cost a penny to have the bird select one of the printed forms which were neatly folded so as to make it easier for the parrot to pick it out with his beak. Invariably, the fortune never changed very much. It would tell you your character and the type of life partner with whom you would secure the greatest happiness. But the monotony of the fortune did not bother the little girl very much for every week she altruistically handed over the penny to receive the same character analysis and the identical caution as to whom to marry. Once a man who had a trained white mouse set up his table a couple of hundred feet away from my favorite "fortune teller," but he didn't stay long in that vicinity. I never could find out the reason for his disappearance from Paddy's unless it was the parrot, for, after all, the parrot had built up a steady trade culled from other dreamy eyed little nine year olds. Some years later I chanced to see the man with the mouse over on Fourteenth Street near Third Avenue. Whether or not it was the same man who years before had threatened the business of the parrot man, I could not determine. I am led to believe, though, that it was, for it is not difficult to conceive that several men would engage in such an odd way of making a livlihood. The man with the parrot? I do not know what happened to him after Paddy's disbanded, but I am sure he will turn up somewhere in Manhattan one of these days. And I have not the slightest doubt but that the parrot will select the same fortune as of old.

Then there was Foley's Tea and Coffee Store. That never changed either. Inside were the black tin bins labeled "Ceylon," "Orange Pekoe," "Irish Mix," "Santos" and all the other teas and coffees, imbued, as they were, with suggestive thoughts of far off islands and peoples and customs so different from our own. At times, the "Ceylon" bin would bring forth visions of mysterious India while "Santos" would transport us all around to the other side of the world where vistas of undulating hills green with coffee trees would loom before our eyes. Foley's was quite a romantic place because with a little imagination one could travel to so many unknown lands, witness countless strange and weird sights and yet experience none of the discomforts or fatigue which real travel imposes. Every Saturday implied a different trip corresponding to whatever geography lesson was then in progress. Towards the rear of the store were kept the spice boxes. They roasted their own coffee and peanuts at Foley's. This store was also the site of a weekly visit and another package went into one of the black oilcloth shopping bags the little girl carried. Sometimes she bought peanuts and once in a while some spices were on the list. Then one was sure that mother was planning to bake the spice cake we all liked so much.

The pork store was always the last place to stop. It contained none of the fanciful products of Foley's, nor did it evoke the extravagant ideas realized by a visit to the parrot, yet it supplied its own compensations. The pork store had been established twenty-five years previously and they are still there though it is another twenty-five years since the little girl crossed the threshold lugging her filled shopping bags. The order hardly varied; Canadian bacon, sausage meat in winter, a smoked pork tenderloin or shoulder and some old fashioned potato salad. This latter was not the mayonnaise soaked variety into which potato salad has been glamorized, or should I say degenerated. No, it was homely, oldtime, down-to-earth potato salad which one doesn't see anymore. The potatoes were sliced and covered with dressing made from oil and vinegar into which the lowly onion had been generously introduced. There was nothing fancy about that potato salad; it wasn't even garnished with the ever-present parsely. But it was tasty.

Paddy's Market didn't confine itself to foodstuffs alone. It was as versatile in its offerings as the pioneer woman who could do all the cooking, sewing, spinning and when the occasion arose drive a covered wagon across the prairie or fire a musket at some skulking Indian bent upon hanging her scalp from his wigwam. Paddy's tendered its prospective customers kitchen appliances along with fruits and vegetables, notions, dress goods, table oilcloth and numerous other items. One saw the same faces and the same wares every Saturday yet the shopping tour never grew monotonous. I imagine that it was because the people all had such an expectant expression on their faces—the customers haggling with the hucksters who, in turn, were trying to outwit the prospective customer.

Paddy's was always crowded on a Saturday, but the Saturday before Christmas would find it filled to capacity. At this time, Christmas trees, holly and mistletoe would appear along with tangerines, dried figs and dates and pushcarts displaying dolls and toys. The din and noise would be terrific. Each vendor would call out his wares in sharp competition with the roar of the Ninth Avenue "el" which passed overhead. Some of the pushcarts had been dragged there by hand; some were prosperous enough to have been able to afforded Dobbins and still others owned trucks. Competition was terrific, eventually resolving itself into a case of the survival of he who could yell the loudest and the longest. At times, it was bitter cold for it seems that years ago the winters in New York were more severe than they are these days. Then, in between their yells of "oranges" or "potatoes" you would see the peddlars blowing their breath on their frozen hands, the warm breath congealing even before it reached their numb fingers.

When Paddy's passed out of the picture, one of the last vestiges of the old Hell's Kitchen was relegated to the past. The tearing up of Eleventh and Twelfth Avenues some years previously and the removal of the Ninth Avenue "el" structure had made drastic changes in the neighborhood, but it seems to me that Paddy's disappearance sounded off the death knell of the old Hell's Kitchen, as I used to know it. And with it went all the luridness, all the anticipated thrill of danger and excitement which one associated with the Kitchen. The entire area is changed. The removal of the Ninth Avenue elevated structure has made the Avenue appear much wider and permits the sun's rays to penetrate into places hitherto unknown. Buses and street cars shuttle back and forth and the clanging of the street cars and the honking of bus horns have replaced the elevated. Even the type of person one meets has been changed. Hell's Kitchen has been so altered in appearance and character that the name no longer applies and like many other things in Mad Manhattan is only a memory of the past.

CHAPTER NOTES

1. Federal Writers' Project, "New York City Guide," p. 159.
2. Federal Writers' Project, "New York Panorama," p. 64.

"The Rialto," TIMES SQUARE, North from Seventh and Broadway

CHAPTER EIGHTEEN

Central Park

"Today I have grown taller
from walking with the trees."
Karle Wilson Baker "Good Company"

THE ordinary New Yorker has accelerated his life to such a pace that there is no doubt but that he would consider walking in the Park one of the best ways of losing time. He does not mind chasing fire engines or standing around idly gazing as excavators dig canyons into Manhattan's crust. But, walking in the Park! Shades of Pan and Thoreau combined! Our sophisticated New Yorker has relegated such frivolity to the era when sleigh bells jingled in gay abandon as they resounded throughout the Park. He would as soon be found garbed in tight knee britches and silk stockings. Very seldom does the warm summer breeze waft its mixed and indefinable scent in the path of Mr. Average New Yorker, leisurely strolling around the Park. He is seldom found under such circumstances. Though once in a while one does see an out-of-towner hail a horse and buggy at the Plaza for an old-fashioned ride around the Park, one must reluctantly concede that the New Yorker would rather go walking up and down Fifth Avenue where the shop windows vie with each other in attracting his attention (and his dollars) than aimlessly wandering in the City's wonderful Central Park.

In Hyde Park or the Champs Elysées one encounters whole families, sometimes three generations, collectively taking advantage of what their cities have provided for their common enjoyment. But in Central Park, the strollers one encounters are, for the most part, children, alone or accompanied by their parents, the parents serving in the nature of unwilling companions. Aside from the children, who make

189

good use of Central Park, there are the ever-present lovers, whom one finds in all cities and in all places, sometimes in such unexpected places as Trinity Churchyard where they stroll absorbed in the present. All too unfortunately, the family as a unit has not learned to appreciate Central Park. Apparently, it never occurs to the Manhattanite of adult age that the Park can provide him with an endless source of wonders, for nothing can be more stirring nor more inspiring than the regularity with which Nature changes her scenery as one season gives way to another, each bringing forth splendors and marvels which, even in this atomic age, man cannot duplicate.

Living in Manhattan, with all its marvels of this post war world, would be tedious indeed, were it not for the fact that Central Park relieves the monotony occasioned by the blocks of anemic stone structures springing out of barren ground. It would be so tiresome that one would eventually succumb to the ennui produced by such a listless isle. Fortunately for all concerned, however, the absence of trees in the residential sections and the terrific traffic noises do not drive the bored Manhattanite to drastic measures. Instead—if he is at all enterprising—he blithely betakes himself to Central Park where the quietude in the midst of majestic trees can do nought but solace his jagged nerves. A compensatory measure, it would appear, for Manhattan veritably teems with noises.

This medley of sound produced by steady streams of surface traffic scuttling along the island's avenues and streets—blatent noises, combining themselves with purring motors, the clang of ambulances and fire engines, after a lapse of time serve to rub the raw edges of one's nerves. Even the droning of airplanes is quite a familiar sound entering into this symphony of Manhattan. But when the noise becomes too annoying and the absence of trees a palling reality, one can always flee to Central Park. There is some quality about the soil and trees which lends it benificence to repairing damages wrought by modern life in a large city. Thus, should the many families who call Manhattan "home" desire to avail themselves of this tract of sylvan charm, they have only to travel a short distance in any direction in which they may find themselves located. Central Park is geographically located in Manhattan's very midst, a most fortunate coincidence.

Yet, the location selected for the Park did not come about as the result of normal negotiations. As a matter of fact, the site was accidentally chosen because of a controversy between a Senator and an Alderman. Had it not been for this controversy, it is questionable as to where the Park would find itself today. The lack of a park had been apparent for some time but it remained for William Cullen Bryant to voice the city's great need for some sort of public recreation ground. Bryant's editorial, appearing in the New York Evening Post for July 3, 1844 urged that the city look into the possibility of purchasing a tract of land for the purpose of providing a pleasure ground to be used by the city's residents. The ground was situated between Sixty-eighth and Seventy-seventh Streets from Third Avenue to the East River and was known as Jones' Wood.

No action appears to have been taken on this suggestion, however and the subject lay dormant until four years later. At that time Mr. A. J. Downing who edited a journal called the "Horticulturist" published his article "A Talk About Public Parks and Gardens" in which he essayed the desirability of a public park. In July, 1849 Mr. Downing elaborated upon his original contention in an article called "Public Cemeteries and Public Gardens" which was also published in the "Horticulturist." In this second article its author sought to convince the American public that the creation of public parks was a necessity and that they would not only provide vast material benefits, but that in the long run they would be self supporting. Downing's contentions fell upon receptive ears and his sentiments were re-echoed in a letter which Mayor A. C. Kingsland directed to the Common Council. His Honor stated, "There is no park on the island deserving the name, and while I cannot believe that any one can be found to advance an objection against the expediency of having such a one in our midst, I think that the expenditure of a sum necessary to procure and lay out a park of sufficient magnitude to answer the purpose above noted, would be well and wisely appropriated, and would be returned to us fourfold, in the health, happiness and comfort of those whose interests are specially intrusted to our keeping—the poorer classes."[1]

This was the first official recognition given to the idea of a public park, though it must be conceded that had it not been for sporadic agitation raised by such public spirited men as Bryant and Downing, in all probability the park would have been much longer in coming.

In the July following Mayor Kingsland's memorable letter a bill was up in the New York State Legislature calling for the purchase of some land to be set aside as a public park. The acquisition of a park for New York City was thus initiated. This parcel, known as "Jones' Wood" was the same land which William Cullen Bryant had suggested in his editorial of 1844, when, after describing its various advantages, he went on, "There never was a finer situation for the public garden of a great city."[2] Jones' Wood consisted of about twelve city blocks, on the extreme easterly side of the city bounded on the north by the Harlem River and one the east by the East River. The Senator from New York introduced the bill for the purchase of Jones' Wood, but his opponent, the Alderman, contended that in addition to the fact that the price was exhorbitant, the acquisition of Jones' Wood was undesirable because it was bounded on two sides by water, precluding the possibility of ever enlarging the park as the city grew. The Alderman also contended that the Senator was personally interested in passing the bill through the Legislature. In an effort to enlist supporters to his side of the controversy, the Alderman called upon General Superintendent of Police Kennedy, who, during the course of examining the maps, suggested the feasibility of the Park's present location. Thus, had it not been for a feud between a Senator and an Alderman, the site chosen would perhaps have been quite different.[8]

The year 1856 had been a severe and disastrous one for the country, presaging the economic and financial storm of the following months. Yet, when panic did sweep the nation, New York City was not too preoccupied with its damaging results to lose sight of the pleasure ground project for which it had been clamoring. Amidst the financial tempest which was brewing, lengthy discussions took place as to the site of the proposed park. In 1856 the city acquired the ground upon which Central Park was eventually laid out. Thus the oft-repeated views of Bryant, Downing and other prominent men of the time bore proper fruit. The property cost $5,169,369.90 of which $1,657,590 were paid by the owners of adjacent lands in view of the benefit they would derive.

The location of the newly acquired Park was ideal. Situated approximately in the center of Manhattan Island, easily accessible to all the island's residents, its hilly terrain offered wide variety as to surface treatment. Landscape architects looked upon the new project with glowing possibilities.

Although this tract may have been ideal from the landscape architect's point of view, as the layman saw it, a more desolate spot on Manhattan could not have been chosen for the city's pleasure ground. One would have to be possessed of great vision to conjure up any semblance to the magnificent park it was planned to construct from the dismal piece of ground the city purchased for the purpose. More than five thousand squatters inhabited the land, living in the crudest of shacks which they themselves had constructed from old pieces of discarded lumber. The squatters lived in the most abject of misery, eeking out a bare existence on the miserable proceeds derived from the refuse and junk of the city.

As though keeping themselves alive were not a sufficiently dreary task to contend with, they are said to have kept nearly 100,000 domestic animals which roamed around the region stripping it bare of any grass and sometimes turning over the earth in search of roots. The main occupations of these squatters were rag-picking and cinder sifting. The legions of domestic animals were fed from the edible refuse of the city and if any bones were found in the garbage, these were reserved for the bone-boiling establishments also located in the area. Swamps and old water courses reeked from decaying organic matter. On the whole, whoever did undertake the transformation of this dismal place would be confronted with many problems, first and foremost being evection of the squatters and their wretched belongings.

The city invited bids for the project of converting this unprepossessing tract into the long dreamed of public park. One plan was proposed by Mr. Egbert L. Viele, the engineer who had surveyed the land. Nothing came of Viele's plan which was fortunate as it was later shown to be cumbersome and could not approach the excellent details presented by the successful plans submitted by Mr. Frederick Law Olmsted and Mr. Calvert Vaux. Olmsted and Vaux's design was selected from among the thirty-three plans which were submitted. The adopted plan, called "Greensward," won for its successful designers the $2,000 prize offered to the winning contestant.[4] The authors of "Greensward" had many handicaps to overcome in addition to dispossessing the tract of its undesirable tenants, it had also to be cleared and drained before any of the walks or parks could be laid out. The first year of work, 1857, the city contracted the services of 3,800 men to demolish the three hundred or more dwellings and bone-boiling establishments before draining out the swamps and clearing the hills.

The designers of "Greensward" sought to carry out their plan by featuring natural beauties while at the same time planning driveways for vehicles, pedestrians and equestrians. Space was to be set apart for botanical and horticultural purposes and the lake was to be used in summer for boating and in winter for skating. The plan, as a whole, had to take into consideration three main requirements if it were to prove favorable. Olmsted and Vaux had to give the public the best Park possible, using the available land for such recreational activities as were proposed and, at the same time, design the Park so as to meet the exigencies imposed by a growing city.

Interest in the project was widespread. Europe was looking on with lively concern at what was being done in the New World and they followed the building of the Park with warm enthusiasm. The City of Hamburgh presented twelve of the swans for which it was famous to the Central Park and when most of these died, in 1860, they sent ten more. London sent twenty-five pairs that same year.

As year followed year other additions were made to increase the Park's usefulness and add to its beauty. Several times it became necessary to emphatically and vigorously resist attempts to divert the Park from the original purposes for which it was intended. All sorts of schemes were proposed, most of them entirely out of keeping and foreign to the use for which Central Park was designed. Some of the proposals were:

> That a street railway be built in the Park;
> That a steam boat and full-rigged ship be put
> in the Park;
> That the Park should be made a burial place
> for distinguished dead of the city;
> That all religious denominations be invited
> to build places of worship in the Park.[5]

From the foregoing, which represents only a partial list of some of the schemes which have been advanced to infringe upon the Park's property, it will be seen that it has been a constant struggle to keep the land unobstructed and used as originally planned.

Once the Park boasted of a lovely sight called the "rhododendron mile" which had been contributed by Mrs. Russell Sage. This "mile" which, in reality was actually only half a mile, won fame all over America for all who saw the rhododendrons in bloom were struck by their individual beauty and the spectacle presented by the magnificent array of colors. The collections, comprising around seven thousand carefully selected seedlings, were imported from abroad. The seedlings were planted along the drive on the east side of the Park between Eighty-seventh and Ninety-seventh Streets.

Ornaments and statues were enthusiastically contributed without discrimination as to whether or not they were appropriate pieces for a public park. There was a time when dozens of useless incongruities which had been donated by generous but misguided individuals were stored in the Arsenal. It would have been a perpetration of one of the greatest esthetic crimes to have placed every piece received in the Park, for there is no doubt but that some of these supposedly artistic efforts were nothing short of monstrosities. These well meaning, but unsuitable gifts were housed in the Arsenal which had been acquired by the city from the state at a cost of $275,000.[6]

Of all the Park's forty-two pieces of statuary, perhaps the most noted is the Obelisk, familiarly known as "Cleopatra's Needle." This latter name, however, is an anachronism for Cleopatra had nothing to do either with its erection or its removal to Alexandria inasmuch as she died in the second year of Augustus while this monumental effort of the pre-Christian era was removed to Alexandria in the eighth year of Augustus. (23 BC) The Obelisk, embodying centuries of Egyptian history in which neither the piercingly hot rays of the sun nor the relentless downpours of thousands of years, have obliterated the

194

original hierglyphics, was presented to the Park by the khedive, Ismail Pasha. January 22, 1881 it was swung into its present position at twelve o'clock to the minute, in the presence of many officials and thousands of New Yorkers eager to see this two hundred and twenty tons of historic stone mounted in the New World. The Obelisk brought to the shores of the New Continent a history rich in adventure and conjecture. It is supposed to have been quarried by Thothmes III being one of a pair erected by that monarch who came to the throne in 1515 B.C. Its hierglyphics relate the stories of Thothmes III, Rameses II and Osarkon I. The Obelisk is also associated with Augustus Caesar under whose instructions it was removed to Alexandria to commemorate his victory over the last of the Ptolemies.[7]

Shortly after the Obelisk was erected gold was discovered in Central Park. Yes, the yellow metal over which men have fought and slaved and even killed, turned up in Central Park! But this discovery, which came about when laborers were excavating for a road near the Arsenal Building, did not bring on any great gold rush. The thrill of the workmen was short lived for it was found that samples of the granite assayed as containing from between $1.00 to $1.75 worth of gold to the ton, cost at least $4.00 to excavate.[8]

The original "Greensward" plan called for four transverse roads to cross the Park from east to west. These roads meander along in such a careless fashion that it would never occur to anyone that they had been planned. Yet, Olmsted and Vaux were far-seeing in their designs for today these roads furnish a direct means of carrying east-west traffic.

A Parade Ground was included in the design which never has been used for military purposes. In 1864 one of the regiments of the First Division of the National Guard attempted to drill there, and this episode was repeated by another regiment. This misconception of the original intention of the Parade Ground or Green as it is sometimes called, was immediately corrected and aside from these two instances the Parade Ground has never served as a military field.[9] There is also a playground which was planned in the original designs. Footpaths were laid out at various intervals and shrubbery planted on the sides to make walking both interesting and an aesthetic passtime. A system of introducing bridges was devised to carry strollers to places of special beauty which would have been inaccessible without the bridges. These carried one over brooks, lakes, stony ravines and even over driveways.

In a few more years Central Park will celebrate its centenary—a hundred years of providing safe relaxation to the city's inhabitants—a hundred years in which it has become dear to the hearts of all New Yorkers. If only for the fact that in summer time one can lie under a tree and listen to the swallow's rapturous song or in winter skate on the frozen lake as fresh gusts of clear air drive past—if only for these two privileges, it deserves a fond place among the things New Yorkers cherish. And it enjoys such prestige for there isn't a born Manhattanite who cannot recall pleasant memories associated with the Park. Boating on the lake, visits to the zoo, feeding the squirrels and birds, May Parties and June Walks—the Park has seen all this. It has offered tired minds and bodies a reprieve from city noises by substituting the relaxing song of the bird for the automobile sirens.

The original cost of the land plus expenses subsequently incurred in connection with the Park's maintenance has been repaid manyfold in the satisfaction derived from its use. Often times cities incur great expenditures to furnish little used facilities, but, despite the fact that New Yorkers do not avail themselves of the full opportunities provided by Central Park, they do enjoy it. It was and is worth all the money expended upon it. It is enjoyed by rich and poor, young and old, alike, and it is too bad that at the present time only a fraction of its possibilities are utilized. The Park affords busy Manhattanites a serene and contemplative respite from the usual active routine which living in a large city implies. And this is as it should be, for coming down to facts obvious in themselves, the life of a city, as regards its necessities, does not differ much from the lives of its residents. Both have well defined requirements which, if they are to grow and prosper, must be supplied. In the case of the city, if it is to progress, maintaining at the time a relative degree of contentment among its inhabitants, it must retain some of its soil as nature intended. Some of its land must be free—except for the vegetation depending upon it for sustenance. A city needs parks and all the things a park signifies, just as an individual needs relaxation and a pause from daily activity. Just as the pause from the regular routine makes for a well-balanced life, restoring one's mental and physical vitality, so do the parks make for a well-balanced city. As evidence of this fact, one has only to observe the behavior of people living near a park as compared with that of those who are deprived this privilege. One notes that there exists more dissatisfaction as well as a greater tendency to lawlessness in those regions of Manhattan lacking the beneficial facilities provided by public parks.

This does not mean that parks are the panacea for what ails the body politic. It does mean, however, that the establishment of parks in slum areas would do much to alleviate many of the ills which brew and infest these localities. Children compelled to find recreation skating along curbs of busy city streets or playing tag in refuse strewn alleys develop an air of furtiveness absent in those whose daily play takes place in the safe confines of a park. They deserve their chance to grow into strong and worthwhile citizens. Parks give them that chance. These sentiments are not new for they were expressed as early as 1861 by the Rev. Dr. Bellows who said in part: "but we do hope that we shall live to know many residents of towns of ten thousand population who will be ashamed to subscribe for the building of new churches while no public playground is being prepared for their people."[10]

Fortunate to record, the City of New York is very cognizant of this fact. Whenever slum clearance projects have been introduced, city engineers have tried to plan that little squares or triangles be left for the enjoyment of those living in the crowded sections.

CHAPTER NOTES

1. Cook, Clarence Chatham, "A Description of The New York Central Park," p. 18. Letter of Mayor A. C. Kingsland to the Common Council, dated April 5, 1851.
2. "The New York Evening Post," for July 3, 1844, editorial, p. 2 c. 1.
3. Smith, Matthew Hale, "Sunshine and Shadow in New York," p. 356, 357.
4. The Central Park Association, "The Central Park," p. 35.
5. "Central Park in the City of New York," an article by Edward Hagaman Hall, published in Vol. 16 of the "American Scenic and Historic Preservation Society," p. 485.
6. Cook, Clarence Chatham, "A Description of The New York Central Park," p. 33, 34.
7. "The World," for January 23, 1881, p. 2, c. 1 & 2.
8. "Central Park in the City of New York," an article by Edward Hagaman Hall, published in Vol. 16 of the "American Scenic and Historic Preservation Society," p. 391.
9. Macatamney, Hugh, "Cradle Days of New York," p. 225.
10. The Central Park Association, "The Central Park," p. 41.

CENTRAL PARK, The Bethesda Fountain, ca. 1900.

Skating in Central Park, Majestic and Dakota Apts. in background, 1894

CHAPTER NINETEEN

Riverside Drive

"A river is the coziest of friends. You must love it and live with it before you can know it."

G.W. Curtis, "Lotus-Eating: Hudson and Rhine"

A Providence which may have smiled upon other parts has not been overgenerous in endowing Manhattan Isle with such natural beauty as to send the beholder into ectasies of admiration. The simple truth is that if one were to eliminate the mighty Hudson, Manhattan would be devoid of any sign of topographical beauty, for Gothamites have removed pleasant little hillocks, buried the cheerful brooks which once gleefully meandered through out the island and generally destroyed many physical charms of the old Manhattan.

Manhattan of yore possessed many topographical features which are practically non-existant today. It seems incredible to contemplate in this day but Manhattan as Henry Hudson first set eyes upon it boasted all sorts of wild game and animals. The soil, from which divers species of trees pushed their branches skyward, was rich and fertile once the phlegmatic Dutchman had set about and cleared it. As the "Half-Moon" slowly plowed its way up the river which today bears his name, Henry Hudson had every reason to be pleased with what he saw. As far as the eye could reach there was the untouched beauty of virgin forests into which no white man had ever penetrated.

Abundant water courses made their way through tracts of forests as they coursed over rocks and between trees, sometimes shielded from the sunlight by the thick vegetation, sometimes sparkling as the sun forcefully penetrated the boughs and brushed the streamlets and brooks with its life giving rays. Many of these water courses remain until today, but now, man in his relentless struggle to progress, has pushed the little streams far below the surface. Once in a while these subterranean brooks try to emerge into their former courses on top of the soil and at such times they thrust themselves through building foundations and even into subway stations; but their efforts in this direction are soon quashed by modern engineering methods and the little streams are again locked in the bosom of Manhattan there to slumber for a few more years.

Hudson knew his discovery was of great commercial value. He reported to the West India Company, under whose employ he had sailed, giving glowing descriptions of the rich land, splendid forests, fish, game and peltry which the new land furnished. Yet, the intrepid navigator considered his mission a failure inasmuch as he had not found the route to China which he had been seeking. At first the discovery of the "great streame" led Hudson to believe his mission had been accomplished, but after exploring our present Riverside Drive section and navigating as far up the river as Albany, he admitted his failure.

Poor Hudson! Had he but been able to look into the future and only partially envisage what has come to pass! Could he but see Riverside Drive with its large apartment houses and great hospitals forming a back drop for the river, his disappointment would have been but brief. Alas and alack! The explorer did not differ from other mortals who desire to bridge the abysmal gap of time separating the future from the present. He had no way of knowing the full importance of his discovery. So he tried again to find a shorter route to China only to discover another salt water strait. For a second time Hudson had a fleeting hope that his journey had been successful. This promise of a triumphant culmination to the hardships he had endured was short lived. His ignorant sailors, terrified of the artic cold, set their captain and his seven year old son adrift to perish in the icy waters of the great bay which we all now know as Hudson's Bay.

Today the great natural benefits which Hudson found on Manhattan have been consigned to the "place of fabulous things." What little was ever left of Nature's wonders has long since been desecrated in man's mad quest to conquer and build, for all who see Manhattan are in one accord—that it is a monument to man's triumphant progress. Not that the result is a disaster! On the contrary, man has achieved something magnificent; something which cannot but help thrill the beholder to the very core, for here is a personality imparted to a city by man, himself. A synthetic personality, one might consider it, which can be broken down into its component parts as surely as water can be separated into hydrogen and oxygen. Yes, Manhattan is man-made and hardly a trace remains of the natural loveliness which Henry Hudson found and the later day Dutch came to appreciate. To be more specific, one might add that nothing remains but the mighty Hudson, for with all the material advancement attained by engineers and architects, they have never been able to entirely infringe upon nature's one remaining gift to the city. The majestic Hudson flows on out to sea just as it has done for thousands of years. We have spanned the river with mighty bridges, shaped its bed into air conditioned tunnels, but still it flows on and on, unchanging, as it sedately embraces Riverside Drive in a final farewell before emptying into the sea.

That is why Riverside Drive is the very essence of Manhattan—because it holds the one remaining natural force which Nature has bestowed upon this magnificent man-made isle, the Hudson. Because of the Hudson the Riverside Drive section can be thought to exemplify the three tenses of Manhattan; as it was, as it is and as it shall be. As it was; because the river continues in its same relentless drive to the ocean carrying the sweet waters of the Catskills on a bridal trip to be joined with the salt water of the oceans. Just the mere speculation as to the time in which the Hudson has been making its way to the ocean transports one into another world in which human ingenuity lay dormant. The Hudson, regal in its splendor, a power and a beauty to be reckoned with, as since time immemorial, it has gently bathed the present Drive's shores, still journies on out to sea.

Manhattan, as it is; because the huge buildings of the island thrust their mortar, stone and bricks into the sky, coming to an abrupt halt when they reach the Drive as though in respectful awe of the Hudson's presence. All over the island huge edifices drive themselves into the heavens, but when they reach the Drive the river compels them to stop.

And that brings us to Manhattan, as it shall be. Who can tell? Will engineers displace some of the river by filling it in? Will they appropriate what has belonged to the Hudson these hundreds of years in order that more land might become available to an already overcrowded Manhattan? The Hudson holds the solution to many things and suggests many possibilities. In it are admirably blended Manhattan's three tenses. Just as when light passes through a prism it reveals the true colors of the spectrum, Riverside Drive imparts the past, present and future of the island. The seven miles of turning, twisting thoroughfare which embrace the Hudson from Seventy-second Street all the way up to Dyckman Street embodies and exemplifies these three stages through which the city has passed, is passing and will pass.

The beneficence of the Hudson is lent not only to the Drive, but the city as well shares in reaping the benefits which the river's presence produces. This winding, turning river flows on its mighty trek to the ocean in blitheful content as it begins its course nearly 300 miles away in the Adirondack mountains and the Mohawk Valley, seeping down through the valleys and hills of New York State until at last it meets its Destiny and the sweet waters of the springs and lakes become as one with the salt water of the Atlantic. It flows through land rich in historical associations and reknown for the wealth of legendary material furnished such gifted penmen as Irving and Cooper. It begins as the merest trickle over a small stone only to terminate its journey as the dominant force which enables gigantic liners to put out to sea or to dock at one of the great piers jutting out into its downtown stretches. Its clear water has lapped against the hollowed tree trunk from which the aboriginal fashioned his canoe with the same equanimity and "savoir faire" that it brushes against the hull of the Queen Elizabeth. It takes all in its stride—from Hudson's "Half-Moon" to Fulton's "Clermont"—flowing on and on as the centuries pass, with never a sign of what has already transpired and giving no inkling of what the future holds. Sphinx-like it courses on, carrying its secrets with it to lock them within the depths of the sea.

One would as leave conceive of the Drive without the river as one would a beautiful woman who had no hair to crown and frame her loveliness. The river is Manhattan's "crowning glory." Without it, Manhattan would be devoid of much that contributes not only to the city's natural beauty, but to its commercial activity and part of the transportation system which makes such activity possible. The Drive without the river would be like any ordinary prosaic street of Manhattan and the sun would rise and set a thousand times and no one would notice anything unusual. But the Hudson washing up against the shores of Riverside Park lends a charm, a touch that only water can render to a scene, supplying Manhattanites with views of unforgettable splendor.

One of these sights is a sunset on the Hudson as seen from the Drive. It is as though after a very busy day, the flaming red ball reluctantly decides to seek rest behind the Jersey hills. But before it disappears, this regal symbol of heat and life emits one last display of strength and beauty. Sometimes the sky is splashed with deep crimson and violent purple; other times the coloring is more subdued and less spectacular. The Heavens are illumined and glow with all shades and hues radiating from the sun in its last impressive outburst of dynamic power. The reflection is captured by the river as though seeking to carry such scenes of dazzling beauty along in its journey to the sea. Every sunset on Riverside Drive is different and each one seems more beautiful and lovelier than the previous one. This is as true in summer as in winter. Sunset on the Drive is not only awe inspiring it is entrancingly beautiful, as the sun drops further and further into the horizon and reflections grow less and less, until the glowing ball of fire is gone and night is left to rule supreme for the next few hours.

It hardly seems possible for one to view such a scene and remain unaffected by its magnificence. As the sun sinks deeper and deeper into the west one cannot help but feel a sense of great power behind the Universe; a power which imbues and touches all things, be they animate or inanimate. In my opinion, if one excludes the Battery, there is no other part of Manhattan where this feeling is so manifest, where this terrific force which regulates the mechanism of all things is so apparent.

Time was when no matter how beautiful a sunset it was destroyed with a sharp realistic pang as the ugly tracks of the New York Central loomed across the scene. There was a time when noisy engines belched huge smoke clouds as they chugged along the veritable labyrinth of tracks which used to mar the Drive's shoreline. The tracks began at Seventy-second Street in what is best described as a maze, untangled themselves a few blocks distant and then ran parallel to the Drive all along the river. They were an eyesore and for years served to detract from the vista which the Drive afforded. After many years of contention a concrete roof was built over the tracks leaving Riverside Drive free to curve and sway far uptown and all along the way as it hugs the Hudson's shore reveal scenes of great beauty. Once the tracks were hidden from view, landscape architects were called upon to beautify Riverside Park as well as the 132 acres added by the tracks concrete roof and the filling in of the jagged edges along the shoreline.

Riverside Drive has for long been distinguished as housing Grant's Tomb and the Claremont Inn. In fact, after the river, they are the two objects most closely associated with the Drive. There are other monuments and buildings, to be sure, like the Soldiers' and Sailors' Monument, International House and the Master Institute of United Arts (formerly the Roerich Museum), but most people, when they come to New York like to see where the great militarist sleeps and where the great colonials entertained.

Standing on a slight promontory at One Hundred and Twenty-second Street and the Drive, the imposing mausoleum in which repose the bodies of General and Mrs. Grant commands an impressive view of the Hudson. The great General, better remembered perhaps in the distinguished role of militarist than that of President of the United States, like most soldiers of all times abhorred the useless waste and destruction produced by war. His oft-repeated maxim "Let us have peace" is inscribed on the parapet wall of the tomb. The tomb was built by public subscription at a cost of $600,000. It was opened in 1897 and contains two reliquary rooms in which various battle flags and Civil War memorials are displayed. The tomb, visible from the Hudson for miles around, is a monument of which the city is justly proud.

Curious as it may seem, Grant's Tomb is not the only tomb on the Drive. Though it is very dignified and is visited by over 200,000 people annually, the massive structure shares interest with a very simple little urn down the slope toward the Hudson. A small iron enclosure has been built around the urn, one side bearing the inscription "Erected to the Memory of an Amiable Child." The "amiable child" was St. Claire Pollack, who was five years old at the time he fell to his death from the rocks below the Claremont.

The property was sold by George Pollack to Cornelia Verplanck, that is, all except the soil wherein rested the small coffin. Upon this spot Pollack erected the little headstone and caused the grave to be surrounded with an iron fence. When the city wanted to purchase the land as part of the Park they encountered this indenture and so that is why we see today the simple little grave of an "amiable child" just north of the impressive mausoleum erected to house the mortal remains of General and Mrs. Grant. And curiously enough, though the monuments are worlds apart, both attract many visitors and arouse unusual interest.

Claremont Inn, now municipally operated as a restaurant, was constructed in 1783 by George Pollack, a wealthy linen merchant who had acquired the land from Nicholas de Peyster. The original Claremont did not have so many verandas as the one we know today and there is no doubt but that its interior must have glowed with the enchanting charm with which wealthy colonials were wont to surround themselves. Claremont was one of the loveliest homes on the island enjoying, as it did, and still does, a superb view up and down the Hudson and across to the Palisades.

Varied were the tenants attracted to this home of the splendid view. Many were distinguished, some ordinary, some spectacular and some mysterious. Each must have imparted some of his own personality to Claremont, and each successive tenant must have left some of his own influence in the manor house overlooking the Hudson. Yet, considering the many owners and tenants who had ample opportunity to modify Claremont, the old residence still retains much of its original colonial charm.

It appears that during the time of George Pollack the land upon which the building rests was known as "Strawberry Hill." There was another parcel known as "Monte Alto" and these two parcels, though conveyed separately previous to around 1822, were later united under the ownership of Joel Post from whose heirs the city later acquired the land and building.[1]

203

One of the spectacular people having title to the site was Michael Hogan. Irish, dominated by a spirit of adventure, Hogan set all tongues wagging when he arrived in Manhattan with the fabulous amount of two million dollars in gold sovereigns, and a dark skinned wife who was reputed to be an East Indian princess. This tycoon was eagerly awaited to be entertained by other nabobs of the era, for it was not every day, nor every year for that matter, that Manhattan saw the likes of the thirty-eight year old figure who had traversed the world in all shipboard capacities, from sailor to skipper.[2] Hogan purchased "Strawberry Hill" from Joseph Alston and renamed it "Claremont" after Claremont in Surrey, England.

The Joseph Alston who sold "Strawberry Hill" to Hogan was at one time Governor of South Carolina. Alston's wife was Aaron Burr's unfortuante daughter, Theodosia, whose fate has been a matter of conjecture since her disappearance at sea in 1812. Many believed that her ship was captured by pirates and that Aaron Burr's beloved daughter was one of the last to walk the plank. Forty years later three men, two in Virginia and one in Texas, made death bed confessions that the crew had mutinied and murdered all the officers and passengers of the boat which was bringing Theodosia to New York to visit her father.[3] Suffice to say that from that day until this there has never been produced any tangible evidence as to exactly what befell Mrs. Alston as once the boat set sail, nothing more was ever heard from it.

There was also a Mr. Courtney associated with Claremont; a somewhat vague personage whose residence at Claremont seems to have been shrouded in mystery. There is no doubt that Courtney occupied the house on "Strawberry Hill" but there is very little to show that during his occupancy Claremont was the scene of any unusual social activity, as was the case with its previous and subsequent tenants. Courtney was so retiring that he provoked the curiosity of his neighbors. One of the chroniclers of that era has the following to say in connection with Courtney's occupancy of Claremont: ... "West of Broadway, between Eleventh and Twelfth avenues, at One Hundred and Twenty-third Street, there was a large country residence occupied by an Englishman, a Mr. Courtney, who, with but one man-servant and a cook, lived so retired as never to be seen in company with anyone outside of this household, and very rarely in public. There were, as a consequence, many opinions given as to the occasion of such exclusiveness. The one generally and finally accepted was that he had been a gay companion of royalty in his youth, and that his leaving England was more the result of expediency with him than choice. The house subsequently was known as "The Claremont."[4] Courtney disappeared from the

American horizon during the War of 1812 when he left the United States and his plate and furniture were auctioned.

At one time the venerable building played host to an ex-King. Joseph Bonapart, crowned King of Spain by Napolean, fled to New York after his brother's defeat at Waterloo. In New York, Joseph took refuge at Claremont which he is said to have re-furnished in a manner befitting an ex-King.

Shortly before the Civil War the villa, already past the half-century mark, was converted into a restaurant. The Claremont is still operating in this capacity—in which respect it is fulfilling the destiny of many famous New York landmarks. Sooner or later many edifices which were once the pride and joy of discriminating families find themselves reduced in station. Fortunately, though, in the case of the Claremont, it is operated by the city and one hopes that it will thus be assured a longer life than it would be under other circumstances.

Twenty or more years ago Riverside Drive was the home of those prosperous burghers who had accumulated enough of the world's goods to be able to afford residences from which they could see the Palisades mirrored in the Hudson. And say what you will—even though these substantial citizens have moved to other parts—the choice was a good one for there are few of Nature's endowments which can substitute water in imparting an aspect of serenity to a scene. The Hudson flows past lovely manor houses all the way down on its journey to the sea, the Drive being the last part where New Yorkers can obtain a view of the lordly river. And so while up-State the homes overlooking the river are further apart, on Riverside Drive they are mostly built adjacent to each other with very few exceptions.

The Drive never reached the reputation of Fifth Avenue as the "socially proper address," but it did gain wide popularity as one of the "best" places in which to live. There was a "millionaires' row" on the Drive headed by the castle-like structure which Charles A. Schwab built. This mansion, modeled after the Chenonceaux castle in France is located on the Drive between Seventy-third and Seventy-fourth Streets and is surrounded by a huge iron fence. Though cold and austere, and exceedingly formal, it is the most prominent single structure on the Drive, resembling some feudal castle in medieval Europe. Lately a very modern note has appeared in connection with the castle for during the last war victory gardens had been planted on the front lawns. It seemed very strange to see this stately and very dignified castle surrounded by tomato plants, cucumbers and radishes.

There were several less pretentious homes on the lower Drive in the early Twenties—homes that today have either been demolished or con-verted into studio apartments. One entered the Riverside Drive homes

205

directly from the street and, as I recall, very few of them were brown stone, most of them being of either a grey or white stone. Some had little balconies with ornate iron balustrades, but they were not large enough to permit their being used as verandas.

Why these former residents of the Drive ever relinquished their charming private dwellings overlooking the Hudson to live in modernistic Park Avenue apartments is more than the average mind can fathom. It could not have been the "help problem" because it requires the same number of servants to care for a ten room duplex apartment as it did to operate a small dwelling facing the Drive. It is more logical to assume that many of these post-Victorian dwellings were closed as a result of high real estate taxes.

Another factor which may have contributed to the conversion of several private residences was the question of fashion. Fashion or style or what is "de riguer"—call it by what term you will—exhibits foolish whims and society blindly follows in an effort to "keep up with the Jonses." Entire neighborhoods have been "made" or ruined by such foibles as thrust Newport into the foreground for a few seasons only to relegate it into nonentity the next. The same process has been going on in Manhattan in a sort of progressional manner and so we have a place like Riverside Drive reluctantly yielding to Park Avenue. Be that as it may and despite the fact that many of the residences have been converted into furnished rooms and apartments, the Drive still has a charm, a contemplative inducement to tranquil living totally lacking in the canyon of gigantic apartments lining both sides of Park Avenue. Nevertheless, if one is to conform to the dictates of fashion, one must be prepared to do many things which appear lacking in what used to be known as "good old-fashioned horse sense."

The city has not allowed the fact that the era of substantial private dwellings is no more, as far as the Drive is concerned, to interfere with its plans for developing the Park. Considerable interest has been displayed in beautifying Riverside Park, and the city is constantly making improvements in this direction. Actually, there are three parks adjacent to the Hudson, Riverside Park only extending as far as One Hundred and Fifty-eighth Street, after which it becomes Washington Park, thence Audubon Park. When one considers that during the Ninteenth Century this land was inhabited by squatters who used to keep their goats there and that as late as twenty years ago I can remember when garbage was loaded into scows from the Ninety-sixth Street pier, one must concede that the city has accomplished wonders.

Camouflaging the railroad tracks was one of the neatest engineering feats performed along these lines. After that, designers could lay out the additional land added and Riverside Park was free to be developed into the charming complement of the Hudson which it is today. The property for the Park was originally acquired by the city in 1872 after which Mr. Frederick Law Olmsted was contracted to design it. Olmsted, it will be remembered was co-designer with Calvert Vaux of the "Greensward Plan" which was adopted for laying out Central Park.

Most New Yorkers and those who visit, too, are of the general opinion that Riverside Park is the loveliest park in the city. I am inclined to agree with this choice. One can appreciate the solemnity of a Wall Street, silent as night reigns triumphant over its abysmal canyon; or the tinsel-like gayety of a Broadway festooned in Mazdas; or even the dignity of the Avenues of Opulence, Park and Fifth, but one must concede that Riverside Drive surpasses them all by night and by day. And what is the reason for its supremacy in this versatile city of New York where each section has some characteristic setting it apart from its neighbors? The Hudson is the answer. One of the most beautiful rivers in America, one has the impression that it serves as a natural barrier to those who would alter the original topography.

CHAPTER NOTES

1. "Old Buildings of New York City," p. 134, 135.
2. Barrett, Walter, "The Old Merchants of New York," Vol. IV, p. 115, 116.
3. "Old Buildings of New York City," p. 131.
4. Haswell, Charles H., "Reminiscences of an Octogenarian," p. 25.

"RIVERSIDE DRIVE, North from 135th Street, Toward Fort George"

CHAPTER TWENTY

Yorkville

*"America is God's Crucible, the
great Melting-Pot where all the races
of Europe are melting and re-
forming! . . . God is making the
America."*
Israel Zangwill, "The Melting-Pot"
Act I. (Produced in N.Y.C., Oct. 1908)

DEFINITELY Central European in character, with its shop
windows advertising their wares in German and Hungarian,
Yorkville is perhaps the only section in Manhattan which has consistently remained populated by the same nationality for over a hundred
and fifty years. The neighborhood is colorful not only because it is
foreign, but also due to the fact that this foreign element is in itself sub-
divided into many nationalities, each of which has its own racial
characteristics. This complete lack of homogeneity is what makes
Yorkville interesting. The area from Fifty-ninth to Ninety-sixth Streets
between Lexington Avenue and the East River provides homes for
several Hungarians, Czechs, Slovaks and some Rumanians, but Germans still predominate and form the nucleous of Yorkville's foreign
population. Some Irish have infiltrated into the region, as indeed the
Sons of Erin have introduced themselves into most localities of the city.
Yet, while Yorkville is slowly being absorbed by other ethnological
groups, causing it to lose some of its Central European atmosphere, the
people from the Rhineland still are, as they were of old, in the majority,
in what was formerly the little hamlet far removed from the city and
known for its salubrious climate.

The Dutch were acquainted with the vicinity and so were the English, since the Boston Post Road entered Yorkville at about the point which we now know as Eighty-third Street and Third Avenue. They knew it as a stopping off place for rest and a change of horses on the tedious journey between New York and Boston. The word "tedious" in this instance seems well advised for up to 1785 it took six days to traverse the distance between New York and Boston and this by travelling from three o'clock in the morning until ten o'clock at night. The Boston stages made the trip three times weekly. It was also familiar to those who did the "fourteen miles round" as the present Third Avenue and Seventy-seventh Street marked the spot where the five-mile stone was placed. The Dutch congregated around the lower extremity of the island and the English extended the city limits only slightly further north. By 1790 Yorkville comprised a scattered settlement of a few Germans who had established little farms. Wherefore, then, the name "Yorkville"—a name typically English and not at all reminiscent of the homelands of these early farmers?

The premise has been advanced that when the British captured New Amsterdam and changed the name to New York, the villagers called their settlement "Yorkville" presumably after the Duke of York, who was later James II.[1]

Two little streamlets coursed through Yorkville at this time; one began around Ninth Avenue and Eighty-fifth Street and ran south, then east, to join another which seems to have originated about Eighty-ninth Street and Eighth Avenue. When they met these two water courses formed the Saw Kill which emptied into the East River near where Seventy-fifth Street now is. Some years later, during the process of grading, the culverts made for drainage of the low ground were poorly constructed and they fell in whereupon the region was subjected to an overflow which sometimes reached the depths of ten feet. As a result of this condition, the area was rendered open to maleria and similar ailments caused by dampness.[2] Thus it came about that Yorkville gained a reputation for being unhealthy; a condition just the reverse of that which the region enjoyed when it consisted of only a few scattered farmhouses. It was not until 1871 that the city finally took measures to correct the situation. The soil was drained and Yorkville was restored to its previous salubrious state which had been one of its main attractions in the days following the Revolution.

Several causes contributed to the subsequent growth of the little farm colony. The city was subjected to annual outbreaks of yellow fever and kindred epidemics which had ravaged entire sections. Coupled with this there were disastrous conflagrations, which left great destruction in their wake. The fire of 1835 alone reduced 700 buildings to ashes.

Meanwhile, transportation facilities were improving and living so far away from the crowded lower regions of the city was no longer the great inconvenience it had been. As it became necessary to rebuild burned areas and as a frenzied populace sought refuge from pestilence, many turned to Yorkville where the shifting breezes from the East River were so pure and the air so bracing that even brief sojourns there were said to be of great benefit in treating certain ailments. By 1840 the village was flourishing to the extent of about a hundred houses, three or four churches and around twelve stores.[3]

It was the merchants of the city who first realized the possibilities of Yorkville. They were the prosperous element of the city, increasing their individual fortunes as the infant Republic progressed. They started the trend for Yorkville as a summer abode after the terrible yellow fever epidemic of 1799 which wrought havoc in the overcrowded lower sections of the city. This was not the first outbreak of yellow fever—nor was it the last, for between the years of 1795 and 1805 the dreaded epidemic broke out annually, each year extracting its toll from the population who were powerless either to control or to combat the scourge. Thousands perished. Those who were not overtaken knew only one defense, to flee the terror stricken city. When the plagues were at their most violent stages those opulent ones who could afford it, and who consisted mostly of merchants then comprising the wealthy class, removed their families to less crowded environs where they could spend the summer in comparative safety. Many moved to Greenwich and Chelsea, but some were attracted to remote little Yorkville which centered around the old Boston Post Road, near the present Third Avenue from Eighty-third to Eighty-ninth Streets.

Archibald Gracie, born in Scotland, philanthropist, patron of the arts, and like many men of his era an exponent of graceful living, was one of the first merchant princes to recognize the possibilities which Yorkville offered in the way of providing a comfortable summer haven. Gracie's ships plied the seven seas. Laden with precious goods, silks, laces and spices and all the other items so essential to the expanding metropolis, they would cast anchor in New York harbor while it is presumed they would sail away with such products as furs and tobacco, two of the principle exports of that time. Gracie, from all accounts, did not devote his entire attention to the plebian task of making money; he also knew how to spend it in such a way that his fellow citizens would derive some benefits. In addition to establishing the Lying-in-Hospital and the Cedar Street Presbyterian Church, he also organized the Chamber of Commerce.

The Gracie House, which now serves as the official residence of the Mayor of New York, is believed to have been built in 1770, and purchased by Archibald Gracie in 1799, whence he had it reconstructed, using part of the original old two story frame building. The house stood amidst the ruins of a Revolutionary fort, and before Gracie could begin the remodeling it was necessary to have all the remaining military equipment removed and the ground levelled off.

Gracie probably did not recognize it at the time, but when he selected this little knoll on Eighty-eighth Street overlooking the East River as the location for his villa, he was actually assisting in the metamorphosis of Yorkville from the small farm settlement into a fashionable post-colonial summer colony. His contemporaries soon came to include Astor, Rhinelander, Schermerhorn and many other well known Knickerbocker families, all of whom were comfortably es-counced in their Yorkville villas, most of which boasted a veranda from which these early Lords of the Manor could complacently smoke their pipes while the then rebellious current of Hells Gate swirled angrily in the distance. Most of these estates were constructed on the river slopes, the residences proper being somewhat elevated—a fact which made it possible for their occupants to enjoy an excellent view across to the shores of Long Island, while the lawns and gardens descended in sweep-ing confusion to the river's edge.

The terrain where earth and water met was somewhat varied as in places rocks covered with kelp and sea moss hid treacherous ledges from which there always lurked the chance to be hurled bodily into the deep channel below. Nature did not employ many such deceptive devices, though, as for the most part land adjacent to the water's edge was rocky and there were miniature coves where the river collected. These coves and tiny inlets contained nothing more dangerous than crabs and succulent lobsters which were very plentiful in the vicinity. As for the woodland above, according to all accounts of the day there was no check upon the complete abundance provided by a prolific Nature, for the woods sustained a great variety of vegetation in addition to an abundance of wild life.

Rhinelander, Prime, Schermerhorn, Ricker, Astor—all had lovely summer homes within site of the river. Yet, today, the Gracie House is the only reminder left of these erstwhile tenants of Yorkville. John Jacob Astor had his house on Eighty-eighth Street. Washington Irving was a frequent guest there, staying sometimes as long as a month. Oh! For days of yore when life was so simple that one could afford month-end guests! Even today the rich cannot afford more than a weekend guest; not so much a problem of money as it is of commodities. Now, in these days of scarcities and dwindling food supplies, a week-end guest is a problem; but when these eminent merchants spent their summers in

Yorkville in dignified opulence, it was very common to have visitors remain for months at a time.

There is no doubt but what Irving found his stays at Yorkville pleasant interludes for his letters frequently make reference to enjoyable days at Astor's Eighty-eighth Street residence as well as to agreeable visits to the Gracie House.

Nathaniel Prime, whose town house was at Number One Broadway, had his summer villa on Eighty-ninth Street and Avenue A. Prime is said to have initiated his career as a coachman for William Gray, the Boston merchant who loaned him enough money to start a small brokerage business. Prime was a very shrewd investor although there were times when he was fooled. They tell the story of his buying a beautiful spotted horse, but at the first rainfall the spots disappeared, being disintegrated and blending with the rain, running off the horse's flanks to the chagrin of the crafty Prime who had so obviously been fooled. Prime, according to Barrett, did not "do unto others as he would have done unto him." Barrett relates that at a dinner party Prime made the remark that "If I had $5,000, I could invest it tomorrow in a manner that would enable me to double the sum inside of a year."

"What security can you give me, Mr. Prime, if I lend you the sum named?" a Georgian planter asked.

"The word of an honest man," said Mr. Prime.

Prime got the money and was as good as his word for within a year he did double it and was able to return the sum with interest to the confiding Georgian. Years later, the planter found himself in straightened circumstances and applied to Prime for a loan of the same amount he had handed Prime years before. After listening to the difficulties which had beset his erstwhile benefactor, Prime is said to have asked, "What security can you give?" The Georgian planter replied, "The word of an honest man." Prime said, "That will not pass in Wall Street," and refused the loan. As a result the planter became a beggar.[4]

Though he was one of the wealthiest men of the city, Prime in later years became obsessed with the idea that he was losing his money. Laboring under this delusion, the old man cut his throat with a razor receiving wounds from which he immediately succumbed. At the time of his death, Prime's Yorkville estate alone consisted of 130 acres showing that old Nat had made great strides since the time he served as coachman to William Gray. It must be remembered, in this connection, that such rise to affluence was not unusual in those days inasmuch as it was a time in which the common man, by dint of sound judgement, perseverance and a small initial captial, was fast rising above his less fortunate brothers.

All these former Yorkvillites had fine villas yet today these old homes, with the exception of the Gracie House, have gone to the "happy-hunting-ground" of old houses and in there stead appears the modern Yorkville, replete with its many beer gardens, each of which possesses jute boxes from which issue militant airs and Viennese waltzes. There is no time for wool gathering on the verandas of the old Yorkville mansions for not only have the old estates disappeared—the very land itself has been monopolized by divers enterprises. Foremost of these is the wonderful Rockefeller Institute for Medical Research. Located on part of the ground formerly owned by the Schermerhorn family, the Institute extends along the East River from Sixty-fourth to Sixty-eighth Street.

In order to make way for the Institute, it was necessary to demolish one of New York's venerable mansions, the home of George Clinton who was first Governor of New York. It is said that during the summer of 1783 George Washington paid a visit to the house at which time he occupied a large room commanding a grande view of the East River.[5]

The Rockefeller Institute for Medical Research was founded in 1901 by John D. Rockefeller. Its objects are to encourage and assist research in hygiene, medicine, surgery and allied subjects. Its achievements in these fields have accomplished much to promote the advancement of science especially in that which pertains to cure and prevention.

The Gracie House is still intact. It stands near the northern extremity of Carl Schurz Park at Eighty-eighth Street overlooking the East River and not far away from the terrible Hell Gate so dreaded by the early Dutch. The bottom of Hell Gate was later blown up by the Government and now its turbulent swirling waters live only in annals of former years. Nearly all distinguished visitors to New York were guests at the House and it was more or less a rendevouz for East River society of a hundred and fifty years ago. Josiah Quincy, who was Gracie's guest in 1805 wrote, "The mansion is elegant, in the modern style, and the grounds laid out with taste in gardens."[6] The Gracie House did not suffer the fate of several New York homes of the pre-Revolutionary period. It was fortunate in this respect as it passed to owners who appreciated the gracefully planned interior and who preserved the colonial building until it finally came into the hands of the Museum of the City of New York in 1923. The Museum had the building repaired in 1927 and in 1934 it was restored as part of the program of the Department of Parks, which after painstaking research had carefully furnished the interior with fine old colonial pieces and then opened the Scotch merchant's former summer villa as a Museum.

213

Visitors to the Museums were few, however, and so, as the Department of Parks states: "... no justification was apparent for wasting thinly spread funds in an unsuccessful competition with the finer exhibits in other large city Museums.[7] It was then restored and set into service as the Mayor's official residence.

The house contains nine rooms and has been renovated to include accommodations for servants in the basement. In restoring the villa great care was taken to maintain its original simplicity and charm and at the same time make certain concessions which its use as a modern home would necessitate. This latter improvement entailed installing central heating and plumbing facilities. From the outside the Mayor's official residence presents a graceful appearance—dignified in its new coat of white paint as it sits upon a little knoll from which one commands an excellent view of the busy East River.

Carl Schurz Park in which Gracie House is located, was named after the Great German Revolutionary who was a close friend of Lincoln. Schurz served his adopted country in many distinguished capacities. He was Minister to Spain and a Major General in the Union Army under the Lincoln Administration while under President Hayes he served as Secretary of the Interior.

The Park consists of twelve and one half acres containing a large playground, a wading pool, some prominades and a few little informal sitting areas where people from the neighborhood may still enjoy what remains of the old surroundings of Gracie House. You see them sitting on benches watching the river traffic plow up and down the river. You see them strolling about the Park; you see them just sight-seeing as I was. If their thoughts ever hearken back to the times of Archibald Gracie their reverie is soon dispelled by the sharp blast of a coal barge or the spiel made by the guide as the "round Manhattan" tour passes and all heads turn in unison to see the Mayor's residence.

Third and Lexington Avenues are two of Yorkville's main north-south arteries. First and Second Avenues also come in for due prominence but for sheer conservativeness and an atmosphere distinctly savoring of the ultra-elite, one must turn to East End Avenue which is strictly residential, especially in the stretch fronting Carl Schurz Park. The most important transverse streets are considered to be Eighty-sixth, Seventy-second and Fifty-ninth Streets. The numbered avenues, especially Third, are the domicile of more antique shops than can justly be visited in a year of Sundays. There are some blocks where every other store sells antiques and these range all the way from purveyors of rare pieces to those who are disposing of Mrs. Murphy's old parlor set. This is an interesting aspect of modern Yorkville which came into prominence only after the establishment of Sutton Place. As soon as the rich started reclaiming the area around the base of Queensborough Bridge and taking up their residences in the reclaimed slums, enterprising antiquarians sprang up in the vicinity like mushrooms after a continued rain. Here they found a ready market for their wares and even though the Colonel's Lady and Mrs. O'Grady were neighbors, the bait dangled by the antique shops was exclusively for the benefit of the Colonel's Lady. Exclusive pieces change hands across these Yorkville counters and in keeping with the merchandise, the prices at times are just as exclusive.

Third Avenue is the habitat of a typical New York custom, probably indigenous inherited from the Indians who fared so badly with Peter Minuit's bargaining. "Rummage Sales" are in progress all along the Avenue. A couple of dollars will pick up a worn gown or costume which may have cost a hundred dollars. Usually, these pieces seem so worn out and soiled, like the old Bowery bum who "may have seen better days" that the on-looker wonders how buyers are ever found for such articles. Yet, one will see a faded yellow white net gown, cut according to the latest 1919 fashion, carelessly flung into one corner of the shop window, only to pass the next day and find that it is gone. Who buys such articles? Surely anyone who has use for an evening gown can afford a new one! But this is one of the most perplexing mysteries of Yorkville, and who killed cock-robbin would be a fitting mate for this conundrum. Rummage sales will produce such a conglomeration of old shoes, family photographs, articles picked up by Cousin Abner when he went abroad, clothing of old vintages, and such miscellaneous junk as ever graced a cob-webbed attic. And markets are found for all these items! That is one of the strangest things about life with the "four million," for these oddities not only find buyers but they yield sufficient profit to keep the rummage sale operators in business.

Modern Yorkville also produces an occasional Gypsy family wending its carefree way into the section. Usually it will be of the Hungarian or one of the Slavic races as the Gypsy tends to set up his camp amongst the people from whence he originally hailed. Thus, a Hungarian Gypsy lives amongst Hungarians, a Russian Gypsy amongst Russians, and so on. This tendency is particularly noticeable in Manhattan where there is a marked inclination to separate into ethnological groups. As a general rule, the Gypsies prefer the lower East Side and a section of Spanish Harlem, but there are times when they are to be encountered lending color and a mysterious quality of romance to Yorkville. Give them an empty store, a few gay pieces of material to use for curtains, and the phrenological chart to hang in the window, and they are all set to tell your fortune by one of several means they employ. They will read the cards, your palm or even the bumps on your head—all with equal complacency. The women Gypsies do the fortune telling and this is the extent of their labor since their housekeeping problems are practically non-existent. The men do no work at all unless they absolutely have to. Traditions and customs of their race are instilled into the young ones and all speak the native Romany tongue, in addition to many others which they may have acquired during the course of their travels.

A few weeks later, or even days, and a tailor rents the shop, or a shoemaker takes over and the Gypsies are gone. So is some of the color from Yorkville and maybe some easy earned cash. In the winter they subsist on home relief augmented by the proceeds derived from fortune telling, but when summer arrives they take to the open road and live as best they can according to their wits. They may never return again for a Gypsy's wanderings takes him all over and seldom does he return to the same place. He may revisit a city but it is unlikely that he will stop in the same neighborhood.

Beer gardens and German restaurants have helped make the Yorkville quarter very popular but I know some who would add another outstanding feature of the former little hamlet, that is, the tendency of pork stores to congregate in the neighborhood. Very few other cities can boast the quantity of pork stores as are established in Yorkville. Ask a Washingtonian where the nearest pork store is and his only reply will be a perplexed look which would be repeated in many good-sized American cities. But in Yorkville the pork stores are an integral part of the neighborhood as much as the "rathskellers" or the delicatessens. Just to scent the strong odor of freshly smoked hams and shoulders and to picture show cases replete with succulent slices of Canadian bacon, liverwurst, ham bologna, etc. overwhelms the absent New Yorker with pangs of nostalgia for the things typical of his native city—things which may not seem very wonderful while he is there to enjoy them, but once he is away from home, however insignificant they may be, they take on a glow and he recalls them with nostalgic longing. Many pork stores also sell "unglamorized" potato salad. This depends only upon onions, salt, pepper, vinegar and oil for a flavor which would be spoiled by the addition of mayonnaise, a deplorable habit which even good cooks employ nowadays.

All this is one side of Yorkville—the Avenues A, B, First, Second and Third where three and four storey tenements provide homes for thousands of people who patronize the grocery stores, barber shops, saloons, pork stores, junk and oddity shops, etc. over which they live. This is the part of Yorkville where the Central European character is most prominent—where moving pictures are exhibited in foreign tongues, where menus are in native languages, where the very air is filled with music so different from the jitter-bugging sounds of other parts. This is the modern Yorkville—a sanctuary to which the eminent merchants of "New York Town" retired for the summer. This is the Yorkville where heavy trucks make up the greater part of the traffic; where an obsolete "el" still rumbles over Third Avenue. This is the section where, though it is modern in some senses, ice is still delivered to many of the tenements and the ice man remains an integral part of the community. Though Lexington Avenue is included in the district, its expensive shops and many storied apartment houses, neither lend nor suggest the atmosphere emitted by its more colorful, but poorer, neighbors.

A new entity is emerging from the old Yorkville. Trolley cars are giving way to buses and the First and Second Avenue "els" have yielded their places, the structures already having been demolished. People who were born and raised in Yorkville are buying their own homes in Long Island and Brooklyn. Entire blocks of rat infested tenements are being razed to make way for improved living quarters. A new Yorkville is in the offing, rising out of the old. This new Yorkville suggests neither the stopping off place on the Boston Post Road where people only lingered long enough to change horses, nor the village of summer manor houses erected by prosperous merchants of Post Revolutionary days. Few of its present day tenents care to hearken back that far, yet, there is a slightly European flavor pervading the vicinity and in this instance, even though it is overpopulated and even though the pace has been somewhat accelerated by time, Yorkville retains some of the characteristics of old.

CHAPTER NOTES

1. Dooley, Rev. Patrick Joseph, "Fifty Years in Yorkville or Annals of the Parish of St. Ignatius Loyola and St. Lawrence O'Toole" p. 5, 6.
2. Ibid., p. 10.
3. Mines, Flavel, "A Tour Around New York and My Summer Acre," p. 238.
4. Barrett, Walter (J. A. Scoville), "The Old Merchants of New York City," Series I, p. 11, 12.
5. "The New York Sun" for October 18, 1903, Section II, p. 3 c. 4.
6. Lamb, Martha, "History of the City of New York," Vol. II, p. 520.
7. Brochure released by the Department of Parks, New York City, May 21, 1942.

View of Yorkville, East 80's, ca. 1885

CHAPTER TWENTY-ONE

Harlem

*"Harlem has a black belt where darkies
dwell in a heaven where white men seek a
hell."*

Alfred Kreymborg "Harlem"

UUQUESTIONABLY, the capital of Negro America is Harlem. It is the Mecca to which negroes gravitate from every far off corner of the earth. Once there, they become part of that black symphony which at time resolves itself into a harmonious grouping of melodious chords; sometimes gay, yet on other occasions so poignant as to render the tune disagreeable. There are instances when the very intensity with which the down beat is struck makes one want to cry out at the sufferings which the race has endured, for no man with an iota of justice in his heart can condone the treatment which the blacks received during earlier history. One asks oneself how it is possible that there is still room for laughter in a heart which, by the white man's standard of measurement, should be a vale of tears. But laughter and an inherant quality of optimistic conformity have been the American negro's richest possession. On these he has progressed. On these characteristics, coupled with education and ambition, he is building his Harlem—his capital of the black world. He is combating superstition and ignorance through education; he is fighting the diseases which decimate his race by providing healthful, sanitary living conditions; he is instilling in his young the desire to progress.

All this not without a struggle for there are many obstacles to overcome and many sour notes to strike out of the black symphony before Harlem can emerge as a creditable captial of the black world. It is still too young, it is still suffering from growing pains. It must be allowed to solve its own destiny in its own manner, presenting, as it does, a problem different from any faced by Manhattan in the various vicissitudes through which this island has passed.

To say that Harlem is unlike any other part of Manhattan would be an understatement. The fact is that it is totally different from any other part of New York; in thought, in habits, in ethnological groupings and in several other ways. It does not reek of tradition and respectable senility like Washington Square and Gramercy, nor cast gigantic shadows of the future New York like Midtown Fifth Avenue: it just goes humbly along in its own tawdry way, the background for an estimated negro population of 298,365. These lives may not be glamorous but they certainly constitute the real Harlem. The streets are of little consequence, the buildings of less. It is the inhabitants who are the primary elements entering into the composition of the true Harlem.

This brings one to the all important factor of the black belt's composition. While it is true that Harlem is mainly black, one must not lose sight of the fact that these negroes may have come from many different countries: they may have hailed from French Africa or Haiti, the British West Indies, Ethiopia as well as from our own St. Helena, Alabama or any other southern state. They came from all over the world converging upon Harlem—people though all the same color in varying hues, nevertheless possessing different characteristics. It was like a current which swept all before it in the rush to its whirlpool. On Lenox Avenue one may hear a southern drawl reminiscent of ante bellum days only to be confronted on the next corner by two West Indians speaking as British as Sherlock Holmes himself. In Harlem all these people of diverse ethnological backgrounds had to be absorbed by the native New York negro and welded into an amalgamous mass, a process which is still taking place, not without friction and difficulties for Harlem maintains its own class separation.

The reasons which brought these people to Harlem were manifold. The accompanying economic and industrial changes which ushered in the present century had their far reaching effect upon the migration of negroes to the Harlem area. Those who were dissatisfied with conditions in the south travelled north where they hoped to find political and social freedom. Those New York negroes who had already established themselves in Harlem prior to 1910 were soon joined by the many southern negroes. But it was not until World War I that the general invasion of Harlem began. Immigration was virtually at a standstill and the demands of war industries were augmented by the lack of man-power. It was the negro's opportunity to improve his status and he took advantage of the higher wages offered him. The trek to Harlem was on. The southern negro came with his genial good humor;

those who were employed in various industrial work on the Atlantic seaboard migrated to Harlem. To these were added large numbers of West Indians who contributed their business acumen to the community. Then there were Spanish speaking negroes from Latin America and even a few French speaking Haitians. They all established themselves in Harlem where it was hoped that the amalgamating process would soon cause them to be assimilated into the general population of this portion of Manhattan. Off hand, this might appear to be a simple matter, but even though the color of all these people may have been the same, they differed radically in characteristics and backgrounds.

Though most people think of Harlem as being the black belt of Manhattan, guide books point out that actually there are three Harlems. These they designate as Spanish Harlem, Italian Harlem and Negro Harlem. Roughly, the boundaries of the three Harlems are from East Ninety-sixth Street to the East River, then all the way up to One Hundred and Fifty-fifth Street on the north between Morningside Avenue and the Harlem River. This is a huge section of Manhattan Island, but, as its division implies, it houses in addition to the negro population of the city, large numbers of Latin Americans and scores of Italians. It is a little known fact that Harlem consists of these three divisions as most people have come to associate the name with the negro section of the city. In fact, when one mentions Harlem the mind conjures a composite picture of the negro's abode—from his elaborate residence on Sugar Hill clear down to the "Alabama Tavern" on Lenox Avenue, where he relaxes amidst the blatant tune of "Stormy Weather" issuing from the jute box. This is the Harlem most people have heard about. This is the famous Harlem of Manhattan.

The exact point at which Manhattan's black belt commences and ceases is actually of little importance, however, as it varies year by year, increasing its area as the population increases. I can remember when negro Harlem did not extend north as far as One Hundred and Twentieth Street; now the northern boundary is One Hundred and Fifty-fifth Street and it is growing yearly. One by one the streets were taken over by negro tenants. This is a continuous process so that the boundaries of Manhattan's negro belt must be always of an elastic nature.

Harlem is credited with being founded in 1658 by that far seeing Dutchman whose remains now lie in St. Mark's In-The-Bouwerie. When Peter Stuyvesant gave his blessing to the little community it was called Nieuw Haerlem (New Harlem) after the beloved homeland. The story surrounding the naming of Harlem is that when the question of a name arose, Governor Stuyvesant was petitioned by a committee each member of which desired that the new settlement be named after his native Dutch town. In order to avoid jealousy and resentment, Stuyvesant wisely decided to call the settlement New Harlem, inasmuch as no member of the committee could claim Harlem as his native town.[1]

On March 4, 1658 the Governor and his Council passed the ordance which brought New Harlem into being. This ordnance read: "The Director-General and Council of New Netherland hereby give notice, that for the further promotion of Agriculture, for the security of this island and the cattle pasturing thereon, as well as for the further relief and expansion of this City Amsterdam, in New Netherland, they have resolved to form a new Village or Settlement at the end of the island, and about the land of Jochem Pieter, deceased, and those which are adjoining to it. In order that the lovers of agriculture may be encouraged thereto, the proposed new Village aforesaid is favored by the Director General and Council with the following privileges: "There followed a series of privileges such as the quantity of land to be received, guarantee of protection, establishment of a ferry near the village, construction of a road, etc.[2]

Accordingly, on the 14th day of August, 1658, the first settlers of New Harlem broke the ground at the foot of One Hundred and Twenty-fifth Street and the Harlem River.[3]

Transportation was exceedingly difficult for these early pioneers due to the fact that the only means of reaching Harlem was by trail. But it attracted some settlers and land was cleared to make way for farms. A curious fact about this early settlement is that the majority of people were not of Dutch origin as one would naturally suppose, for we find that in 1661 at least one half the population consisted of French.[4] At the end of 1672 amidst great excitement and jubilation, a very crude wagon road was opened which passed through Haerlem. A monthly mail started to Boston which gave an added impetus to the progress of the little community.[5]

It grew in extent and in population but remained farmland for nearly one hundred and fifty years. It was noted for its delightful climate and because of its remoteness from the lower part of the island, which then was considered to be all ahustle and abustle with activity, people moved to Harlem to spend their summers. Mrs. Ella Graffin in her booklet "Reminiscences of Old Harlem" tells us that her family moved there so that a delicate brother could benefit by the country air.[6] It was a great farm section where rich fertile earth produced good crops. James Roosevelt, President Franklin D. Roosevelt's great-grandfather owned the land east of Fifth Avenue between what is now One Hundred and Tenth Street and One Hundred and Twenty-fifth Street which he used as farm land. In 1825 this parcel was sold for $25,000.[7] In the 1850's and 1860's Harlem consisted of beautiful summer homes surrounded by well kept gardens. Not a trace remains in

221

Harlem of this earlier role, giving credence to the off repeated statement that New Yorkers are prone to disregard the past.

This is essentially true in Harlem, where there appears to be no past and a future to which only scant consideration is given by the majority of Harlemites. There is only the ominous present—the daily grind and struggle for existence which seems to be more intense in Harlem than in other sections. But no matter how drab the present may be, it is always relieved by the geniality of the Harlemites, for the inhabitants of Harlem always manage to see the brighter side of things.

Harlem has its poorer sections where vice and the underworld hold sway, but it also has its influential sections where the rich reside in luxury. Contrasting with all its "hot spots" where entertainment of a variety which sometimes has to be of the "off-the-record" sort is freely supplied, are the places where intellectual negroes meet to discuss the problems confronting their race. Compensating for every fakir and for every swindler who prey upon the gullible Harlemites, one has only to read of doctors, lawyers, teachers, nurses and journalists whose work in their respective fields shall always be a credit to Harlem.

Those successful Harlemites reside over on Edgecomb Avenue, locally known as "Sugar Hill." There, in well kept apartments one part of Harlem looks down upon the other, for the windows fronting Edgecomb Avenue command a view of all Harlem. Emphasizing the affluence of "Sugar Hill" are the expensive automobiles always found lining the curb. Directly in front is the playground which contains a swimming pool, spacious game courts, and in the summer time that so necessary escape from drabness into green surroundings. "Sugar Hill" is to Harlem what "Knob Hill" is to San Francisco or "Beacon Hill" to Boston: aristocratic, cultured, perhaps affluent; the pinnacle to which those below aspire. It is the Park Avenue of Harlem with its luxurious apartments and their well-to-do occupants. Every Harlemite's dream is to reside on "Sugar Hill."

Though negroes have lived in New York City since its settlement, as the records of 1628 show there were negro slaves in New Amsterdam[8] it was nearly three hundred years before they "discovered" Harlem. This came about as the result of the negro problem of securing better housing. Until recent times, even at this date, the negro has always been allotted the poorer paying jobs. This economic situation required that his home be the cheapest he could locate. West Fifty-third Street used to be the center of negro activity, but when this section became too crowded the trek to Harlem began. This was about 1910. The Lenox Avenue subway had not yet been constructed, so that transportation facilities to the east of Lenox Avenue were very poor. As landowners

222

were finding it difficult to rent their property, they accepted negro tenants. This move was fostered by negro realtors.

Here the colored tenant found better housing facilities than he had ever known, and though often there was friction between the white and colored residents, the section of Harlem was gradually released to the new arrivals. During the war there was a general invasion of Harlem.

With such an influx of immigration, it was not surprising that within a few years Harlem became overpopulated. Congregated in an area of two square miles the greatest part of New York's 500,000 negroes live in overcrowded tenements and remodeled private homes. Harlem is one of the most densely populated regions in the world. The City Planning Committee in its 1935 survey found the most densely populated street in Harlem to be between One Hundred Forty-second and One Hundred Forty-third Streets from Lenox to Seventh Avenues. In this city square block there were housed at that time 3,871 souls which corresponds to the population of many a rural village.

So pressed are the Harlemites even for sleeping space that many beds are occupied by two tenants; one who sleeps by day and a second occupant who rents the same bed by the night. In 1916 it was estimated that every house in Harlem contained at least forty people, and overcrowded conditions prevalent there today would no doubt reveal an even greater number.

When people are herded together in close quarters lacking even the elementary factors conducive to sound minds and bodies, it is to be expected that public health is not of the best grade. The rapid accumulation of so many people in such limited space was not without its accompanying assortment of problems. Education facilities had to be provided, health centers had to be planned and set up: there was a dire need for the services of trained social workers to meet the special needs of the large percentage of those who were maladjusted to their surroundings. In establishing such aids as the new community should require, consideration had to be given to the fact that all the people who flocked to Harlem were not of the city: they were recruited from agricultural regions of the south; some came from the West Indies and Cuba; some were holders of college degrees while others were illiterate. All these factors had to be considered in setting up any community assistance. Harlem was transformed into a seething melting pot from which it was hoped that the mass would be amalgamated into healthy, useful citizens. With such limited facilities as the community actually did provide, it was a hopeless task and one is led to wonder that the results were not worse than they really were.

Mortality among the negro population of New York City is exceedingly high, while infant mortality is nearly twice as high as that for

223

the rest of Manhattan. Tuberculosis among negroes is more active than it ever was in the old tenement days of the lower East Side. This fact was greatly emphasized when the Federal Emergency Relief Administration began its activities in Harlem. Harlemites were found virtually starving, a condition brought about not only by the catastrophic depression, which left devasting results in the poorer sections of every large city in the United States but it was also produced as a result of the tendency to discriminate, it being commonly known that in times of depression the negro is the first to lose his job.

Because Harlem is so over-populated, rents have grown disproportionately higher than in any other part of the city. Rooms that would rent for forty dollars a month elsewhere, cost at least ten dollars more a month in Harlem. This is as true today as it was before the negro invasion of Harlem began. Forty years or so ago the negro inhabited that portion of Manhattan below Twenty-third Street on the West Side. Thus we find: "We have a tenement on Nineteenth Street, where we get $10 for two rooms which we could not get more than $7.50 for from white tenants previously."⁹ But, one is led to inquire, how can the average negro worker afford to pay such high rentals? Very simple. First, there is the expedient of having many people share the same apartment or room, thus reducing expenses. This, of course, leads to the overcrowded conditions generally found prevailing throughout Harlem. Then, there is another method of meeting the rent, which, though not so common nowadays, was very much in use during the 1930's. That was the "Rent Party."

When the time approaches for the rent collector's visit, the tenant very complacently invites all of his friends to a "Rent Party." Everyone admitted must pay a set admission fee, the aggregate sometimes reaching beyond the necessary amount needed to meet the rent. A good time is had by all, the landlord is satisfied, the host is assured of another month's lodging, while the guests have had good entertainment at little cost. "Rent Parties," originally devised due to necessity, have been discovered by many Harlemites as an expeditious way to pay their rent and at the same time enjoy themselves.

So acute has the negro housing problem become that the Federal Government has given its consideration to alleviating the condition. The Harlem River Houses, a P.W.A. Project, was the first step in this direction, for on the banks of the Harlem River is a giant apartment house constructed according to the latest methods of sanitary housing where three rooms may be had for twenty dollars. The building consists of five units and provides modern housing facilities for 574 families. When news of the project was first published, 11,000 applications for rooms came pouring in. Here, surrounded by green gardens, and in

224

rooms where the sun can really be seen, it is hoped that the negroe's chance for health and contentment will be far greater than it has ever been.[10]

Remedying the housing situation is one visible improvement in conditions in Harlem. However, for the most part the average white "out-of-towner" never really sees the true Harlem. He is never entirely able to penetrate beneath the veneer which he thinks is Harlem, or for that matter, to even scratch its surface. Usually the visitor is sidetracked by a few night clubs and perhaps a walk up Lenox Avenue where he is impressed by the number of orators who, with a step ladder for a rostrum, originate, discuss and settle myriads of unimportant questions.

However, real New Yorkers know that although externally it presents a dismal appearance, life in Harlem is not too drab. This is due more to the inhabitants rather than to the environment, as most negroes are happy and cheery regardless of their surroundings. Very seldom does one see a negro suffering from melancholia. This does not mean that they are not affected by the dolorous and tragic events which come into everyone's life. It means, rather, that the negro, with his simple philosophy is able to overcome such happenings and to relegate them to the back of his mind, thus removing the possibility of such troubles assuming gigantic proportions. In my opinion, this quality is a great asset and one which has done much to sustain the negro race over difficult periods in its history.

No matter how late it is one never finds the streets wholly deserted. In truth, the visitor receives the impression of a city where no one sleeps. The fact is that in this part of New York there reside two shifts of workers. There is a large army of workers employed in daily occupations, but there is also a vast number of night workers. This latter group, coupled with those who are out to enjoy themselves constitute the number of people one encounters throughout the Harlem night.

One Hundred and Twenty-fifth Street is the nucleous of activity in Harlem as well as a pivotal point in Uptown Manhattan. It contains the leading shops and theatres of the district. On the west end of the thoroughfare is the ferry to New Jersey, while on the east end is situated one of the arms of the Tri-Borough Bridge. Between these two ends One Hundred and Twenty-fifth Street runs, a seething teeming center of motion. In the day time it is the shopping district, but when night falls it becomes transformed into Harlem's amusement world, in short, an Uptown Great White Way. And night life in Harlem can be very gay. Cabarets, theatres, movie houses and burlesque shows beckon the passerby to see "the finest show in Harlem."

In most theatres nearly all colored help are employed and on the stage the cast consists of colored stars supported by a bevy of dusky

225

chorines. Many dances are originated by these Harlem "stompers"—it is no exaggeration to say that most of the newer dance steps are born north of One Hundred Twenty-first Street. Although the Big Apple owes its inception to a Columbia, S.C. church dance, it remained for dancers at the Savoy Ballroom in Harlem to give it enough momentum to speed it into the dance craze of 1937. A combination of the Suzycue, Charleston and Trucking, the Big Apple was just an example of what Harlem can do with a dance when it really "goes to town."

Amateur Night in the Apollo is a unique feature of Harlem's night life. The contestant is required to "suzycue" over to the microphone then do his act. If he does not live up to expectations the audience is not long in revealing the fact. It is then the duty of the stage manager, Puerto Rico, to shoot the offender with blank cartridges, to the uttermost delight of the audience. On the other hand, when a performer is good the audience perform with him, stamping their feet to the rythymical beat of the orchestra and from time to time shouting a "Yeah, Man" or a "Swing in there, Boy!" The audience shout back and forth to one another and comment to their neighbors, just as though they had all been properly introduced. They become like one big happy family.

Another very great socializing force in Harlem are its churches; the negroe's innate craving for religion is evident throughout the sector. One finds churches all about the neighborhood. All denominations are represented including effanescent sects never heard of before they appeared in Harlem. At one time there were one hundred and sixty churches in the district, many of doubtful origin. They are located in apartments, furnished rooms and even in vacant stores. According to Mr. James Weldon Johnson at least one hundred of these churches could be closed without inflicting any serious damage upon the religious life of the community, as the majority are fakirs preying upon the hardworking negro who supports them.[11] It may readily be seen, therefore, that religion in Harlem is of two kinds; that which presupposes adherance to accepted creeds or denominations and that which professes belief in the unorthodox. Fortunately, this last is the minority group notwithstanding that the percentage of adherants is calculated to be relatively high. This includes the practice of voodooism, hoodoism and many other "isms."

One reads, shudderingly, of voodooism in Haiti and some parts of Africa: yet voodooism and conjurism still exist in Harlem. Picture a dimly lighted room over on Lenox Avenue furnished in the modern style, including radio and refrigerator and the latest mechanical devices where a conjure doctor grimly exhorts his followers to take part in primitive African rites—sacrifices which many people believe confined to the jungle and not taking part in a civilized metropolis like New

York City. Here you have a throwback to darkest Africa, land of mysticism, of superstition, a land where voodooism was, and still is, as indigenous as the African soil. Miraculous cures are promised, many negroes consulting their conjure doctors before a licensed physician is called. This is one of the greatest evils of Harlem, creating a condition which the police find it difficult to control. It is estimated by a reliable negro doctor that at least 30% of Harlem's population practice some sort of hoodoism.[12] Such a percentage is not an overestimate, for the police will tell you that almost every negro prisoner searched carries some sort of charm or amulet as a protection against evil forces. Magic powders and miraculous roots and herbs are sold openly at fantastic prices. Thus religion goes rampant in Harlem where some will pay as high as five dollars for a ten cent box of supposedly sacred or lucky incense.

As a general rule, though, the majority of Harlem negroes are solid Baptists or Methodists, devout and serious in their beliefs. A curiously interesting fact in connection with religious sects of this district is that it harbors a group of very little publicized negro Jews. There are an estimated 3,500 negroes professing this faith and they are located principally in Harlem. Around 900 of this number are Phalasians or Falashas. According to this latter sect, they are the only real Jews since they claim to trace their descent back to the union of Solomon and the Queen of Sheba.[18] The negro Jews of Harlem maintain two synagogues, The Commandant Keeper's Congregation at Eighty-seven West One Hundred Twenty-eighth Street and another synagogue located at One Hundred and Sixteenth Street.

On the other hand, a group which has received wide publicity during the course of the last few years are the Divinists. As the name implies, these are followers of Father Divine, whose rise to his present standing has been nothing short of phenomenal. Some years ago the self-styled Father Divine was known as George Baker in the South from whence he hailed. He and his wife took over a house at Sayville, Long Island from where they dispensed such services as the operation of a free employment agency and clothing and feeding the needy. When he signed the deed on the little house in Sayville, George Baker had become "Major J. Devine," thus starting the career which, aside from whether or not one agrees with his precepts, has served to raise the erstwhile George Baker to one of the most spectacular religious leaders among his race. The "Major" was soon replaced by "Reverend" and the "e" changed to "i" and Baker had become the fabulous Father Divine.[14] Today, Divine is one of the most influential men in Harlem. He is spiritual leader to hundreds of negroes and whites, not only in Harlem, but throughout the world. He operates seventeen Peace Missions in New York City, has

227

branches in twenty-five states and correspondents in Australia, Hawaii, Canada, Switzerland, England, Panama and the British West Indies. According to his own statement, this is only a partial list of "Father's connections," because the exact number is unknown.[15]

The Mission owns several parcels of real estate and operates a variety of enterprises. The past decade has seen a definite rise to affluence and influence of the former George Baker, yet, the source of his wealth is as mysterious as the disappearance of Judge Crater. Where the funds come from no one has been able to ascertain, but Father Divine explains it thus: "The Spirit of the conscious of the Presence of God is the Source of all Supply, and it will satisfy every good desire." Or again, "Aren't you glad! Everything automatically comes. To me it is attracted and drawn and it shall be throughout all eternity."[16]

To his followers Father Divine is health, happiness, joy, peace, life, wealth and love.[17] His disciples abide by precepts which he dictates, even forsaking their proper names for such cognomens as "Faithful Mary," "New Heaven," "Patience Joy," "Love Joy" and various "Angels." The fabulous Father has coined lasting catch phrases like "Peace, it is wonderful" and "Aren't you glad" which are bywords throughout Harlem.

Today he ministers to the spiritual needs of thousands of adherents, whites and colored, alike, located in every corner of the globe. His dynamic personality has penetrated to places where he himself has never been. What strange anomaly of human nature impels these disciples to follow this little man, who, seemingly to offset his slight physique, capitalizes everything connected with himself? One can explain the rise of the Rockefellers, the Carnegies, and the Mellons, but Father Divine's success story involves a combination of inexplicable circumstances. Aside from the fact that he supplies an innate craving for religion, which is inherent in the negro race, there are other less tangible aspects connected with the Father's Peace Movement. There are other factors surrounded in mystery, notably the perennial question as to the source of the Mission's wealth. This vast supply of material goods, which neither dwindles nor disappears during depressions, baffles everyone who gives the matter a little thought, inasmuch as Father Divine has often declared: ". . . even as I refuse to accept compensation, remuneration, donations, take up collections in any of our public meetings anywhere or change fees, for MY Spiritual Work and Service to humanity."[18]

A few years ago when Father Divine was arrested, his followers swarmed to his defense. They claimed the law could not touch God, and when he was released all Harlem was jubilant and his One Hundred and Fifteenth Street Mission rang with the Hosannas and the joyful

Hallelujahs of his followers. God, seated in a Rolls Royce and accompanied by his staff of lawyers and prominent followers, rode triumphantly from the Tombs to his One Hundred and Fifteenth Street Mission.

Charlatan, Messiah or as "Faithful Mary" called him after their dispute, "the religious gigolo of Harlem," the dynamic Divine fulfills a specific need in Harlem and if the negroes did not have his Missions or "Heavens" to attend, there is no doubt but that in many instances they would spend their time and money in less wholesome manifestations.

One must not come to the conclusion that the residents of Harlem devote all their spare cash and talent to churches. Much attention is given to business enterprise and to the various arts. An appraisal made some years ago by a leading Harlem realtor, John E. Nail, placed negro land holdings in Harlem as reaching a value between fifty and sixty millions of dollars, a figure which would be relatively higher today in view of present values.[19] There have been instances where single fortunes amassed by enterprising Harlemites have reached astounding figures.

There was Pig Foot Mary, for instance, who, through her particular way of preparing pig's feet was enabled to purchase a five story apartment house.[20] Then there was the famous Mrs. C. J. Walker who popularized a negro beauty formula. The proceeds from this formula were so lucrative that until her death Mrs. Walker lived luxuriously in her own mansion at Irvington-on-the-Hudson.[21]

Of late, Harlem has made liberal contributions in the fields of art, music and the theatre. For a long time large deposits of latent artistic talent lay dormant in the negro race, but the last two score years have witnessed intense cultivation of this cultural reserve, Harlem playing a major role in its development. Racially, the negro is capable of keen artistic expression. This is as true in the fields of art and literature as it is in music and dancing. Harlem, as the center of negro activity in the United States stands out as the place where much of this latent ability is brought to the foreground. One has only to recall the phenominal success of Williams and Walker, or of Florence Mills, all of whose popularity has outlived them. Who can watch Bill Robinson perform his inimitable taps and not appreciate the part Harlem is playing in molding popular dances. There is Paul Robeson whose triumphant success in the title role of "Othello" is well remembered and Countee Cullen whose "Heritage" vibrates with all the power of race prejudice. Marion Anderson's voice is familiar all over America and in many other countries where this talented singer has given concerts. Cab Calloway and his orchestra brought Harlem's version of jazz into many homes, and so did the late Fats Waller, who originated his own style of piano playing

229

and singing. Art, music, and literature, Harlem is contributing in every field. It is supplying proponents to each branch; irrefutable evidence of the importance of the Harlemites in this formidable kaleidoscope of things that are New York.

CHAPTER NOTES

1. Shackleton, Robert, "The Book of New York" p. 270, 271.
2. Pierce, Carl Horton, "New Harlem — Past and Present," p. 14, 15.
3. Ibid., p. 1.
4. Wilson, James Grant, "Memorial History of New York," Vol. IV, p. 375.
5. Ibid., Vol. I, p. 355.
6. Graff, Mrs. Ella, "Reminiscences of Old Harlem."
7. Federal Writers' Project, "New York City Guide," p. 256.
8. Williams, George Washington, "History of the Negro Race in America," Chapt. XIII, p. 1.
9. Riis, Jacob A., "How the Other Half Lives," p. 151.
10. Federal Writers' Project, "New York City Guide," p. 394. "The New York Times," for August 19, 1937, p. 21, c. 6. "The New York Times," for August 27, 1937, p. 17, c. 8.
11. Johnson, James Weldon, "Black Manhattan," p. 163.
12. "New York World Telegram," for February 15, 1937, p. 17, c. 6.
13. Federal Writers' Project, "New York City Guide," p. 261.
14. Hoshor, John, "God in a Rolls Royce," p. 30, 31. Parker, Robert Allerton, "The Incredible Messiah," p. 4, 5.
15. "The New Day," for February 24, 1945 A.D.F.D., p. 46.
16. Ibid., p. 7, c. 1. Ibid., p. 8, c. 1.
17. Ibid., p. 11.
18. Letter from Father Divine to the author, dated April 4, 1945.
19. Johnson, James Weldon, "Black Manhattan," p. 154.
20. Ibid., p. 154.
21. Ibid., p. 282, 283.

Columbus Theatre, exterior photo, 114 E. 125 Street

CHAPTER TWENTY-TWO

Washington Heights

He comes! —the Genius of these lands—
Fame's thousand tongues his worth confess,
Who conquered with his suffering bands,
And grew immortal by distress.
  Philip Freneau, Occasioned by General Washington's
  Arrival at Philadelphia.

ALL Manhattan is richly associated with Washington, to such a
large measure that it would be difficult to ascribe major import
to any one particular locale. Yet, were one special spot to be dedicated
to the memory of the great general, it appears that the area to which the
name "Washington Heights" has been appropriately given would come
in for a high share in that honor. It was on this hilly portion of the infant city that Washington suffered his greatest defeat in the cause for
American independence—the loss of Fort Washington. It was here that
Washington and his soldiers, many of whom were untrained, were
routed by the British and after a most discouraging battle, the cream of
the American troops—nearly 3,000 in all—had to surrender the Fort.

Reminders of the Fort's existence are still to be found in the
neighborhood as occasionally the earth yields some mute evidence that
soldiers once tramped the ground. Old fashioned bullets, buttons from
soldier's uniforms and such objects as soldiers mess pieces, crockery,
etc. often have been unearthed in the vicinity. Several of these relics are
on view in the Jumel Mansion or Roger Morris House, as the Mansion
was known when Washington made it his headquarters. The site of Fort
Washington is today commemorated by a tablet which James Gordon
Bennett, the Empire State Society and the Sons of the American
Revolution have placed there. Bennett owned nearly half of the land

231

upon which the Fort was located. In 1903 he deeded it to the city in memory of his father and it is now known as Bennett Park. Part of the Fort, consisting of an irregular wall, has been reproduced in the Park—otherwise the scene of Washington's crushing defeat has been obliterated by the passing of years. Only Washington's name has remained to connect this place with early Revolutionary history.

The year the Fort fell was a disastrous one for the cause of American Independence. The Continentals sustained one loss after another until Fort Washington was the last American stronghold on Manhattan Island. But on November 16, 1776, after a terrific battle, this, too, fell to the British, whereupon Manhattan became an island of prisons. The conquerors found themselves with nearly 5,000 prisoners on their hands, however, little concern was given as to how to care for these charges, as the annals of that time show that the prisoners fared very badly. Every available public building in the city—churches, halls, warehouses—all were commandeered to imprison the men who had dedicated themselves to the then lost cause for liberty.

The men who had fought so assiduously for liberty were themselves deprived of the bare necessities of life. Conditions which prevailed in these prisons were such that General Washington himself protested to the British commanding officer. The records show that the General's complaints went unheeded for there were days when the sun never set until it had cast its final rays over a common grave into which dozens of bodies had been thrown. The old Sugar House and the prison ships yielded up their daily quota of victims. Prisoners died in such large numbers that there were mass burials, yet, to call them burials would be a desecration of that word. Whatever clothing the men were clad in at the time of their deaths was left on them and then their bodies were piled ignominiously into collective graves, oft times without the burial service. The foul hulks they called prison ships disposed of their dead in like manner. The Poet of the Revolution, Philip Freneau, was held prisoner on one of these prison ships. He has vividly described his sufferings in his poem "The Prison Ship" a few lines of which follow:

"Hail dark abode! What can with thee compare?
Heat, sickness, famine, death and stagnant air—
Swift from the guarded decks we rushed along,
And vainly sought repose—so vast our throng.
Three hundred wretches here, deny'd all light,
In crowded mansions pass th' infernal night.
Some for a bed their tattered vestments join,
And some on chests, and some on floors recline;
Shut from the blessings of the evening air,

232

Pensive we lay with mingled corpses there;
Meagre and wan, and scorch'd with heat below,
We looked like ghosts, are death had made us so."[1]

Some years later the bones of these nameless patriots were all re-interred in Trinity Churchyard at the head of Wall Street. Inscribed upon the stately Gothic monument which rises to their memory are the words:

"Sacred to the memory of
Those brave and good men who died
Whilst imprisoned in this city for their devotion to
The Cause of Independence."

Many patriots who were unfortunate enough as to be taken prisoner fell into the hands of the brutal provost marshal, Cunningham, of whom it is said that not content with allowing many prisoners to starve to death, he actually poisoned some, continuing to draw their rations which he sold. Cunningham, it will be remembered, was the same officer who tormented Nathan Hale, a fact for which he was censored by the Americans as well as by his British fellow-officers. Some years later a fate which had been long in approaching finally caught up with Cunningham. His day of reckoning came when he was convicted of forgery in London and executed. Before his execution he confessed to the murder of many prisoners who had come under his jurisdiction while he served as provost. Indeed, it was often his boast that he had disposed of more "rebels" than the King's Army.[2] It was of the events leading up to this phase of the Revolution that Paine wrote "These are the times which try men's souls." Paine's words remained true during the entire time of the Revolution for there were occasions when even the inclement weather seemed to favor the British.

Fort Washington played its part in these "times which try men's souls." The tragic memories of Washington's defeat, of the suffering endured by his soldiers and of their ultimate incarceration in prisons hastily set up by the British—are all part of this hilly region which to-day takes its name from the Fort and is known as Washington Heights. This section includes the district between St. Nicholas Avenue and the Hudson River from One Hundred and Thirty-fifth Street to Two Hundred and Twenty-fifth Street, notwithstanding the fact that the United States Ship Canal physically separates this upper portion from Manhattan. The entire tract is hilly—ascending and descending in all four directions. The terrain is so irregular that streets had to be laid out in conformity and so if one approaches Riverside Drive from downtown, it is necessary to travel uphill while the same is true to reach the easterly part of the district.

Years ago this then sylvan area of hilly woodland between One Hundred and Fifty-fifth Street and One Hundred and Fifty-eighth Street, from Broadway to the Hudson, was known as Carmansville. It is particularly of note that the famous naturalist, John James Audubon, established his family in this wooded area from which one could enjoy a superb vista of the Hudson. Many still recall that Audubon called the little region Minnie's Land—Minnie being the Scotch word for mother and the name by which he generally addressed his wife.

Audubon built two homes on the property and later his sons added to the number of Audubon houses in Minnie's Land. As the first one outlived its usefulness to the growing Audubon family, the naturalist constructed a newer and more pretentious home which adjoined the original house on the south. The first Audubon home was once the residence of Samuel F. B. Morse, and the basement contained a laboratory from which many early experiments in electrical transmission of messages took place. The Audubon property was known as Audubon Park. It contained around twenty-four acres extending from Tenth Avenue down to the river slope. One half of the property was level ground while the other formed a gradual slope in the direction of the river; a topographical feature which is indicative of that section even today.

It was in this thickly wooded area, filled with feathered friends of the great naturalist, that Audubon spent his final days. He enjoyed nothing more than the hours he passed roaming the vicinity to observe the habits and sounds of ornithological specimens. Usually Audubon took these walks before the other members of the family had risen. After breakfasting he would transfer the likenesses of the birds he had seen to canvass. Surrounded by his sons and grandchildren, his ever-faithful Lucy never far from his side, the failing naturalist thus enjoyed many happy days in Audubon Park, days which, as it turned out to be, just preceded the twilight of his life. As his sight and mind began to fail, his wife remained constantly by his side, until death took him from her.[3]

Late in life Audubon began selling small parcels of Minnie's Land, a procedure which was carried on by his heirs. It was not long, therefore, before the woods in which the famous ornithologist roamed in silent commune with the birds of which he was so fond, was converted into a settlement of many houses and the region which had yielded much material for Audubon's "Birds of America" became depleted of some of its specimens.

By 1890 many distinguished people had gravitated to the Park. This wooded region of an earlier day was a popular setting for cultured and

234

prominent men and women of the time. While the rest of New York was gay—for it was the "Gay Nineties"—Audubon Park attracted the intelligentsia of the city who found in this verdant spot an ideal place for the quieter pursuits of life. Strolling along its tree lined paths and streets, with an admirable view of the Hudson in the distance, these residents of fifty or sixty years ago enjoyed such tranquility as was unknown in the lower city.

Two years ago the "New York Sun" published some interesting letters concerning these former residents of Audubon Park. One of these letters, written by Charles Griffith Moses, furnishes a good account of the people who lived in the Park before the end of the last century. Mr. Moses writes:

"I can recall most of the families living in Audubon Park during the 1880s and 1890s: Charles Francis Stone, eminent lawyer, one of the firm of Davies, Stone & Auerbach, owned and occupied the original homestead. Killian Van Rensselaer, of the well-known Knickerbocker family, lived in the second house built by Audubon. The house to the north of the homestead was for many years the home of Eugene Jerome, whose very beautiful sister became the mother of the famous Winston Churchill."

"The next large house was known as the Stockwell house. Mrs. Stockwell was the daughter of Elias Howe, inventor of the sewing machine. Then came the Sheppard Knapp house at 158th street. These four houses took in the entire river front of the park except for two on the northerly side of 158th street, which, though not strictly in the park, were closely linked to it. One of these was built by William A. Wheelock and the other by William Foster. The latter was a prominent New York citizen who built and financed the Ninth Avenue Elevated Railway, the first elevated railway to be built in New York.

"Other owners and residents of the park were Charles H. Kerner, proprietor of the exclusive Clarendon Hotel on Union Square; Joseph and Harvey Ladew of Fairweather & Ladew, the leather tycoons of the time; Wellington Clapp; William Grinell and his son-in-law, Newell Martin, well-known lawyer and founder and first executive officer of the Title Guarantee & Trust Company.

"All the houses mentioned were outstanding, impressive mansions, surrounded by well-kept grounds and beautiful old elm trees. The smaller, but none the less attractive, villas, mostly on the slope of the hill and nearer to Broadway, were those of Edward P. Griffin, well-known leather merchant; Andrew Soulard, president of the German-American Title Company; Henry Hartman, Assistant District Attorney under Col. John R. Fellows; Irving Putnam of the publishing house; Royal S. Crane, lawyer; Honorable Seth Hawley, whose house

235

was built and presented to him by Commodore Vanderbilt; James G. Wilson, an Englishman who introduced the Venetian blind to America, and then, a little later, the artist Philipatoux, who painted the cyclorama, "The Siege of Gettysburg"; the Very Rev. Milo Hudson Gates, then rector of the Church of the Intercession and afterward Dean of the Cathedral of St. John the Divine; Walter Stabler, Comptroller of the Metropolitan Life Insurance Company, and Reginald Pelham Bolton, antiquarian and historian."[4]

Some of the culture of these former Audubonites has been transmitted to the present day neighborhood. It now possesses no less than five cultural establishments which are housed together in one group facing a common court opening on Broadway. They owe their inception to the generosity of Archer M. Huntington, a poet and scholar. Huntington used the fortune left him by his father, the railroad magnate, Colis P. Huntington, to establish not only these five museums, but eight others as well. The group represents the nation's most distinguished cultural societies and museums, comprising, as it does, the Museum of the American Indian, American Geographical Society, Hispanic Society of America, American Numismatical Society and the American Academy of Arts and Letters.

The Museum of the American Indian devotes itself solely to preserving cultural material relating to the aborigines of the Western Hemisphere. Among the exhibits on display are included a collection of shrunken human heads. The American Geographical Society which is the oldest geographical society in America contains a library of over 100,000 volumes together with a large number of atlases and maps from which those engaged in geographical research are permitted to work.

The Hispanic Society is devoted to promoting Spanish and Portuguese culture and in line with this project, it maintains a good-sized library of related material together with various exhibits such as sculpture, pottery, tiles and metal work to show the influence of various conquerors on Hispanic culture. It contains a very good collection of Spanish paintings among which such prominent painters as El Greco, Goya, Velásquez, Zuloaga and others are represented. Some very rare editions of Don Quixote and a sizeable collection of old manuscripts, treaties and other documents make the Hispanic an ideal place for the bibliophile.

The American Numismatic Society was established to preserve an interest in the art and history of coins. The American Academy of Arts and Letters limits its membership to fifty who are elected for meritorious achievements in the arts.

Modern Washington Heights includes every facility man could require from birth to death. If he needs medical attention the Columbia

Presbyterian Medical Center, a twenty acre site extending on Broadway from One Hundred and Sixty-fifth to One Hundred and Sixty-eighth Street is equipped and available to dispense some of the finest medical attention in the United States. Further downtown is City College. This seat of learning is as well known for its Lewisohn Stadium as it is for the wide range of subjects covered by its curriculum. The stadium offers popular priced concerts during the summer at which time it is a mecca for music lovers of the city. For those interested in baseball, the lower Heights houses the Polo Grounds and to completely furnish man's needs up to death, there is Trinity Church Cemetary for a final resting place. Thus are supplied the complete necessities for the span of a man's life.

A superficial glance at the Heights reveals it as a modern entity of Manhattan, yet, as in most sections of this fabulous isle, it possesses some landmarks or links between the past and the present. The Fort is practically a memory, but the Heights retains two old mansions where in contemplative reverie one may return to times before and after the Revolution. The Hamilton Grange and the Jumel Mansion are the oldest houses in this part of town. Hamilton Grange is now in a sad state of neglect, yet beneath its tarnished interior and its weather beaten exterior, the country manor house which Hamilton built still evinces vestiges of its former grandeur. No less an architect than McComb, who also worked on the plans for City Hall, designed this home for the First Secretary of the Treasury. When it was built, in 1802, it was two blocks further north, having been moved to its present site at 287 Convent Avenue in 1899. Timidly, it sets back from the Avenue, rendering an appearance of gloom as an apartment house blocks the light from one side and a church casts its shadow from the other. Despite its aspect of neglect, Hamilton's old home is in no sense dilapidated. It needs only a few coats of paint and some minor repairs to restore it to the lovely villa it was during Hamilton's day. Its illustrious builder once owned all the land from One Hundred and Thirty-eighth to One Hundred and Forty-fifth Street, and though it was very far out in the country at that time, Hamilton and his family occupied The Grange as a year-round residence. The Grange cost £1,550 to build, the great financier himself supervising many of the details in connection with construction.[5] In addition to his many other accomplishments, Hamilton is reputed to have had some knowledge of gardening. He had a hand in laying out the gardens surrounding The Grange, the thirteen gum trees which he planted on one side and in front representing the thirteen original states. These trees lived for many years and some of them even continued to thrive in the spot where Hamilton planted them long after The Grange had been removed.

237

The Hamiltons enjoyed a pleasant life at The Grange until that fatal day when the First Secretary of the Treasury went forth to Weehauken to stop the bullet aimed from Aaron Burr's gun. Mrs. Hamilton was a daughter of the distinguished old General Schuyler and when some of the Schuylers were not at The Grange, the Hamiltons could be found up in Albany visiting Mrs. Hamilton's family. It was from The Grange that Hamilton left to keep his disastrous encounter with Burr. He never returned.

Of a far more cheerful mien is the Jumel Mansion at One Hundred and Sixty-first Street east of St. Nicholas Avenue. It has an air of romance about it, too, and well it might. It is the perfect setting to which lovers of bygone days would have repaired to enjoy the magnificent view. As it is situated on a hill one could "command an extended view of the Hudson, of the East River, the Harlem River, Hell Gate and the Sound. In front is seen the city of New York, and the high hills on Staten Island, distant more than twenty miles. To the left are seen Long Island, Westchester, Morrisania, and the village of Harlem with its cultivated surrounding fields."[6] Visitors to Jumel Mansion today do not see the same scene. The Hudson is blocked from view by large apartment houses and the beauty which was the Harlem River is marred by gas tanks and chimneys which rear their ugly hulks skywards. The waterways are spanned by bridges and boast of a heavy traffic. Mme. Jumel, even in her later years, never looked down upon such a scene as one sees today! Yet, though the "cultivated village of Harlem" has become a thriving metropolis in itself, replete with all equipment of a city, the scene is still beautiful—in another sort of way. It represents the city, teeming with a people each of whom has his own personal problem. The vista pulsates with the hopes and woes of New York's millions; it hums with the sound of its mechanical devices, invented to make life easier but serving at the same time, to complicate and harass man's existence. Yes, the vista is still beautiful: in a mechanical sort of way.

The surroundings may have changed, but not so Jumel Mansion. It is as charming now as it was in 1765 when Col. Roger Morris built it. This fine old Georgian Colonial mansion is now owned by the city and operated as a museum under the asupices of the Daughters of the American Revolution. Here is a house with a definite personality. Entering it, one senses that this is a place where people of distinction once lived amidst the best to be had. Roger Morris who was the mansion's first occupant, had married into the eminent Philipse family, his wife being Mary Philipse. Mary Philipse Morris was reputed to have been very beautiful and well educated. Before her marriage to the British Colonel it is said that Washington was romantically interested

238

in her.[7] The story goes that Washington proposed and was refused but this has never been established as an historical fact. Col. Morris and Washington once served together under Braddock but when the break between England and the Colonies came, Morris cast his allegiance with the British. He fled to England and the handsome home was confiscated along with the rest of his property.

The Roger Morris house was used by Washington as his headquarters during the tedious days of the battle of Harlem Heights. The great general was probably beset by many worries during the time he occupied this house. In all likelihood, his memories of the place were far from pleasant. It comes more or less as a surprise, therefore, to find that shortly after becoming President he invited his cabinet members and their wives to a supper which was served at the Roger Morris House. It was a July day in 1790 when President Washington invited Vice President and Mrs. John Adams, Secretary of War and Mrs. Knox, Secretary of the Treasury and Mrs. Alexander Hamilton and Thomas Jefferson, who was then Secretary of State, to a picnic lunch at Fort Washington. It seems strange that Washington should have selected the site of such bitter recollections for his picnic. Stranger still is that after the picnic Washington and his guests drove over to the home where Mary Philipse Morris once presided as chatelaine. Here the supper was served. It must have been a day of memories for the Father of His Country but what those memories were—of disappointment and chagrin, gaiety, despair or triumph, no one will ever know, for historians do not tell. One can only conjecture on such matters.[8]

Jumel did not acquire the old Morris house until 1810. Stephen Jumel and his wife can best be described as an aspiring couple; she socially and he financially. They had interesting personalities and the French merchant had attained sufficient capital to indulge whatever outlets their personalities should pursue. The interest of both husband and wife apparently centered on the Roger Morris house. Fortunately, the Jumels had excellent taste. Each trip to Europe they acquired more beautiful pieces which were used to furnish the mansion. The former Roger Morris house became one of the elegant homes of the era. Possession of one of the most comfortable and tastefully furnished homes in New York, however, did not necessarily signify that the Jumels moved in the best circles. Many years were required before Madame was socially accepted in New York. The old established families looked askance upon her somewhat shady past and those who did cross the threshold did so more out of a sense of curiosity than of friendship for the hosts. It was not until after the couple went to Europe where they were entertained by royalty that New York society let down some of its barriers. Then the Jumels began to repay some of the hospitality they had received across the Atlantic. Prominent statesmen and members of royal families appeared at the estate in Washington Heights: life at the mansion centered on a very high plane. Housed with elegant furniture and objects d'art which the Jumels brought back from France, and frequented by the keenest intellects and most distinguished people of that time, the Jumel Mansion attained fame on both sides of the Atlantic as a place one had to visit in New York. Among its guests were Louis Philippe, Lafayette, Tallyrand, Joseph Bonaparte and Louis Napoleon.

Jumel died in 1832 and the erstwhile belle of New York's stage came into possession of the mansion and the grounds surrounding it. The widow Jumel, who had had three names before acquiring that of the French merchant, was not long in adding still another name to the growing list, for within a year along came Aaron Burr suing for the land of the wealthy widow. His dreams of empire dispelled in the far distant past, for he was then nearing his eightieth year, Burr pleaded his suit and the ceremony took place in the Jumel Mansion.

The odd pair were very ill matched: Madame Jumel was fifty six years old while Burr was not far from four score. The marriage was extremely unhappy. Burr, who all his life had had a way with women fared badly with the mistress of the Mansion. The marriage lasted but a year during which time Burr lived at the Jumel Mansion. There is a room on the second floor which he occupied and where his trunk and desk-table are displayed. Burr died in 1836 but the bride of his old age outlived him by twenty-nine years, passing on into final sleep in 1865.

The lady known successively as Betsy Bowen, Madame de la Croix, Eliza Brown, Madame Jumel and finally as Mrs. Burr had reigned as mistress of the famous Colonial Mansion for a period of fifty-five years, a period which embraced the progress of the infant republic from the War of 1812 until Civil War days. From her manor house in the Heights, Madame Jumel had witnessed the city of New York grow strong and robust under the administrations of twenty-two mayors.

Madame Jumel was buried within walking distance of her home, in Trinity Church Cemetary. This is the largest cemetary in Manhattan, more in keeping with a final resting place than that surrounding Trinity Church in Wall Street. Many distinguished people lie in eternal slumber in Trinity, notably John James Audubon to whom the surrounding ground was once as home and Clement C. Moore, the Chelsea poet who endeared himself to childhood by his poem "A Visit from St. Nicholas." The son of Charles Dickens is buried there and so are Astors, Van Burens, Schermerhorns, Bleeckers and many old Dutch families. The cemetary is divided into two parts by Broadway and runs

240

from One Hundred and Fifty-third Street to One Hundred and Fifty-fifth Street.

CHAPTER NOTES

1. Freneau, Philip, "The Prison Ship."
2. Ulmann, Albert, "A Landmark History of New York," p. 136.
3. "Life of John James Audubon," edited by his widow, p. 435-437.
4. Moses, Charles Griffith, in a letter to "The New York Sun," dated August 25, 1945, p. 6, c. 2.
5. Hamilton, Allan McLane, "Intimate Life of Alexander Hamilton," p. 344.
6. Shackleton, Robert, "The Book of New York," p. 272 (taken from an advertisement for the sale of the Roger Morris House which appeared in 1792.
7. Jenkins, Samuel, "The Greatest Street in the World," p. 318. Callander, James H., "Yesterdays in Little Old New York," p. 48.
8. Shackleton, Robert, "The Book of New York," p. 274.

WASHINGTON HEIGHTS — Washington's Headquarters, view north from "Death Gap", 183rd Street west of Broadway, 1904